Kings, Queens and People's Palaces

Kings, Queens and People's Palaces

AN ORAL HISTORY OF
THE SCOTTISH VARIETY
THEATRE,
1920—1970

Vivien Devlin

Polygon
EDINBURGH

© Vivien Devlin 1991

First published by Polygon 22 George Square, Edinburgh.

Set in Perpetua 12/12½ pt by Alden Multimedia Ltd, Northampton
and printed and bound in Great Britain by Page Bros Ltd, Norwich

British Library Cataloguing in Publication Data
King, Queens and People's Palaces.
1. Great Britain. Variety shows, history
1. Devlin, Vivien
792.70941

ISBN 0-7486-6097-6

The publisher acknowledges subsidy from the
Scottish Arts Council towards the publication
of this volume.

'The music hall was a natural world, an unselfconscious world that did not see the need for any pretence . . . here are the cross-talk men, and trick cyclists, jugglers, tumblers and comic singers, the men and women who had nothing but themselves, a song and a backcloth.'

J.B. Booth, *The Times*, March 18th, 1932.

'To watch a truly great comedian perform is just as exciting, if not more so, than watching a fine Hamlet. The comic lives dangerously, he is always on the razor's edge. His audience . . . they are sitting there, waiting. Laughing – and waiting.'

Sir Laurence Olivier, *On Acting*, 1986.

'The House of Terror was the Glasgow Empire where the audience would say to English comics, ''awa hame and bile yer heid''.'

Ken Dodd, BBC Radio, June 1990.

'If Variety theatre came back, I'd be the first in the queue. It was the war which brought people together, to be entertained with a community spirit of laughter.'

John Nelson, Edinburgh theatregoer.

In memory of my Grandmother, Madge Fenton-Smith

Contents

ACKNOWLEDGEMENTS

Without the generous co-operation of all the contributors to this book, who so willingly agreed to discuss their life and work, this oral history could not have been written. I visited many people throughout England and Scotland and was always given a warm welcome and marvellous hospitality. I thank everyone for their time and particularly for their patience during my long hours of questioning.

I especially wish to thank Jim Friel for sharing his vast knowledge of the Glasgow music hall and Glasgow life. His unstinting advice has been enormously helpful as has his assistance in researching stories, theatre listings and reviews. If the telephone rang at around 11pm on a Sunday, it would always be Jim, with another wonderful anecdote.

I wish to acknowledge the following for permission to use copyright material:

The BBC for extracts from archive recordings and other radio interviews.
BBC Enterprises Ltd. for a quotation from *Oh Yes It Is*, by Gerald Frow.
Cork University Press for a quotation from *The Irish in Scotland*, by James Handley.
Richard Drew Publishing for quotations from *Music Hall Memories*, by Jack House and *The Bedside Book of Glasgow Humour* by Stanley Baxter.
Methuen, London for quotations from *A Good Night Out* by John McGrath.
Motherwell District Museum and Fiona M. Neale, Museum and Heritage Officer, for the extract from the George Clarkson interview transcript.
Frederick Muller at Century Hutchinson for the extract from *The Glasgow Story* by Colm Brogan.
The Open University for extracts from course material.
Weidenfeld and Nicolson Limited, for a quotation from *On Acting* by Laurence Olivier.

I wish to thank the following people for supplying me with photographs and programmes:
Isabelle Dick, Denny Willis, Mae Stevely, John Robertson, Archie Foley, W. Finlay, Ilona Ross, Aileen Vernon, Dorothy Trewhitt, Philippa Mackay, Carey Wilson, Marjorie O'Donnell, Bunty MacLeod, Rory

Gordon, Johnny Beattie, David White, Walter Carr, Alex Rodger, Betty Barr.

Every effort has been made to contact the copyright holders of material used in this book. Where this has not been possible, I apologise to those concerned.

Grateful acknowledgement must also be given to Mr William Irwin, Promotions Manager, and Mr R. D. Orme, Marketing Manager, of Scotrail, who supplied me with complimentary tickets to visit contributors in Glasgow, Aberdeen, Perth, Dundee, Arbroath, Ayr and Scotlandwell. I would like to thank them for their generous support.

INTRODUCTION

When I began to research this book on the Variety theatre in Scotland, I discovered that most of the books on the music hall dealt entirely with England, and that the vast majority of references to the Scottish Variety theatre consisted of biographies about or memoirs by the ubiquitous Harry Lauder.

There is limited material concerning Scottish entertainment after the Lauder era of the turn of the century up until the thirties. Indeed, I frequently came across comments such as that in Peter Bailey's book *Music Hall: The Business of Pleasure* '. . . we could find no-one with work in hand on music hall outside England. These . . . deficiencies . . . clearly constitute opportunities for a further collection of studies'.[1] Furthermore, in *The Historical Development of Popular Culture in Britain*, Bernard Waites makes the point that: 'Unfortunately the provincial hall has been particularly badly served by historians and, to my knowledge, nothing exists on the Scottish halls'.[2]

This apparent lack of published source material and background information on the Scottish music hall was both heartening and daunting. Heartening, because I realised I would not be going over old ground which had been written about before; but at the same time, the prospect of working in an unfurrowed field was initially daunting. The book began to take the form of an oral history, which would draw upon the memories, experiences and the dusty, faded scrap-books of the people who knew the Variety theatre best: the comedians, stage managers, dancers, singers, acrobats and also the men, women and children who queued nightly for the 6d gallery.

I interviewed dozens of people, each with their stories of back-stage and theatre life, and together they form as broad and contrasting a view as possible of the Variety theatre of Scotland. Here are the anecdotes of chorus girls, coping with rats in cold, damp dressing rooms; the experiences of an Aberdonian theatrical landlady who cooked beef pie suppers at midnight and rose at dawn to buy the best fish at the market for her entertainer guests, and observations by the stagehands at the Glasgow Empire, regarded as 'the best stage staff in the world', who had seen it all. And since it is *their* voices, these stories are related with honesty, pride and a great deal of affection.

The time-scale covered in this survey is from the early nineteen twenties to the late sixties. This is an appropriate period on which to concentrate because at that time social, cultural, economic, and racial influences and changes produced and shaped a distinctly Scottish Variety entertainment.

The history of the music hall has been well documented elsewhere and notable studies are listed in the bibliography. Perhaps it will be sufficient to say here that Music hall entertainment originated in London song-and-supper rooms, pubs and taverns during the 1830s, where an all-male clientele would be treated to bawdy jokes and songs. Within ten years, in an effort to improve standards and attract a better class of patron, publicans and entrepreneurial businessmen acquired licensed halls, arranged professional programmes of entertainment, charged an admission price which included some refreshment, and allowed women to attend. In London, the growth of music halls was extremely rapid, but it also quickly spread to the North of England and Scotland. It is no coincidence that this new entertainment developed alongside the expanding urban communities of the working class population. This was an extension of the local public house, where people regularly congregated for a drink with congenial company and a song. By the 1880s:

'The music hall was predominantly working class, both in the character of its audience, the origins of its performers and the content of its songs and sketches . . . The artisan, tired with his day's labour wants something to laugh at . . .'.[3]

At a time when the Chartist movement was losing strength and the standard of living and work conditions continued to be deplorable, this new people's entertainment could at least serve as a 'culture of consolation'.[4] With its basis in a growing socialist solidarity, music hall humour depicted a working-class consciousness, dealing with poverty, work, drink, marriage and the misfortunes of the backstreets, contrasting with the leisurely life of the upper-class 'toff'. The mass following of the music hall reinforced values and provided, through parody and satire, a barometer of political opinion.

Many of the songs and sketches expressed national and even blatantly patriotic fervour such as MacDermott's 'We will not fight but by jingo if we do', popular during the Boer War. This was replaced in the First

World War by Harry Lauder's sentimental ballad 'The Laddies who Fought and Won', and then in the Second World War by the comic caricature of the A.R.P. by Dave Willis, and his song, 'In My Wee Gas Mask'. On the one hand, the music hall united its audience, but on the other hand, each performer observed the cultural differences between regions, and adapted his material to suit Yorkshire miner, Lancashire textile worker or Clydeside shipbuilder.

From an original cheap and raucous, male-only entertainment, there gradually developed by the turn of the century, class-divided, custom-built theatres, each with a three-tier price system providing a 'clean' family show of music, dance, magic and comedy. The prestigious Moss Empires, by now established in Edinburgh and Glasgow, and the Livermore Palaces in Dundee and Aberdeen, were comfortable, professionally run and provided a nationwide platform for the leading London music hall stars of the day. But it was the period from the end of the Edwardian era, until the 1930s, when every small town and seaside resort in Scotland was building its own local Pavilion or Alhambra, which brought an opportunity to nurture specifically local talent. The sheer number of theatres created an ideal touring circuit for Scottish entertainers and soon provided sufficient work fifty-two weeks of the year.

There has often been confusion between the terms Music hall and Variety theatre. Some social historians have suggested that the change of name came about with stricter legislation and the banning of food and drink from the auditorium in 1914. It was also said that Sir Oswald Stoll, by opening the London Coliseum in 1904, made music hall respectable enough for a gentleman to take his wife to, and this kind of light entertainment was soon referred to as 'Variety' theatre. However, the Glasgow theatre critic, Jack House, regarded the two names as interchangeable.

The traditional 'bill' of varieties with the pattern of individual song, dance or comedy acts continued particularly through the national Empire chain, and the smaller local theatres. Meanwhile independent producers began to come on the scene, form their own variety companies, book a theatre season at one theatre or arrange a tour around the country, where they would stage a professionally co-ordinated concert party or revue. To many performers the term 'Variety' only meant the turn-by-turn acts which were unconnected with each other, in contrast to being part of a company production. In this type of show the performers had their own spot as well as working together in ensemble musical numbers and comedy sketches.

The book focuses on every area of the theatre business from the viewpoints of entrepreneur, producer, performer and audience, and examines the origins, content and the need for Variety entertainment.

I asked my contributors to reflect on such questions as – the importance of personality, patter, and catch-phrase in the making of a successful stand-up comic; the tradition of man as Pantomime Dame or the double act and the role of foil; what is particularly *Scottish* about Scottish light entertainment and the reasons for the demise of the Variety theatre circuit in Scotland when the pantomime is still as healthy as ever.

John McGrath in his exemplary study of popular theatre, *A Good Night Out*, identifies nine ingredients making up working-class entertainment. These include Comedy, 'working-class audiences like laughs, middle-class audiences in the theatre tend to think laughter makes the play less serious'; Music, 'live and lively, popular, tuneful and well played'; Variety, '[the audience] . . . seem able to switch from a singer to a comedian, to a juggler, to a band, to a chorus number, to a conjurer, to a sing-a-long . . .'; and, Immediacy, 'the meat of a good comic is the audience's life and experience'.[5] These and other components build up into a clear-cut relationship between performer and audience, the one knowing what to offer in terms of entertainment, the other with a precise expectation of what will be given.

The legacy of the Variety theatre continues today in the 'legitimate' theatre in Scotland with the touring companies, such as Wildcat and Borderline. Wildcat is the foremost exponent of small scale music-theatre, presenting revue-style shows, always topical, often with a political message, which tour around the fringe theatres and community halls throughout Scotland. David MacLennan, founder and director of Wildcat, acknowledges the Variety influence: 'I think there is a great love of Variety in Scotland, and it's a very dramatic form. Music hall and Variety are the main traditions on which we draw our strengths. We have no stock formula, just several songs in different styles, knockabout comedy, but the one thing in common is that we talk directly to the audience, which brings enormous vitality to the show . . . When people go out for a night's entertainment they want songs, and laughs and they want to be made to feel happy and sometimes made to feel sad . . . .'.[6] That final comment neatly echoes the comment made by the artisan going to the music hall, over one hundred years ago.

Moreover, it is particularly the perennial love of pantomime in Scotland which illustrates that music hall performance is still a real native art. As Colm Brogan wrote in his book *The Glasgow Story*, in 1952: 'It may be objected that pantomime comics are hardly culture, as the word is understood by the architects of the *Third Programme*, but they are "culture" in the wider and more tolerable sense. They come much nearer the truth of the Gorbals, than any dialectical exposure has ever done'. Today, the brash, burlesque showmanship of pantomime in

Scotland continues developing this unique blend of traditional folk-tale and contemporary idiom.

Finally, I would like to endorse the comments of Max Tyler, Historian of the British Music Hall Society: 'It should be remembered that for every one performer who left his or her mark, there were some two or three hundred artistes who, whilst good performers in their day, left little or no records behind. There have been many books written on the subject of Variety and music hall but they nearly all tend to deal with well known names. The same old anecdotes and incidents keep on cropping up and getting passed on'.

Among the contributors in this book are the names of several star performers of the Scottish stage, but the majority are the unsung heroes and heroines of chorus line, back stage and pit, whose work was equally valuable. It is their story which should be told and that is also one of the purposes of this book.

Vivien Devlin
Edinburgh, 1991.

"Gilroy's Entertainers."

Lex McLean and Company

Chapter 1

'EVERYONE WANTED TO BE AN ENTERTAINER'

STARTING OUT IN THE BUSINESS

Sunday Mail; 22nd July 1934
The Williams Brothers:
'Claude Williams the conjurer used to work with his ten-year-old brother Dave in an act known as Claude Williams and Funny Clive. Their first big date was around 1905 at the Panopticon Music Hall, Trongate, Glasgow. He put Dave into a page boy outfit, painted the end of his nose red, and let him fool about with the props during the conjuring act. There were four shows a day, 2 pm, 4 pm, 7 pm and 9 pm and they worked like fury for the money. Trouble arose for Claude when he had to square things with the school authorities as Funny Clive was supposed to be at school. Clive was sick each afternoon with unfailing regularity'.

Despite, or perhaps as a direct result of such truancy, Funny Clive grew up to be widely regarded as one of Scotland's most original and popular comedians, Dave Willis, (1895–1973). Charlie Chaplin remarked that he was Britain's greatest comic.

DENNY WILLIS

Born Glasgow 1922. Comedian and the son of Dave Willis.

'I was taken on stage by my father when I was about nine. The famous Houston sisters, Renee and Billie, had a third sister and she was about my age and somebody got the idea of putting us on together, and as two little tots – we were about nine – we had to jump through a paper hoop and do an Irish dance. So I was mixed up in the theatre to that extent in the summer holidays. Then I was back to school again, but the touch was there.

'When I was a youngster down at Ayr where Dave Willis did summer season after summer season, for five years, I used to go down there for fun and learn a bit of juggling, or dancing or conjuring or tight rope walking, whatever they were doing that week, and it was fun. I don't think children would do that now, even if the chance was there, I don't think they would bother trying'.

GEORGE CLARKSON

Born Motherwell, 1894. Dancer with the Five Jocks and later producer of G. B. Bowie's Summer Shows.

'I was the youngest boy of eighteen of a family. Ma parents had eighteen children, although only nine survived, so it was a big family. Ma father was a railway man on a very small wage and how ma mother and father carried on bringing up a family Ah'll never know. It must have been very hard on them. But ma father must have been very ambitious and he just said to me when I was a young boy, you're going to be a dancer whether you like it or not. I was sent to a dancing master in Glasgow and so ma father had to pay ma fares every night, from Motherwell to Glasgow for me to see Mr Kelly – Jimmy Kelly. Then when I was about ten or eleven Mr Kelly had a troupe of dancers called the Douglas Troupe and I was one of them. We toured all round the church and community halls at the time.

'So that's how I became a dancer and as a boy entered competitions and took part in many of the Highland Games and the Braemar Games. I won quite a number of medals and cups for ma dancing. Ma favourite dance was the Sailors' Hornpipe and I picked up many a gold medal for the Hornpipe. The unfortunate part about all this was that every medal and every cup I won, I could only see from the Saturday to the Monday because it went missing on the Monday. Later I discovered that ma father had pawned them and he never redeemed any of them. By the time I was fourteen I was getting a bit cute about this and knowing that if I won anything it would just go the same way so I was up at the Douglas Highland Games one Saturday afternoon and won a gold medal for the Irish Jig and the gold medal for the Hornpipe. When I came home I thought to myself they're not going to know anything about this. When ma father asked what did I win, I said nothing at all, so I got a clout around the ear for going up to the competition and not winning anything at all! I'm glad I kept those two medals – they are the only ones I have to show I was a champion Highland Dancer as a boy.

'I always wanted to go on the stage and knew that I had something to offer and I liked the glamour of the footlights. Ma father would never allow me to go on the stage without learning a trade first. He put me into French Polishing so I had five years of agony as a French Polisher. I was just counting the days and weeks till five years was up. Then I said I'm off to the stage and ma father said, don't put away your brushes and apron because you'll be back in a fortnight and you'll need them again to start work!

'I went down to the Partick Star Palace and was given a trial week. I appeared under the name Ian Lawson, because I thought if I was going to be a flop it would be Ian Lawson that would be the flop, not George Clarkson. On the Monday night I had just finished ma dancing act – and it was a good act though I say it maself – and there was a knock on the dressing room door. A fellow came in, and the first thing I saw was that he had a big cigar in his mouth. I was more fascinated by the cigar than by who he was. He asked what I was doing the next week and I said if I don't do well, Ah'll need to go back to my trade. He said that he could find me work. He returned on the Thursday and said he had booked me a thirty-seven week tour finishing up with a London show date at the Newcross Empire. That thirty-seven week booking allowed me to finish my French Polishing job all together. Many a time when things were going bad with me I felt like coming home but I said no, I just wouldnae do it. It was through determination at that time because it was tough to begin with. It took me eight years before I got to the top of the bill. I was eight years struggling'.'

MAE FARRELL

Born Pollokshaws, Glasgow, 1906. Taken to the pantomime as a child and trained in Highland, Irish and tap dancing from a young age.

'The first time I ever went on the stage and sang was at the Pollokshaws Burgh Hall when I was eleven years old. The Corporation at that time ran what was called a Kinderspiel; it was a sort of big children's concert and I was taking part with the Wylie Troupe of Highland dancers.

'The Wylie dance rehearsals were held in a large loft above a bakehouse – all we could smell was the baking of bread. We had to pay a shilling a night for our dancing lesson and we were never paid for our performances as we were only children. We didn't do it for money, we were so thrilled to go out and dance for people. The Wylie troupe of dancers was very well known. The music to our dancing during rehearsals was simply Mr. Wylie whistling, but it was excellent training.

'A. E. Pickard ran the Panopticon Theatre near Glasgow Cross and in my day it was quite the thing for anyone with a talent to sing or dance, to perform there. Nobody was paid but anyone who thought they had an act would go along, like *Opportunity Knocks*. My father was a slab dancer and used to dance the Irish jig on a stone slab without coming off it. So he took me along there once. And if the audience wanted to get rid of an act, it wasn't always money they threw on the stage, it was old peeled tomatoes and all sorts of fruit. The theatre was near the fruit market. Eventually a hook was used to pull the unlucky people off the stage and some were bold enough to stop and pick up the coins before they walked off.

'Then I saw a wee advert in a local paper asking for artistes. It showed how naïve one can be, not knowing what you are taking on. It was a concert party, but because I was an experienced dancer and had been on the stage at a very young age, it didn't hold any terrors for me, I was an awfully funny wee person. I answered that advertisement and it turned out to be *Harry White's Frolics* in Partick. I went along to Harry White's house for an interview, and amongst all the other hopefuls an unknown Jack Anthony was there. It was Jack's first time too, he had answered the same advert: Jack Anthony aged twenty-one, from White Street, Partick. From there on Jack and I were in that concert party right on until I was married in 1932. My first professional work was as a soubrette and dancer in a variety show at the Maxwell Picture House, Pollokshaws. This was 1920 when I would be fifteen. I had already started full time work in a photographer's shop when I was fourteen, because I was just with my mother and we needed the money.

'As well as my day job I was rushing away on a Friday night and going over to Rothesay to do the Saturday show and then having to get back for work on Monday morning, when there were no steamers at that time on a Sunday. We had to get one of those cutters and travel back to Greenock, no matter what the weather was like, and then catch the train to Glasgow. These were charity concert parties for the British Legion and I was there nearly every week. The show came together as a combined effort, but Harry was the boss, and Billy Nelson, our pianist was a wonder. They were Partick people. Jack Anthony was West End, and later Alec Finlay joined us who was from Cathcart and I was from

Shawlands, but we all merged together and met to rehearse in the piano shop in Sauchiehall Street. They let out their rooms so that we could use the pianos and have the whole place to ourselves.

'What amuses me now is that Jack Anthony couldn't dance a step, but I taught him to dance. We always ended up our act with the little Dutch dance and the soft shoe shuffle. Any steps he continued to do after I stopped working with him, they were mine. Jack Anthony was a light comedian, like Jack Buchanan, and dressed immaculately with a silver topped cane. When he left the *Frolics* it was also my songs he took with him. They were my music and songs: 'Little Mister Baggy Breeches' and 'All over Nothing at all'. These songs had been written a long time ago and I must have heard my father sing them. I gave them to Jack because we had sung them so often together'.

Sunday Mail, 9th December 1934

Robinson Crusoe: with Dave Willis, and Jack Anthony. A big future is predicted for Jack Anthony, playing second comic at the Pavilion. Horace Collins, the producer says 'In two years he will practically be where Dave Willis is now.'

FAY LENORE

Born Newcastle upon Tyne, 1928, the daughter of Leon Dodd, theatrical producer, and Babs Gordon, singer and comedienne. First appeared in 1930, aged eighteen months old in her parents' summer show.

'I was almost born in a trunk, but not quite. My parents were running a concert party in Whitley Bay, from 1930 until the war. They decided to try something different to bring people in and began the idea of having al fresco shows to give people entertainment without them having to go inside and lose the sunshine and fresh air. I think there were al fresco shows at Portobello, on the Pier some time ago. As a young child I was encouraged to perform. Having to change the programme every other show to keep the holiday makers coming back, I would be pushed on: "There's a gap there, go on Fay, get on and sing a number". So that was my beginning. I was told just to get on and do it. I had to do everything; comedy sketches, dance, sing, pull the tabs, which are the curtains, make the props and also carry the "bucket" as there was no loo at the back of the theatre.

'My mother came from Edinburgh and she and her little sister Lena used to stand on the corner of Bread Street and sing for pennies. She started off in Cooke's Circus which was on the site of the old Palladium Theatre. My grandmother Poppy and her three sisters, Beattie, Daisy and

Julie were known as the Four English Rosebuds in a variety act. They had come up to Edinburgh where later my mother and her sister went into showbusiness when they were very small. They really had a very hard time because they were actually bought by a woman called Lady Mansell, who found talented children to put them in a troupe. But they were treated very badly and Lena, who was four years younger than my mother, would have blood pouring from blisters on her feet from wearing tap shoes.

'My mother was determined to leave the troupe and one night climbed down a drainpipe and ran away to Pickard's Panopticon Theatre, where she successfully auditioned for the show, *Morgiana and the Forty Thieves*. She saved up enough money and rescued her sister from Lady Mansell's troupe. They then went out as a sister act, the Gordon sisters – Bunty and Bijou Gordon. On the variety circuit she met her future husband, Leon Dodd, who had started out in 1910 as a Lost Boy in *Peter Pan*. They married and ran shows and pantomimes together. Dad was a very good Dame and Mother, Florence Dodd, a beautiful Principal Boy. So you can virtually say I was born in a trunk behind the stage.'

WALTER CARR

Born 1925, Larkhall, Lanarkshire. Taken to the Hippodrome Theatre, Hamilton, to see variety shows and pantomime as a child. At seven years old he played the part of the plough boy in an amateur musical revue at the Swinhill Miners welfare near Larkhall.

'I always wanted to go on the stage as far back as I can remember. I did have previous members of the family in show business, a great aunt called the Mighty Divine, who was quite a big star at the turn of the century. At six years old I was playing on a rope swing and the swing broke and I injured my foot. There was much discussion on what to do about strengthening this foot. I had a cousin who was being taught tap dancing and although we lived out in the country I took up tap dancing as well to strengthen my left foot. That was where it started – the rudiments of learning professionally to dance and sing. I have always loved that area of theatre.

'There was a little variety theatre called the Ritz in Irvine which many people may remember. I was a boy then, only about thirteen or fourteen, but I was always tall for my age. I went along to the theatre and blatantly asked if there was anything I could do and they said "What can you do?", and I said, "Well I dance and sing a bit", and to cut a long story short I used to go there and play on a Friday and Saturday. We did two shows on a Friday, two shows on a Saturday for which I got paid £5 which was a lot of money in those days. And I worked with old comics like Bert Bendon and that really was my first taste of professional variety.

'One had to take part in the sketches and I had to play an American and all sorts of characters like that. There was one sketch in particular where the comic would say to me, ''What's your name?'' and I, as the feed, would then say to the comic ''What's yours?'' and he would say ''I'll have a double whisky''. People still do that sketch. But then there was a point when I got wise to it and I turned the gag round and of course I didn't know how we got out of it and he would say, under his breath, ''For goodness sake, say so and so, and such and such'', to twist the gag to reach the punchline and get the scene finished. It was all a wonderful experience and very funny.'

CATHIE MACDONALD

Born 1924, Edinburgh, the daughter of M. J. McHale who ran concert parties, *The Melody Makers*, and the *Tartan Follies*, between the wars.

'Edinburgh travelling variety shows started off with my father, Michael McHale and a friend, Sandy Chapman, with the *Tartan Follies*. That would have been just after the First World War. Then when I was a child, in the late twenties, my father started out on his own and started *The Melody Makers*. These were charity concert parties, or as an entertainment put on for football clubs, either in halls or the shows might be pageants travelling around Edinburgh by lorry. Betty Brandon was a well-known dancing teacher at the time and she would recommend and supply dancers which was always good experience for her pupils. There was one girl, Evelyn Trill, who was excellent, and could put her body into all sorts of positions, she really was double-jointed. Then there were the Graham Sisters, the Jenkin Sisters, and Ella Wood the vocalist who was a lovely blonde with a really rich voice. One of the comedians was called Spud Thomson and there was a dancer, Isobel Lorimer.

'When they were very young, and just starting out, Robert Wilson, The Henderson Twins, Maidie Dickson and Chic Murray all used to appear in my father's shows. Years later when they had become successful, my father would remark, ''Ay, they're good, but they started with me!'' My father was always on the look out for talent. In Portobello they had a sort of Opportunity Knocks affair, *Carrol Levis and his Discoveries*. Young entertainers would be ''discovered'' by him and then they joined my father to get their grounding. It worked very well. He used to audition too, and he'd have people dying to come into his show but he was strict and would say, ''Well, I'll put your name down and send for you if we need you.'' He wouldn't take anyone. It was a breeding ground for the few who really had talent. He had to see you and see your act and the Melody Makers was THE show. It wasn't a case of just anyone getting in.'

MAIDIE MURRAY

Born Edinburgh, 1922 (née Dickson). Accordionist and singer. Later in double act with her husband, the comedian, Chic Murray.

'As a child I don't actually remember *not* being in the business. My parents had me as a toddler going to concerts, and all sorts of shows in Leith at the Capitol and the Regent, possibly out every night of the week. There was never any time for play. I came home from school, got washed and away to the concert. I think I was the first child performer to go on at the Capitol in the thirties. My parents weren't in the business, not at all. My mother sang very well and I believe she wanted to run away with some troupe, but she never did do anything professional. They were both interested in music, and that is how I started to learn. When I was twelve I went into pantomime in Newcastle at the Palace, with a man called Pete Davis. He was a producer in Scotland. It was back to school after the pantomime but when I was fourteen, I went on tour with Pete Davis to Bangor, for a summer season. Then home again and out on tour throughout Scotland and England around all the variety theatres. That was my training for the profession.'

DOROTHY PAUL

Born Glasgow; singer, actress.

'I had been trained as an operatic soprano, my mother was a wee bit of a stage mother and was always putting me in for things. In 1955 my mother put me in for the Carrol Levis Competition – so I was a Carrol Levis Discovery, originally. Looking back it was all rather ridiculous. My mother was telling me things like, "Now you stand up there and show the man all you've got". Naïve! I would try and explain that I was too nervous and didn't want to go in for it. She however just continued being very supportive towards her daughter, by simply saying "Aye, you'll go!"

'I was invited to the finals and asked down to Mr. Levis's room and he was a repulsive man. I mean repulsive, hairless and fat. He started to chase me round the room, saying, "If you play ball with me, I'll play ball with you. I'll adjust the clappometer in your favour". And he started getting nasty so I punched him. Well, I didn't win the competition. A lassie who was a contortionist won, but that's how I started.'

ALEC FINLAY

(1906–1984). Renowned comedian and character actor, he was billed as Scotland's Gentleman, and was a versatile singer, musician, and comic in seaside revue, and pantomime. In a BBC archive interview, Alec Finlay described how he had begun his stage career.

'It started at ten years of age, during the First World War. Every month the Band of Hope had a children's night and we entertained ourselves and once somebody put my name down and I got the fright of my life when I was called out. I walked onto the stage and began a monologue ''Napoleon's Farewell to his Granny''. All I said was, ''Ta ta Granny''. The superintendent got me by the back of the neck and said ''No nonsense, you've got to entertain, you've got to sing''. Well my grandfather had an old fashioned gramophone, and I learnt all Harry Lauder's songs – I didn't know who he was but I loved his songs and patter. I just sang ''Roamin in the Gloamin'' and I think I ended up singing four or five songs that first night. The superintendent then asked to me to come with the Senior choir around the hospitals; they used to entertain the wounded soldiers. This was fine and the soldiers seemed to like me and so that is how I started.

'I wanted to see the world and all my uncles were engineers and because I wanted to be an engineer I went to G. and J. Weir's in Cathcart, to serve my apprenticeship. But my father was encouraging me with my stage work and he thought I could be a success. He said, ''Keep your concerts up in the evening, Alec, and when your time is out, you can go to sea and see the world, but if you make a success in show business, you'll see the world anyway because you'll be invited to all these other countries''. So I took his advice and I worked very hard. I was working from eight in the morning to five at night, then home for a quick cup of tea, but sometimes straight to the theatre, or cinema because ciné-variety was common in those days. I would do two shows, and home to bed and away back to work at eight the next morning and so it went on.

'Playing in what you might call a rougher cinema, I was a bit too refined for them and I got the bird on many an occasion. I would come home broken-hearted. My father would say, ''Why are you disappointed? I was there tonight, I thought you were great. Every time I see you, you are improving''. Now I didn't know he was there, he just quietly turned up and if it wasn't for his encouragement, I would have given up many a time.'[2]

BARBARA McCALL

Variety theatre regular in Edinburgh and Portobello, where her husband was manager of the Marine Gardens Dance Hall, 1923–39.

'Nearly all the comics started at Letta's Pierrots at Portobello. André Letta always wore a carnation in his button hole, which he got every morning from Rankins, in Elm Row. Letta's Pierrots was in Bath Street, where there is now Bingo, and it was packed every afternoon and night. It was such a good opportunity for young people to get a start. If you got into Letta's, you were made. Whenever my husband and I saw the singer Donald Peers, I said, "This fellow is going to go far". I knew it. He wasn't a common sort of fellow, he was a gentleman. We spoke to him and he said he was a soldier in the army but that he enjoyed singing. We helped him find some suitable songs to sing and whenever I heard 'By a Babbling Brook', I knew that it was perfect for Donald Peers and bought a copy. We took him this sixpenny songsheet that night and he sang it. From there on he bought himself out of the army, continued getting experience at Letta's Pierrots, married, and then he was away to London. The next thing he was at the Albert Hall making a huge amount of money, with that song, "By a Babbling Brook" becoming his signature tune. At the same time as Donald Peers started at Letta's, Dave Willis was there, just a young comedian. They all started down at Portobello – Tommy Morgan, Charlie Kemble from Rothesay, and Peggy Desmond, well known in the West, who actually married Letta after she came down there, although he was much older than she was.'

Portobello with its pier, lavish dance and concert hall, swimming pool, and a number of variety shows on offer, was a popular holiday resort and soon became known as the Brighton of the North.

Evening News, 14th August 1934

Letta's Show: 'A large holiday crowd showed warm appreciation of the programme at the Pavilion, Bath Street, Portobello last night. The comedy note was predominant and demands for encores were frequent. Mr Dave Bruce and Miss Peggy Desmond again led the way, ably assisted by Mr Jack Radcliffe. They presented a number of entertaining burlesque items, including a skit on Italian Opera. The Saxon ladies provided popular singing and dancing interludes' while at the same time, down at the Portobello Prom Palace, 'Mr Tommy Morgan and his entertainers continue to attract crowded audiences. Tommy Morgan causes great laughter, assisted by Tommy Yorke who has a rich vein of humour. There was much to admire in the skilful dancing of George Clarkson and Joe O'Rourke, a tenor, sings catchy melodies'.

MAY MOXON

Born 1906 in Glasgow, into a theatrical family. She and her two brothers were trained by their mother for the stage. The act was known as the Four McLeans and their first performance was in the Glasgow Casino Ciné Variety theatre, when she was ten and her brothers, twelve and fourteen. The Glasgow Casino, Castle Street, was in the Townhead district on the north side of Glasgow and was owned at one time by A. E. Pickard who owned the Panopticon.

'The first time you go on the stage, you don't forget it. I came from a theatre family and it was common for children to go on the stage, although there were strict laws and children needed a licence. You still had to go to school if you travelled away from home to work in the theatre. My mother worked with us, my two brothers and I. We didn't sing much, it was really a comedy sketch with some dancing. At that age we were just learning. At fourteen I joined the Henglers Circus. Every year this circus came to Glasgow, which was a major event. It used to be where the Cannon cinema now is in Sauchiehall Street. There were all the famous circus acts, and the clown Doodles. At the finale there was a magnificent water scene and the horses even jumped into the water. That was where I came in. I was the young girl who was kidnapped and taken away as part of this little drama they performed in the circus ring.

'At that age you don't think you are working; you think it is fine and you haven't known anything different. Mind you, I don't know how my mother had the nerve to go on with three children. I was just ten. But she must have thought we were of a good enough standard and the theatre managers accepted us. We did do well.

'Ciné-variety was the thing in those days. We weren't performing in the big theatres then. But you could get fifty-two weeks work a year in the ciné-variety. The programme would be a big feature film, then a couple of acts on the stage so that it was certainly a varied evening's entertainment. It wasn't a lot of money but they were happy days'.

INA HOWDEN

Née Hill; born 1921, Leith. A regular theatregoer in Leith and Edinburgh from childhood.

'As a child our mother was a Highland dancer in Leith. She was in the sixteen Leith Lassies. She performed at the Gaiety, Leith, and there used to be Codona's circus showground. When my mother was a girl of thirteen in 1908, she went inside a basket and was then carried by a man who walked the tightrope.

'My mother was mentioned in the local Leith newspaper. She was called "the pluckiest girl in Leith". She was just thirteen and she must have had great courage to do that. So it was through Mother's love of the theatre that we enjoyed it too. When my sister Agnes went in for a competition when she was twelve, it was a *Go As You Please* talent show, she sang and danced to that song, "She's my lady love". She was very popular and got half-a-crown and went back the following week and got half-a-crown again. We were so proud of her. She also did acrobatics, just with a gym tunic on, with black stockings, tucking her tunic up. She did cartwheels, and true acrobatics. This was at the Alhambra, Leith, but they had these shows all over the place, the Palladium, and the Capitol.

'These shows wouldn't have been every week, but perhaps for a spate of three or four weeks and it was always crowded. Just a talent contest and the best act won half-a-crown. My sister was so sharp, and keen to learn that she joined in with the older lads who at that time used to tap dance at the corner of the streets. She used to pick up the steps in a minute, and came home to practice. My aunt sent our cousin Jean for dancing lessons and she eventually joined the *Half-Past Eight Show*. We were poor, and although my mother had been a dancer, she couldn't send us to lessons. Money was for other things, even though my sister had something there, a real talent. I took part and sang, but you couldn't hear me behind a newspaper. I was so in awe when I saw that sea of faces. But my sister had pluck — she wasn't frightened of it. I am sure she could have made something of her dancing and acrobatics, if she hadn't got married'.

LENA NICOL

Née Sweetman, born Edinburgh, 1922. Trained with Adeline Calder, at the Madame Ada school of dancing, Edinburgh. Her late husband was the popular comic Hector Nicol, who died in 1985, aged 65.

'I first performed aged nine with my brother in a concert party for charity. All my three sisters and two brothers were trained to dance, because our mother had wanted to become a dancer but wasn't allowed to perform on stage. My first professional performance was as one of the Babes in the pantomime, *Babes in the Wood*, with Harry Gordon and Bond Rowell at the Theatre Royal, Edinburgh, in 1936. I then worked for twelve years as a dancer in Scottish variety shows, and revues. I even partnered Bruce Forsyth in Carlisle in 1947, until he was called away to do his National Service. He was a wonderful dancer.'

Evening News, 18th January 1937
Babes in the Wood: Theatre Royal.
'The Royal pantomime has much to commend it, in the matter of singing, spectacle and dancing, but its especial appeal is humour and Mr Harry Gordon, jumping into his stride, gave the audience every good reason to rejoice in his clever comedy, and wit. Misses Betty O'Rourke and Lena Sweetman are appealing babes and the John Tiller girls add pace and loveliness to a pantomime to please the most expectant.'

ANNE FIELDS

Born Dalmarnock, Glasgow. Singer and comedy actress.

'I was born into a theatrical family. My father was part of a double act called Clifford and Clinton, a song, dance and comedy act. He came out of showbusiness and only took part on odd weekends when the family was growing up, as he couldn't be away from home so much. My mother had a good voice, but didn't go into show business. The talent went down the family line though and my cousin was the first to go into the business: Margo Henderson was an impressionist. Then my brother tried his hand but after a year at the Metropole he didn't fit happily into the routine of working every evening. There was no life outside the theatre. I went onto the stage at a young age, and my sister, Sally Logan, followed, who now performs with her husband Joe Gordon, and their son, Scott, who plays the accordion and drums.

'I first performed at the age of eight at the Pavilion, Perth. Then at twelve I was in the summer season at Rothesay and had to get a special licence from school. Then when I was still only fourteen I left school and joined the summer season at Barrfields Pavilion, Largs. This was a seventeen week season with a change of programme twice a week. You were not allowed to repeat songs, or costumes so that you had to come with twice times seventeen different acts and dresses. I was so young and just starting out. My music had to be transposed because I sang so deeply. I had a white strapless bra and a white slip, as well as a black bra and slip. Then with five yards of tulle, and tacking thread, I put together my costumes and alternated between white and black dresses, adapting as I could each week.

'I was called "the sweet singer of sweet songs" at that age. I was a crooner and also did a bit of dancing. And at fourteen and a half or so I was also having my first taste of comedy sketches. The comic that year was Tommy Lester and I was told to walk on and when he produced a pair of ladies' panties, I was to slap him on the cheek. I was so nervous and instead of a gentle pat with the right hand, I brought up my left fist and walloped him so hard on the side of his jaw that he was knocked out, and fell flat on the floor. That was my first comedy sketch. Luckily it was not my last.'

JOHNNY BEATTIE

Born Glasgow, 1926. Comedian.

'I was an electrician in the Glasgow shipyards, and it's a strange thing, because so many of the Glasgow comics came from the Glasgow shipyards. Billy Connolly, Lex McLean, Tommy Morgan, Russell Hunter, and would you believe Nicholas Parsons — he once worked at John Brown's Clydebank, in the drawing office. I suppose it is understandable because there was such a tremendous number of people working in the shipyards, it was the industry in Glasgow. I often laugh when I hear the phrase today, the ''comedy workshop'', for all these alternative comics, and I always say the Fairfield shipyards must have been the original comedy workshop, because they were all comics, and the patter was flying about all day long. I suppose you had to be fairly quick on your feet if you wanted to survive.

'I actually wanted to be an actor at one point. We formed an amateur concert party which we modestly called the Star-Gazers. I then got involved with helping a friend, Walter Butler with the Glasgow University Revue, *College Pudding*, which they put on every year for charity. He was actually in a bit of a fix, as he had no material, so I helped him in that. An agent in Glasgow saw me and suggested I go along to talk about going into the Variety theatre. At that point I wasn't too sure. The following year, the same thing happened. Robert Wilson, the producer and singer, who was known as the Voice of Scotland, wanted a young comedian and asked if I was interested.

'I always remember going along to a Sunday night concert in Broxburn and I did a ten minute spot, and Robert offered me six months work touring all round Scotland. That was 1952. He offered me £15 a week, which was an awful lot of money in those days, and I found out eventually that the actual going rate at the time for that kind of thing, was £12. This man, who was a thorough gentleman, he really was, put us all up in the best hotels, albeit in small towns and villages in Scotland, because he liked the company to be together; he didn't want any of this nonsense of looking for cheap digs at the edge of town. So that was a great opportunity although I was getting married at the time the show was starting to tour. But Robert Wilson said get married and then join them. Kitty and I were married on the 3rd of May, 1952 and I joined them a fortnight later. Monday 19th May, 1952, was when I started as a comedian and they still haven't found me out. If I get my equity card, they'll be no holding me back!'

JIM FRIEL

Born Glasgow, 1941. His parents were great music hall goers and he remembers shows and pantomimes from childhood. Favourite haunts were the Pavilion, the Metropole, the Empress, and the Queen's. In later years he frequented the Empire, Alhambra, King's and Theatre Royal.

'I was brought up in the last generation before the influence of television. We did not have a television until I was thirteen. I was brought up in the Garngad district of Glasgow. This was a very Irish district and parties and sing-songs were regular occurrences in houses in those days.

'It was a Garngad man, John Croall, who discovered the comic Tommy Lorne, whose real name was Hugh Corcoran. He worked at the Blochairn Steelworks which stood where the city fruitmarket stands today. At that time a Cork priest called Father Edward Lawton was parish priest at St. Rochs Church on Garngad, now Royston Road, near the steelworks. He ran Sunday night concerts in the parochial hall and it was here that the young Hugh Corcoran first appeared. Others who appeared at these concerts were Tommy Morgan, Tommy Yorke, The O'Rourkes, Charlie McGonagall, (later Naughton of Naughton and Gold) who came from the Anderston district of Glasgow, Jimmy Donoghue and many others. Donoghue, whose real name was Jimmy McAree, came from the Garngad area. His original partner was another Garngad man called Billy Cosbie, and they were known as Donaghue and Sands. They later split and the act became Donaghue and Ramsay. They appeared in many of the smaller theatres for a long time. Father Lawton became a great friend of Tommy Lorne and indeed was the confidante of many show-biz people. He was known as their unofficial chaplain. It was he who conducted the Requiem Mass at Lorne's funeral in 1935.'

ALEC RODGER

Born Alloa, 1928. Stagehand, Metropole Theatre.

'I was just eleven at the time, in 1939, when I joined the theatre, working what we called the limes, the spotlights, because all the regular men had been called up for the army. A friend of my father's was stage manager at the Metropole, Stockwell Street and when the boys were called up, they had no stagehands. So that's why I began in the theatre at such a young age. The limes were operated from the balcony. They were made

— 21 —

of two carbons, and you had to make sure they were burning well and not crossing one another. They had to give a perfect light. There were two of us in the box, doing the spots. Then I took the switchboard job on. I was friendly with Alec Frutin the theatre manager, who was very good to me.

'On one occasion, Tommy Morgan was playing at the Metropole, in a pantomime, *Clairty in Blunderland*. Pete Davis, the producer was taking the show on tour to Stockton on Tees and it was good experience because I went with the company, staying in digs, but living off ration books so that you just got a half slice of bread. That wasn't much good for me, a young growing boy. However we had six Scots lads, four pipers and two drummers in the band. While we were away a lady invited us to her house on Hogmanay and I have never seen such a spread in all my life. I don't know where she got it all, so you can imagine how we all tore into that. We had a great Hogmanay down at Stockton, with the boys piping up the street after the party. I also toured to Rothesay, Forfar and Galashiels.

'There was a lot of talent around. Youngsters would try their luck, showing their act at the Panopticon Theatre on the Trongate, which we called the ''Pots and Pans'' because all the workmen used to go in with their billycans of tea. It was a tough talent show, and if you were no good, there would be a hook to pull you off!

'But this was the era when the Variety theatre was extremely popular. There was no television in those days and everyone wanted to be an entertainer'.

The Gaiety Theatre, Ayr
Copyright *The Ayrshire Post*

Chapter 2

'THE FIFTY POUND CLOUD'

THE SUMMER SEASON AND THE TOURING CIRCUIT

The popularity of family seaside holidays and day trips to the Scottish coast was at its height in the years between the wars, when increasing numbers of employees had the benefit of annual paid leave from work. During the twenties and thirties, small beach pavilions and halls were built along the promenades of every tiny resort down the Clyde coast, along the Firth of Forth, and up the East coast. Brass bands, Pierrot shows and concert parties would entertain the crowds. One of the regular summer journeys was to take the train south from Glasgow to Wemyss Bay, and board the steamer on a thirty-minute crossing over the Firth of Clyde to the Isle of Bute. The destination was the popular holiday town of Rothesay, described as the 'Madeira of Scotland', which curved around a wide, attractive bay. The summer shows at the Winter Gardens on the Esplanade won a high reputation. The theatre was large, seating 1,200 people, and it was the resident company there, the Rothesay Entertainers, which became the training ground for such performers as Jack Anthony, Dave Willis, Tommy Morgan, Alec Finlay and Robert Wilson. All around Scotland most comics, singers and dancers began their careers during long summer seasons beside the sea.

ROSS BOWIE

Entertainment Agent, son of G. B. Bowie, Summer Season producer.

'It was 1932, the year I was born, when my father launched his first seaside summer revue and that was at the Beach Pavilion, North Berwick. My mother ran the box office while my father produced the show for eight weeks that summer. That was his first rented premises from the local council and from there it developed up to the time he was running fourteen different summer shows in the one year, such as Dunbar, The Barrfield in Largs, Carnoustie, Montrose, Arbroath, Inverness, Aberdeen, Saltcoats, The Cosy Corner in Dunoon, The Cragburn in Gourock, Winter Palace, Rothesay and so on. In the winter he would dabble with other shows like the Roxy Theatre, Falkirk, on Friday and Saturday nights, or the Granada Theatre, Hamilton at the weekends. Basically it was summer seasons. These pavilions had been there for many years, and were owned by the local council. Once my father had made his name as a successful producer, different council representatives would go and see his various shows and see if this was the kind of entertainment they wanted for the next year. Looking back he did put on some very good shows.

'At that time the biggest theatrical agent in Glasgow was William R. Galt. Galt's Agency was synonomous with showbusiness. My father and Willie Galt were quite friendly so he knew who was up and coming, who was starting out. He would also audition people but mainly he knew the acts, knew what he wanted and he would go to Willie Galt and say, for instance, he needed an accordion player for Arbroath, and Galt would look through his papers and recommend one. But my father didn't have much to do with the production of the shows, after casting the company. He had a producer in each place who was totally responsible for what went on, although he was out every night to see the shows. Normally the season ran for anything from ten to fourteen weeks, with a change of programme twice a week, Monday and Thursday.

'In England, the summer shows they had at the end of the pier had four programmes during the whole summer. If you brought an English act up to a Scottish summer show, and told them we ran for fourteen weeks so you will need twenty-eight acts, they usually wanted the first train back saying, "I don't have twenty-eight acts". So they were told, "Well, you will have by the time you leave!"

'The main responsibility my father had was for getting the costumes from A to B. A gypsy scene in Arbroath on a Wednesday and opening in Rothesay on a Thursday is not easy. It was all packed into big wicker hampers and sent by rail or in our old grey truck we used to transport all the bits and pieces of scenery and costumes. Then you would find that the Mountie costume which had fitted a six foot tenor in Montrose, didn't necessarily fit the five foot four chap in Rothesay.

'In the dancing troupe on these small stages there were usually four girls, maybe six for the larger stages. You always had the principal comedian who ruled the roost, and he had his comedy team with him. You always had your tenor and your soprano, your accordionist, maybe a three-handed musical act, or a three-handed vocal act, so you could finish up with about fifteen, sixteen people.

'It was twice nightly, 6.30 and 8.45 were the average starting times. There weren't many matinees, but what we did have sometimes were midnight matinees in places like Rothesay and Inverness. They were very popular – you did your two shows and then another one starting at midnight. Good weather was no use to us at all because if it was a sunny night, or if it had been a warm day, nobody wanted to go inside to a theatre. So we used to come out and see if we could spot "fifty pound" clouds coming across the horizon, hoping it was going to rain by six o'clock! Obviously if it rained the theatre was where people aimed for because there was nothing else other than sit in the boarding house or hotel.

'Everyone started in the summer shows, it was the only place to perfect your trade and where you learnt the business. The wages were comparable with a shop keeper's wages at the time. All things being equal. I remember the chorus girls getting about five or six pounds a week, but they were living in digs with full board for two pounds ten shillings a week. No fares were paid. If you were booked for a season at the Beach Pavilion, Aberdeen, you got a letter to say that rehearsals started on Monday the such and such and you had to get there. Not like today where they have to pay your rail fare and see that you stay in the best hotel. In those days it was very hard work. They had rehearsals every morning starting at ten and with all the comic sketches and production scenes, they didn't finish before one o'clock, back into the theatre at five o'clock for the first performance at six thirty. You didn't get out of the theatre until eleven o'clock at night, back to your digs, have your supper, get to bed and don't be late for the rehearsal at ten o'clock. So it really was a strenuous routine.

'I remember Rothesay during Glasgow Fair, when you couldn't move in the place. People used to send their luggage down two or three days before they came and in those days the porters had white caps and wheelbarrows and you would see them running round the town delivering people's luggage. The place was absolutely chock-a-block. That was Rothesay in its heyday.'

ANNE FIELDS

'Just when I was finding my feet in the business, my sister was coming up behind me and I introduced Sally to G. B. Bowie for an audition. He accepted her for a summer season but was going to pack her off to Saltcoats in her first year but I persuaded him to let her stay with me in Largs and he agreed.

'G. B. Bowie was a lovely man. You didn't see much of him as George Clarkson was the producer and G. B. Bowie only came down once a week to see that we were alright. He would ask if there were any problems, and would very gently enquire, "Come on, my girl, you can tell me". Even when he was an old man, he would come down to the Ayr Gaiety where I would be performing with Johnny Beattie. He would arrive and send up a message, "Tell her to come down because I'm too old to climb up those stairs".'

The place to be in the summer months was 'Doon the Watter' even if you could only afford a day trip. In the early fifties, day rail excursions were popular at the weekends, at around eight shillings return from Edinburgh to Troon or Ayr, and eleven shillings to Rothesay. Many families, however, thronged to the coast in July and August for a week or a fortnight.

In June 1938, the *Evening News* advertised package holiday suggestions from Edinburgh, with travel, bed and board, for a week in Dunoon at £5.5s, to Aberdeen at £6.12.4d, although it was cheaper to enjoy the amusements at Blackpool Pier for £6.5.6d. Holiday accommodation in Ayr in the summer of 1946 was being offered with 'Bed, breakfast and light supper at six shillings, daily, and a high tea if arranged'. In July 1951 a guest house in Rothesay catered for 'Bed and Breakfast, high tea and supper at 11/6d daily, with gas fire and wash basin'.

GEORGE CLARKSON

'I had twenty-five years producing for G. B. Bowie and of course later on in life for Ross Bowie, who took over from his father. Twenty-five years is a long while to stay in one firm but I was always sure of my grounds so far as George Bowie was concerned. No matter what happened in the show, if it was wrong or if it was right, George Bowie always said to artistes, "Look, take your instruction from Mr. Clarkson. He's the gaffer, the guvnor there and no matter whether it pleases ye or not just take your instruction from him".

'It was a strenuous summer season because as producer I had to find eighteen different acts; we had eighteen separate scenes in each performance with a completely fresh programme every Monday and

Thursday with only two days to rehearse the new show. On Tuesday and Wednesday I had to produce another eighteen items. The producer's brain had to work fast to find ideas for different scenes and company ensembles! We hadn't much time to ourselves during the season.'[1]

DOROTHY PAUL

'Where I really served my time, where I learnt the business was when I did a summer season, in the late fifties, with Gracie Clark and Colin Murray. That was G. B. Bowie's show, with the Rothesay Entertainers and it was very tough work, absolutely. And for £12 a week, and all the pies you could eat. It was beyond the call of duty, looking back. People really don't work as hard as that now. It was a twice weekly change for twenty two weeks. I did the opening, a scene, my own soprano act, finishing the first half, comedy sketches in between, opening the second half, sketches and the finale. Grace Clark was a hard task master. I mean she demanded that you were on the ball, because she was on the ball. I learned how to time comedy and everything. If you made a mistake she nearly battered you, she nearly went for you. I used to think that she was too hard on me, but now I realise that I really learned the business with her.

'Then wherever you toured, there were the digs. My mother, she was always taken to do things for me, as I was only eighteen and still very "raw". "I'll get you good digs. Auntie Iza and I will take a day trip". So they did that and came back and said, you're starting in Aberdeen on Monday and you've got great digs. £2.10 a week for bed, breakfast, lunch, tea and supper. Wonderful I thought. So I got up there and it was a wee woman who lived near the Silver Sands and she seemed a very nice woman and she made me a lovely lunch and let me settle in. She seemed to be a widow with two children, but before I am in the house five minutes she starts telling me all the details of her sex life. I was shocked. I thought if my mother knew this! She kept talking about her boyfriend who was away from home. Anyway I stayed on and one day there was this fellow there, with a very white face, and a big coat on, looking most odd. This was the boyfriend, just out of Peterhead Prison! So my wonderful mother, with her "I'll get you good digs" remark. But in those days you took people at face value and my mother was very naïve.'

JOHNNY WILLIAMSON

Born Perth, 1914. A theatregoer from a young age.

'I can remember back in the early twenties, when I was dragged every week to the local shows in Perth. The programme changed every single week. The price was a shilling for a seat inside the little theatre, which was built of wood with a verandah, where you could stand and they would take a collection after the show. This was called "bottling the crowd". Inside you got a seat but it would be a shilling. Each week was a different programme, starting on a Monday to Saturday, with afternoon performances as well. We enjoyed every minute of them. It was the Pierrot show at the North Inch in Perth, we had in these years. First of all comedians, Mark Denison, he did all the hard work, with Eric Victor, then we had May Wills and Will Adams, they sang and played the piano. Then we had a soubrette, Queenie Forbes, she latterly married Jimmy Currie. Queenie Forbes was a dancer and light comedienne, and Eric Victor was a straight man to help the comic. Most of the work went to the comedian, he was there all the time. The same people went week in and week out. The same people came along on the same night every week to pay their shilling.

'They were there all summer, the same company. Then they took the building down in the winter. As well as seeing the Pierrots, we had shows in Carnoustie, in Broughty Ferry, Monifeith, and in St. Andrews, where a Mrs Leo Bliss appeared for many years, and she never told us what she was going to sing but in the programme it said she would sing "Songs from her repertoire". Then we had Johnny Devlin in Carnoustie, he was a comedian. Here it was the same set up as in Perth – a wooden hut with a collection taken for those outside, or a shilling for a seat inside. At Broughty Ferry I saw Jack Tripp, a comedian, and here it was the same idea, seats inside or stand outside. Then Charlie Kemble, he was a comic who sang songs about people in the audience. As a child, I even had a song sung about me, which went like this:

There is a wee boy over there,
He has a nice wee pair of panties,
I doubt they are his own,
I think they are his aunties!'.

ALEC FINLAY

(From a BBC Archive interview)[2]

'The summer shows were at their peak between the wars. Every seaside town had a summer show because there was so much talent in Scotland at the time. I was at Ayr with Charlie Kemble who was a great local comedian, a very spontaneous man, a marvellous ad-libber. He was principal comic and I was second comic. There was a comedienne, a soprano, a tenor, my wife Rita was the solo dancer, and there was a pianist. Going on with Charlie, there was no script. He just blethered and you had to keep going, otherwise the thing would have flopped. I learnt to be an ad-lib comic through Charlie Kemble and I am terribly grateful to that man.

'Every show was the top show. You had to believe that. You lived the stage life, you breathed the show from morning to night. You rehearsed in the morning and in the afternoon you would be thinking about it until you were into the first house on a Monday. Then you might add a wee bit for the second house. Tuesday you got an idea, inspiration for a sketch, and with Charlie you could say anything and, although he was always smarter, he encouraged you.

'Millport was the first show I was principal comedian in. I was very young at the time and the man who ran the show was Leslie Linn, a great comedian himself. There were no curtains across the stage and most sketches were kitchen scenes with a table and three chairs. There were no lights for blackouts and we had to run three times around the table and then off, which was the climax of the piece. There was always this chase. On the first night it seemed to be going alright, people were laughing but I only ran round twice and off. Leslie came to see me in quite a state, saying I had spoilt the whole sketch because I had only run around twice. He used to stand and watch me every night to see that I ran round three times. I used to have to count it carefully. One night for devilment I ran round four times and then got a telling off for that as well. But I learnt a lot from Leslie Linn. It was a terrific atmosphere. You weren't really working for money and it was almost a surprise on Friday when you got paid, because we would have worked for nothing, we were so happy.'

W. FINLAY

Born Glasgow, 1936. Daughter of Alec Finlay and Rita Andre.

'In those days most people went to the Scottish seaside for their holidays. Rothesay was a thriving place during July and August and the theatre would be full every night with two shows. It was about a shilling to get in and three and six for the best seats. It was simply good family holiday entertainment. My mother was a soubrette and was also in the business, and the only times I saw her on stage were in the summer shows at Gourock, Dunoon, Largs and Rothesay, which were my father's haunts. She would "feed" him, and by that I mean the comedy scripts, the cues. She fed him at home too of course, but she acted as a sort of comic's foil, and took part in the sketches. It would occasionally be a bit fraught, with a high level of tension on first nights, I do remember as a child.

'I have the impression that the break in my father's career came after he returned from his South African tour of 1938. Whether it was professional maturing or an improvement in his confidence but whatever it was things were very good when he came back to Scotland. From then on he began to run his own show, at least he would have the show named after him, *Finlay Frolics*. It gave him the independence to do the work he wanted and the freedom to select the company for the season.'

Alec Finlay in *Finlay Frolics* at the Cosy Corner, Dunoon Summer season 1947: Opens 7th June, with a change of programme every Thursday.

'The enthusiastic applause that greeted the end of each act in the Cosy Corner last night was proof of the general opinion that Alec Finlay has done it again. He has gathered together a cast of artistes who are not only masters of their own particular art, but who blend well together to complete a show that sparkles from beginning to end. Alec Finlay is an outstanding comedian, ably aided and abetted by Cliff Harley . . . Florence Hunter is a soprano of no mean ability while the well-trained Millie Jackson Girls and the music of Billy Rose round off a well-balanced and entertaining show that would be hard to better.'

EVELYN HENRY

Born Aberdeen. Soprano.

'When I started, in the mid-forties, the resident season was in its heyday in Scotland. You would rehearse the week before opening and after that, once the show opened, the programme changed every week. The artistes all took part; you were contracted to take part in all the scenas, sketches, whatever and your own solo spot. For your own spot, you dressed yourself, in those days, and as the show might run for twenty-two or even twenty-six weeks, you had to have a change of wardrobe all the way through. You had to have a change of music, and supply the music for your own spot, decide what you were going to do, and it had to be timed. As a soprano, I might have five or six minutes which would be two songs, one longer than the other. You were expected to have proper orchestrations for the band. You came in on the Monday morning and put your music down at the side of the stage, and took it in turn to have your own band call, and rehearse with the orchestra. As a soprano, I tended to choose something quite straight. Depending on the audience I might put in an operatic aria, but selected something popular and suitable which would, I hoped, get applause. And the producer would have booked me because he had seen me somewhere else and knew my style, so you couldn't do anything too outrageous.

'The show would open on a Monday, with Band Call in the morning – acts first, then Production scenes. Then you would iron your own costumes and hope that the costumes with which you were supplied for the scenas, fitted. If not you had to get those fixed, and more often than not fix them yourself. There would then be two shows that first Monday night. The next day you would have off to recover, then Wednesday, Thursday, Friday you would rehearse for the next week's show. Saturday was usually off. Rehearsals would normally be from 10.30 am until lunchtime, and then have the afternoon off, before coming back for the two evening shows. It really was very hard work, continuing like that week in week out, for a long summer season, yet we all seemed to thrive on it. When Scottish theatre was in its heyday, there were so many theatres, the artistes didn't need to go out of Scotland, there was enough work. You could go round and round the circuit.

'People may have thought the theatre life was one big party, but in fact you never had time to speak to each other because you were tearing up and downstairs all the time doing quick changes.

'The summer season at Largs was great, and it was really quite straightforward. Two shows a night, and it was regarded as one of the special shows on the Clyde. It was very nice. Leven was quite different, and amazing when I look back on it, because we changed the programme twice a week. Changing the show once a week is hard work, but twice a week is absolutely horrific. The amount of material one had to have ready, by way of songs and dresses was tremendous. Then we heard about a midnight matinee which I thought was a joke at first, but it was true. People came in droves, buses were put on to bring them in. It was for the miners, who were on the back shift, and the atmosphere was electric. They were really wonderful. To begin with we had all thought, how dreadful to have to do a midnight matinee but it was so rewarding because of this wonderful reception.'

JOHNNY BEATTIE

'When I started out in the business there were summer shows on every street corner. The Clyde coast for a start, there was a summer show at the Pavilion Gourock, Barrfield Pavilion, Largs, Rothesay, Dunoon, Millport, Saltcoats, Girvan, Ayr. It was amazing all those summer shows. I suppose the point is there were all these places for the young people to learn their trade. Where do they go now? That is the big problem really.

'My first summer season as a comic was at North Berwick in 1955 in The Harbour Pavilion, and we were called The Pierrots. And we changed the show twice a week, two shows a night, and we played for thirteen weeks. They wouldn't let us repeat so we did twenty seven programmes. I remember saying to the comic Wally Butler one night "What are we doing?" He said "We'll just go on and talk to each other". It's easier for singers to change, obviously, they just choose songs. But to do comedy! That was hard going. You would literally put one show on on a Monday night, and went away back home, and you would think what will I tell the company in the morning, to rehearse? My wife used to say 'put that light out' but then she would wake up in the middle of the night and I would actually be sitting there, asleep with the pen on the page, about four in the morning. You'd have been rehearsing all day, done two shows, programme on, next morning thinking what the hell are we going to do, and that night you're trying to figure it out. You wonder how you survived it! That was my first year as principal comic.

'I did five consecutive summer seasons, 1960 to 1964, at the Ayr Gaiety. Eric Popplewell was the man who ran the theatre and their slogan was "The Gaiety theatre, the family theatre, run by a family, for the family". He wouldn't let me say Damn or Hell. If I'd said Bloody, he would have dropped the curtain on me. I was doing a series for BBC Radio, and they wouldn't let me do gags about drink in the late fifties. I couldn't do gags about pubs. I said to the producer "Are you denying the existence of pubs? Have you walked along Parliamentary Road, there are more pubs than houses". "Oh yes, I'm sorry, but they don't want any mention of that." I am talking about almost thirty years ago, but it gives you an idea of how dramatically it has changed.

'Bob Hope had a lovely gag once, some years ago on television, he was talking about the films they were doing in those days. He says, "Gee", he says, "they do things on the screen my wife and I won't do in the bedroom. Unbelieveable".

'I have now actually done 14 summer seasons at the Gaiety. I have done more summer seasons at the Gaiety than any comic in its history, and am delighted to be in the Diamond Jubilee *Gaiety Whirl*. I love the Gaiety. It has such an intimate atmosphere, it's like having your own wee model theatre. It really is, it's wonderful. By and large they have tried to keep going that summer family show tradition.'

BERNARD COTTON

Manager of Ayr Gaiety since 1973.

'In 1902 the Ayr Gaiety was built in Carrick Lane. On the site, there had been a public house with a garden and in that garden there was a tent. Entertainment provided in that tent was doing so well that they decided to build a permanent structure and the pub and garden was demolished.

'It was very much a second-rate theatre. There was a mixture of live shows and then cinema when that was popular. By the twenties it wasn't doing so well and there were periods of closure. In 1928, Ben Popplewell decided to purchase the theatre. Ben Popplewell was a Yorkshireman who had been coming up in the summer seasons working in the Ayr Pavilion, and he obviously saw some potential in this theatre. In 1930 he started a new policy of bringing in top stars, English and Scottish entertainers, like Florrie Forde, Will Fyffe and others. That saw an upsurge and he suddenly realised, as I still see today, that the more you speculate, the more you accumulate. He found success there in shows of a better standard, and these *Gaiety Whirls* soon became very famous summer shows. They ran from May to October, so they must have had much better summers in those days to merit such a long season. Ben was a marvellous man from what I have heard, who seemed to design the *Gaiety Whirls* around some of the bigger popular shows which were going the rounds at the time. He must have kept abreast of what was being produced in London and in fact went to New York occasionally. These shows had large casts, and were quite spectacular with marvellous scenery and costumes. He even brought the Tiller Girls in, twelve Tiller Girls were brought up for the show. Into the thirties and during the war business was good. The very habit of theatre-going had improved and he went from success to success.

'Tragically there was a fire in 1955, yet it was the insurance policy which paid for the refurbishment of the theatre, with new seating, new carpets, new flying tower, lighting rig, which allowed them to continue the theatre for the next twenty years.

'So the Popplewell family continued until the seventies, when things were not so good financially. In 1973 they finally decided to close the theatre, and it was sold to Tesco for a car park space. But there was quite an outcry from the people who used the theatre: the locals, the amateurs, and the artistes, the Johnny Beatties, the Andy Stewarts, and literally they started a campaign to save the Gaiety. This was successful not so much by the fact that by linking hands no bulldozer would touch the Gaiety, but it was rather astutely done by a lawyer who went off to Edinburgh and saw some gentlemen there whom he persuaded to come to Ayr with a view of putting some sort of preservation order on it. The architectural gentlemen came and were rather intrigued by the interior plasterwork and they agreed that it would be a great shame to destroy all this and promptly slapped a Class 3 preservation order on it. So they couldn't pull it down. The town council, reluctantly, bought the theatre back from Tesco, and it was from 1973 that it became a civic theatre and I arrived to take over as manager just two weeks later. The council has continued to run it and subsidise ticket prices, while the theatre is fortunate in that it is commercially successful.

'The Summer season today is not quite as popular as the old days, running from May to October, but we still manage thirteen, or fourteen weeks. In June we are expected to have light entertainment on, a summer revue, and we are still expected to have some show on through September. This year, 1990, the Diamond Jubilee of the *Gaiety Whirl*, we will have the well tried format of a traditional revue with Johnny Beattie, the Alexander Brothers, the dancers and the musicians. We will probably have a company of about sixteen whereas Popplewell had twice that number. He didn't have Equity minimums in those days!'

While the holidaymakers stayed in hotels, B & Bs or rented accommodation, the company of entertainers, away from home for three months or more, could only afford digs. But the best theatrical digs would specifically cater for their erratic hours.

MRS GREEN (GREENIE)

Cleaner and theatrical landlady for the Beach Pavilion and later the Tivoli Theatre, Aberdeen.

'I would rise at about half-past three and go and do the cleaning at the Pavilion. Then come home and make breakfast for my children and send them off to school. The artistes didn't have much of a breakfast and they didn't take a big lunch but they loved a late supper. When the show was finished, many hotels wouldn't give them a late meal so this was one of the attractions of theatrical digs that I would make a hot meal. Some landladies wouldn't have a meal waiting. I always gave them a cooked meal for them coming home. I would be working and clearing up until about two in the morning, and then I had to get up at half-past three again. I did that for seven years, but it hasn't hurt me. I am now ninety-two.

'I charged about £3 a week for full board, in the thirties and forties. Food was cheaper then, stable prices. They were only being paid between five and ten pounds, depending on the performer, and out of that they had to keep themselves and pay for digs. I didn't make a huge profit, just a turnover. I was thrifty and cooked well. It was half-past eleven when they came home. I made soup then maybe a beef steak pie, a roast, or battered fish and chips. I was a great batterer and it was all good home cooking. They enjoyed their meal at night. Sometimes one or two of their friends from the company would come back to see if they could have a meal. They would say they were going up to see Greenie, I was never Mrs Green, always Greenie. "Let's go up to Greenie's for a meal".

'I knew that Robert Wilson loved tripe and one day I had cooked tripe for his evening meal. This particular night he phoned to say he would be late back. I said just go into the kitchen and help yourself. Well, he ate the whole potful of tripe; three pounds. This turned into quite a joke and the next night he mentioned the story of the tripe on stage. I was quite often spoken about by the artistes. When I was in watching the show, the comics or singers would often make a point of saying something about ''Greenie''. It was all very affectionate.'

ANNE FIELDS

'The best digs were when I stayed with Greenie in Aberdeen. From the age of sixteen or so, she was a real mother to me. It was a home from home. I was just a young teenager and first of all I was in digs where I wasn't happy. It was another girl, Greta Hagen who was staying with Greenie, took me there one night for tea. Greenie was sorry for me and said that I must stay with her. She was amazing in the way that she would always give you your favourite food and do so much to make you feel at home. If you said you liked beetroot, then you got it for breakfast, lunch and dinner. I once said I enjoyed Kit-Kats and found I was being offered them for breakfast. She would be up at 5 am in the morning to go down to the fish market. Food was still being rationed in the early fifties and she was determined that her guests would have the best available meat and the freshest fish. When we arrived back after the evening show at 11 pm, there would be our hot dinner ready waiting.

'She would be so concerned about me, asking how I was, where I was going, what I was doing. If we went on a trip with the company, she would always hint that she wanted to come too. She became so fond of her theatrical guests. Her sons, Stanley and Billy were like brothers to me. I virtually lived with the family from the age of sixteen to twenty because I would do summer shows, and pantomimes at the Tivoli, Aberdeen.

'I was once in a show for twenty-six weeks at the Ayr Gaiety. It started in May and went on to November. Then I had to get permission from Mr Popplewell to leave the show because I was due to join Jimmy Logan to begin rehearsing the pantomime!'

And after perhaps a three month pantomime season it would be back to Aberdeen or Arbroath, Troon or Ayr, for another strenuous but enjoyable season, year in, year out, as the show went on:

From 14th July, 1934
Rothesay Entertainers: Charlie Kemble, Jack Anthony, Bond Rowell, Peggy Desmond and Dave Bruce.

Sunday Mail, 22nd July, 1934
Dunoon Pavilion: *Whirl of Laughter* with Tommy Lorne
Prestwick Beach Pavilion: Tommy Hope, Scotland's newest find.

Daily Record, 19th July 1935
Barrfields Pavilion, Largs: Harry Kemp's *Jubilee*, 6.45 and 8.50 with Bert Bendon leading the laughs, Betty Jumel, the bundle of fun, Bond Rowell puts over the song hits, and Jack Radcliffe, light comedy.

Sunday Mail, 20th May, 1940
Cosy Corner, Dunoon: From June 24th, Summer show with Bert Denver and Mary Lee.

Sunday Mail, 2nd July 1956
Gaiety, Ayr: *Gaiety Whirl* with Jack Milroy, and Cormack and Sharp.

Daily Record, 18th June 1962
Barrfields Pavilion, Largs; G. B. Bowie's Summer Show with Billy Rusk.

Gaiety, Ayr: 33rd *Gaiety Whirl* with Johnny Beattie, Anne Fields.

5th July to 29th September, 1990
Gaiety, Ayr: The Diamond Jubilee Production of the *Gaiety Whirl*, starring Johnny Beattie, Anne Fields and the Alexander Brothers.

RUBY TURBERVILLE

Dancer, and later journalist and broadcaster. Woman's Editor, *Aberdeen Evening Express*.

'People talk about the glamour of show business. But they forget about the grotty digs which you often had to put up with, and living out of a suitcase, mending fishnet tights, and sewing ballet shoes, and washing your costumes over the weekend. The glamour was on the stage when the lights came up; the rest of it was hard grind. But we did seem to thrive on it.'

GRACE MACKAY REAY

Dancer, choreographer. Daughter of dance act, Pagan and Ross.

'I joined my mother in a double act when my father was ill after the war. We appeared as a sister act, Babs Ross and Grace. We did a lot of touring where I enjoyed the experience of choreography and performing. Sometimes you played one night stands, like a concert party, in a church hall, which was a soup kitchen during the day, and the dressing rooms might be the two kitchens, the men in one and the women in the other.

'When you moved up a bit it was either weekly variety or a season of about two or three months. In between you used to fill in with odd weeks so that you could easily work fifty-two weeks in the year. If you played Rothesay for three months in the summer, then you might go on to Largs for two weeks, and then Gourock. Other shows might go out on the road when they would be weekly in each place. When you were moving about, the costumes all had to be folded carefully and put in baskets and if you were leaving them for a time, you would put hot water bottles in amongst the clothes in case they got damp in cold weather. We also took tap mats with us because when you arrived in a new theatre, the stage might be all lumps with knots of wood. The tap mat was like a wooden corregated mat, but rolled up and was easily transportable. Like a slatted trellis, with wire between, it allowed movement rather like a spring base to give bounce. There was the odd theatre with a tap mat fitted into the stage – I think Paisley had one – but you always took one with you when touring in case you needed it.'

MAIDIE MURRAY

'Millport was a famous Summer season. I played Millport on my own in 1946, the year I got married. You would be there for perhaps twelve weeks from the end of May to August, changing the show twice weekly. Chic used to row over from Largs in a boat to see me. I never played with Chic at Millport but together we were in G. B. Bowie's show, the *Rothesay Entertainers*. Years later we went for a season to Largs and took the children with us, because Douglas was three and Annabel was only one. My mother came with us to look after the children.

'We played the Beach Pavilion, Carnoustie; Barrfields Pavilion, Largs; The Victory Theatre, Paisley; the Electric in Falkirk. In Dundee it was the Palace, and the Adam Smith Hall, Kirkcaldy. We were booked by Galts, the famous agency: William R. Galt, at 13 Sauchiehall Street with his assistant Nellie Sutherland. Otherwise, if you were out of work you would hang about Lauder's corner. Near the Pavilion theatre there was a pub called Lauder's, hence Lauder's Corner. Right opposite there was Green's Playhouse and we used to go up there for coffee while we waited to find work. There used to be lots of smaller variety theatre agents who booked the Church Halls on a Sunday. There was a man called Wee Fergie, who booked St Francis on a Sunday. That was known as a Three Half-Crown job. He used to place three fingers on his left chest meaning he would pay three half-crowns.

'For regular work you would go up to Galts to see if he had anything for you. Nelly Sutherland would open this wee window and she spoke in a nasal voice: ''Ah've got nuffin for you the day. Nuffin for you the day''. If you were in luck it was maybe the Gaiety, Leith, the Palladium, Edinburgh, or the Greenock Empire. These were for either one week variety bookings or for a revue perhaps running for six weeks, where you would change the show every Monday.

'Work was all touring and living out of a suitcase and when you didn't have a car, you had to take the train. Sunday meant travelling and looking for digs. We used to keep a notebook listing all the recommended digs, although when you got there they would either be full or second rate. You would be in the theatre all day Monday rehearsing and then get the ironing done; that was important. Because of fire restrictions you weren't supposed to iron in the dressing rooms but I used to travel with an iron which you could screw into a light socket.

'Mondays were a shambles because you had your band call to do, ensuring that you had all the band parts – you were responsible for your own props, gags and your own music. The producer was responsible for the ensembles and the comedians for the sketches. So band parts, make-up and you had to be there on time. You couldn't be late, the curtain goes up whether you are there or not. "Twice Nightly, Twice Brightly" as they used to say at the Ayr Gaiety. The Ayr Gaiety was a wee step up from the Metropole, and the Glasgow Queen's. The Victory, Paisley, that was something else! Your clothes used to get damp from the river because the dressing rooms were downstairs there. The Opera House, Dunfermline, that was another theatre Galt booked. You would come home for the weekend and travel over there for the Monday morning, buying a hot pie at the bakers across the way from the theatre, to keep you going through the long day's rehearsals. I was pregnant with Annabel at the time and I remember sitting in the dressing room making shirts for a Hillbilly act. It was a yellow shirt with black pockets for Chic.'

Despite the constant weekly touring, few people in the theatre business would have been able to afford to buy a car in order to travel comfortably and conveniently from Edinburgh to Dundee, or Dunfermline to Ayr for the next booking.

Motorworks in Edinburgh announced in the *Scotsman* of December 1938 the arrival of new 1939 cars, such as a Sunbeam Talbot at £485, or a Vauxhall Saloon, at £198. The *Evening News* of 20th February 1951 advertises a reconditioned, secondhand 1940 Morris 8 at £325. From the same paper, under situations vacant, 'Salesman required at £350 per annum guaranteed on salary and commission basis', and 'Clerical Assistant with shorthand and typing: £100'. For the majority of people, working in or out of the theatre business, during the forties and fifties, and earning a moderate weekly wage of less, often much less, than five pounds a week, a car was out of the question.

MAY MOXON

'The summer shows were exceptionally good fun. G. B. Bowie – what a nice man, a great man he was. There was a wonderful atmosphere in those small companies of his coastal resort shows. That is where I always put my young girls. I mean there would be two experienced and two partly-experienced dancers. Then I knew by the end of the season if they were going to be any good and then they would become my regulars.

'There was William Galt, the theatrical agent, but no one ever actually saw him. Nelly Sutherland was his assistant and she was quite fierce. She would be the one who would interview you. If you went in to see if there was any work she would say, ''Come up tomorrow''. And you would go up again and sit in the waiting room and see if there was any work. ''No, but I want you to come on Wednesday''. After a few weeks of this coming and going I got quite friendly with her and I said to her, ''Nelly, why do you tell people to come back on a certain day when you haven't got anything for them?'' – And her answer was, ''Something might turn up, you never know''. Which was a lovely philosophy. That was Nelly Sutherland.'

JIM FRIEL

'Nelly Sutherland was a legendary figure who ruled the roost in the booking agency for several theatres. One pole-vaulting act almost pleaded for a week's work somewhere, anywhere. After enquiring about the various Roxy's, and Palaces and Pavilions, he said to Nelly, ''What about Paisley?''. ''Nothing at all'', said Nelly. As he was going away, she opened the half window and shouted through loose false teeth, ''I've telt ye fore, yer pole's too big for the stage at Paisley''.'

ALHAMBRA

Howard and Wyndham's

"half-past eight"

PROGRAMME

6d
PLEASE
THAT T
SEAL
UNBRO

Chapter 3

HALF-PAST EIGHT

Life begins at Half-Past Eight,
In Good Old Glasgow city,
Now's the time for fun,
With jest and song we'll pass time along.
Tell your friends, how good we are,
Your sisters too, and dear old Ma,
Forget your sins, for life begins,
At Half-Past Eight.

STEWART CRUIKSHANK PRESENTS
HOWARD AND WYNDHAM'S
HALF-PAST EIGHT

A bigger and brighter than ever, Song, Dance and Laughter show.

Due to the increasing popularity and demand for summer shows in the seaside resorts, during the thirties and forties, with more beach pavilions and theatres opening up each season around the Scottish coastline, it was common practice that the city theatres closed for up to two months between June and August. In 1933, Howard and Wyndham's managing director, Stewart Cruikshank, decided it would be worth experimenting with a summer season in Glasgow along the lines of the seaside entertainment. It would be once nightly at half-past eight; thus a shorter show at a lower ticket price. The first performance opened on June 5th, 1933, described as "an after-dinner liqueur of song, mirth, and melody, designed for summertime at summertime prices". The *Glasgow Herald* the following morning reported that "it is simply an experiment in switching over to music hall entertainment for a season. In its manner it is quite an attractive and often amusing entertainment and the audience last night enjoyed it, and notwithstanding the fine weather out of doors, was one of considerable popularity. The production might well go on for a fairly long period''.

The Lancashire comic Jack Edge headed the *Half-Past Eight* cast and the show continued for fourteen weeks. The following year Billy Caryll and Hilda Mundy led the *Half-Past Eight* team for eleven weeks at the King's, Glasgow, while Jack Edge moved to Edinburgh in 1935 to try out the summer show experiment there. After unenthusiastic reviews and poor box office the show closed within six weeks. While Glasgow continued the *Half-Past Eight* habit in 1935 and 1936, the Edinburgh King's remained dark, until the arrival of Charles Ross and his daughter Ilona who were invited to Scotland to produce the pantomimes for Howard and Wyndham.

ILONA ROSS

Dancer, ballet mistress, and co-producer of the *Half-Past Eight* shows with her father, Charles Ross, for twenty years from 1937.

'My father was appalled at the thought of closing the Edinburgh King's in the summer. What a waste of theatre space it seemed to be. Stewart Cruikshank said that they had tried it once but that he wasn't interested. My father kept on at him again and again and eventually, I think in sheer exasperation, he said, "Alright, you have made a success with the pantomime, I will give you four weeks. Four weeks and no more and then the notice goes up". That meant he would close the show.

'The first problem was to find a good comic. There wasn't one really suitable. My father went everywhere in Scotland to every theatre and show imaginable, and he finally went to a small theatre in Paisley and there he saw a young comic called Dave Willis. He went back to Mr Cruikshank and said that he had found him a star for the show. And so we began the show. In the first week, if we had a handful of people in we were lucky. In the second week we had two or three handfuls. We changed the show every week, except for the opening and the finale, because they were lavish numbers. By the end of third week the notice for the end of the run was put up. Mr Cruikshank came to my father and said that he was very sorry, but I told you so. But then the miracle happened. The people began coming in, and they started queuing for advance booking. It was unbelievable; by the Thursday we were almost sold out, Friday was a Full House, Saturday two shows, standing room only and we were booked right into the next two or three weeks. Word of mouth had gone round and the notice announcing end of the run was taken down again. We had a very good run, into September, so it was about three months. So that's how our *Half-Past Eight* shows all began.

'Dave Willis was certainly the funniest man I've seen; no one has made me laugh so much. He was such a grotesque little soul with his arms too long and his legs too short, there has never been anyone quite like Dave Willis. He really was quite brilliant, with a sense of irresistible fun that you couldn't help laughing at, he really was a natural.'

As leader articles in the newspaper commented during the summer of 1937 on the impending grim political situation in Europe, proclaiming, 'There shall be no war', and the national gossip continued about the Duke of Windsor's abdication and marriage to Mrs Wallis Simpson, people turned for light relief, to summer entertainment at the King's.

From 31st May, 1937,
King's Theatre, Edinburgh
Half-Past Eight: Dave Willis in the Summer Time show. An after dinner light revue fare of song, dance and laughter, with Cliff Harley, Florence Hunter and the Charles Ross Girls. 3/6d; 3/–; 2/6d; 1/6d; 1/3d; Gallery 6d.

Evening News, 15th June 1937:
'Any show featuring Mr. Dave Willis is certain to succeed in Edinburgh and when the popular little comedian surrounds himself with a talented company, this summer show is not to be missed. It is practically a continuous performance on his part and his new burlesques are among the best ever done, and he has a splendid foil in Mr Cliff Harley, who can also be serious as Darnley in a Mary Queen of Scots episode. Miss Florence Hunter is a sweet singer. Dancing has a prominent part in the show and swift-footed tap dancers, Miss Ilona Ross, Ballet Mistress and the Charles Ross Dancers make the most of their opportunities.'

Dave Willis starred in the Edinburgh show for five years while its popularity continued to grow, with seasons running for twenty-eight weeks in 1939, twenty-two weeks in 1940 and again twenty-eight weeks in 1941. When Dave Willis moved to the Glasgow edition, Harry Gordon took over for three years, and subsequent comedians were Stanley Baxter, Rikki Fulton, and Jimmy Logan.

ILONA ROSS

'A typical programme began with the opening which was usually a lavish affair, as an introduction to the cast, to the chorus, to the show, and it usually lasted about six minutes. After that it was usually quickies, fast quick-fire, comic gags, with black-outs between the scenes. Then generally a bright number, a popular topical song, with a couple of tap dancers. After that, a comedy sketch. Quite often we had a serious interlude such as the Mary Queen of Scots sketch, which my father wrote, during which the audience would be in tears. After that, perhaps an excerpt from opera. Then another comedy sketch followed by the first half finale, which quite often was a selection of musical numbers. One of my favourites was when 'Singing in the Rain' was popular. We had a set of big staircases, and we used a medley of songs from the show, running into one another, with different artistes, on different staircases, and the dancers moved right round the stage, with wonderful lights going on and off. The whole scene finished with Harry Gordon, who came on carrying an umbrella, singing 'Singing in the Rain', coming down the central staircase.

'Then we had another one celebrating Gershwin, in which we had Jimmy Logan at the piano, playing 'Rhapsody in Blue'. He had to practice like mad for that finale, but it was quite spectacular. Jimmy Logan could play the piano well and he was an excellent dancer.

'The second act was more or less the same, although it took me three years to talk Mr Cruikshank into letting me put on a scene from a classical ballet and he was pleased when he saw it. But it had been a struggle, and he kept saying, people don't want to see ballet, this is a Revue. But they did, and after that it was a must. Jack Spurgeon and June Tucker were my principal dancers for years.

'We rehearsed for two weeks before we opened and then during the run every morning and afternoon, opening the new show on Friday night. The bulk of the audience were regulars, and they would book for the season, knowing they would see a new show every week.

'The first show in 1937 was quite wonderful. We were really quite certain that we had failed after three weeks, and the notice of end of season had gone up. Yet those people who had come must have told their friends to go and see the Dave Willis show and gradually it accelerated, and it ran for months. It is quite a story now that I look back on those days.'

BERYL REID

Comedienne and actress. Appeared in the *Half-Past Eight* shows, of 1946 and 1947.

'I owe a great deal to Dave Willis. I did 427 sketches with him and never had anything written down. At that time I didn't drink at all but had to go to the boozer to find him to rehearse — something he didn't want to do. We did five sketches every week. I would ask him what are we doing next week? "You just come in and say such and such, and I'll reply and just keep it going, do yer patter and the punch line will find its way in". It was mostly ad libbing, making it up as we went along, and it stood me in good stead in my future career.

'Dave would say, "Don't bother putting the costume on at the dress rehearsal, then we can have a good laugh on the night!". It was a hard school indeed. On a Friday we got paid and went to the Aperitif, which was regarded as a very grand cocktail bar and restaurant in Edinburgh at the time. I would have a Pimms which cost half-a-crown. We worked hard but we played hard. We were young and had parties many an evening, banging the dustbin lids late at night so that we must have caused a bit of a stir. One of the company, Hope Jackman, got a little tipsy one night and decided to slide down the bannisters believing there was a knob at the bottom. There wasn't and she fell off the end. The next day the stage doorman said to her, "Hello Hopey, are you dopey?" They really were delightful, fabulous days. I lived in Tarvit Street, just behind the theatre and was called The Belle of Tarvit Street. It was all a great adventure. Dave Willis never made it in England which was a shame. He had no ambition and he didn't want to learn new things. He was a master of the craft and taught me everything. Dave had a little touch of the genius about him, like Max Wall.'

Evening News, 4th June 1946
King's Theatre, Edinburgh: *Half Past Eight*
'To the average theatregoer, one of the most attractive features of a resident show is that one knows in advance what type of entertainment to expect. The basic mixture is of light-hearted fun and the large audience would indicate a public who love it. Dave Willis is excellently supported by Beryl Reid and Jimmy Plant.'

'In 1947 I came back to the Half-Past Eight show and this time it was with Harry Gordon, which was a totally different kettle of fish. He was script bound and set me back really. I was used to free speaking with Dave and working in such a different way was destructive to my training. I didn't understand Harry Gordon's sense of humour. He was a good technician but it was not a style of comedy for me.

'I would love to work in Scotland again. I spent so much time there in my young days. I'd love to do a drama, or a television play. It would be wonderful.'

BEN WARRIS

Comedian and half of the double act, Jewel and Warris, 1934–70.

'For the *Half-Past Eight* shows with a new programme every week we had to dig into our collections of sketches to provide new scripts for every new show. We played the *Half-Past Eight* show in Glasgow in 1941, and it ran for twenty-seven weeks, so we couldn't have been too bad. We had great fun there and in fact I met a young lady and if circumstances had been different I would have married her. But at that time, my job was touring theatres and she lived in Glasgow. Glasgow was a long way to travel from London and the south and it just couldn't have worked out.

'When we first worked in the *Half-Past Eight* show we did get a hostile response at the King's in Glasgow. The audiences were unsure of English comedians and were used to the likes of all the great Scots comics: Tommy Morgan, Will Fyffe, Jack Anthony, Jack Radcliffe and Harry Gordon. It was not a kindly reception at first. But we soon warmed to them. Mr Cruikshank, the boss of Howard and Wyndham, was wonderful to us. We had a five year contract with him for Pantomime and summer shows.

'We didn't alter our style of comedy at all coming to Scotland. They still had their own Scottish comics who could do their thing, and we were just as popular doing our double act. Timber was a popular sketch and I remember when that was written – all our own work too. It was Jimmy Jewel's initial idea and he got it at half-past three in the morning when we were in Melbourne, Australia on tour in 1936. He thought of this episode involving a net of timber falling all over the stage and we worked on that sketch out there and brought it back to perform from 1937 onwards.

'I remember going to the Pavilion to see Tommy Morgan. The gags were all about stairheids, and jaikits, and I couldn't really understand a word he was saying. Humour through dialect is of course very local, but fortunately we had a very general style of quick-fire gags and sketches which worked everywhere.'

Evening News, 9th May 1942

'Last evening a crowded audience, at the King's Theatre, Edinburgh, gave Jewel and Warris a wonderful reception. There is never a dull moment from the time they rush through the auditorium announcing their ''unexpected'' arrival, and in scenes such as ''Timber'' and ''Tripe'', they are at their best. They have a style of humour all their own. They are the highlight of a really first class entertainment. Betty Jumel adds to the hilarity; The Charles Ross girls dance well in chorus specialities and the orchestra under Ellis Midgeley provides bright and up-to-date music.'

The *Half-Past Eight* habit had truly caught on and the title remained the same despite an earlier start during the war years so that people could get home safely due to buses and the blackout.

After the war the show often kept to an eight o'clock start, sometimes a seven-thirty, and later a five-past eight curtain up. This confusing oddity brought about an amusing incident at the Braemar Highland Games one year when the *Half-Past Eight* company were playing Aberdeen during the normal departure from Edinburgh during the Festival in August. At the Royal games, Harry Gordon was introduced to King George and Queen Elizabeth. "Oh, Mr Gordon, now you are with the show are you not that is called *Half-Past Eight* and starts at Five-Past?" Harry could only reply with a smile, "Yes, your Majesty". As Ilona Ross recalls, "It was a joke with us for a long time. It was years before anyone thought of changing the title, because it was so well known as *Half-Past Eight*. The leaflet and the poster was of a clock, and the hands were that of a dancer pointing to half-past eight which was our logo."

The logo did change so that the dancer's long stockinged legs, bursting through the paper clock, pointed to five-past eight. As the Glasgow *Evening News* pointed out on May 27th, 1955,

'The Biggest and Best Howard and Wyndham summer show Glasgow has had in the long series. That is the inevitable verdict on *Five-Past Eight* which opened last night (note the change of time). Expert direction by Michael Miles, and very lovely dressing. Jack Radcliffe is joined this year by Jimmy Logan, an experiment so tremendously successful in a comedy sense. The highlights? Jimmy Logan as Churchill, interviewed within a huge TV cabinet. This is a triumph; a large company of many talents. *Five-Past Eight* could run not only through the summer but practically indefinitely'.

The show in fact ran until October.

STANLEY BAXTER

Comedian. Performed in *Half-Past Eight* shows from 1952 until 1958.

'For the 1958 show I dreamt up the idea of Francie and Josie for Rikki Fulton and myself. We got a man called Stan Mars to write it for us. He christened the boys and wrote all the stage scripts. I had to persuade Rikki first of all to spend the money on the Josie teddy-boy suit. He said, "Supposing this doesn't work, does it mean we will be left with suits on our hands?'' Well it was the best investment Rikki made in his life because after we had done that season, I left to come to London and Rikki continued with Jack Milroy in the Francie and Josie sketch both on stage and on television. It was then that it became nationally famous.'

From the Programme of *Five-Past Eight*, 16th June–12th July, 1958.

Interval
8. A Traveller Returns
9. FRANCIE AND JOSIE:

An American teenager	Ethel Scott
Mon	Marjorie Thomson
Francie	Stanley Baxter
Josie	Rikki Fulton
Nurse	Fay Lenore
Patients	Peter Bentley and Irene Claire
D. Krepit	Stan Mars
Doctor	Clem Ashby

RIKKI FULTON

Comedian and actor.

'I worked for the Gateway Repertory Theatre in pantomime, Rep. Romps as they were called. I was given the opportunity to write material and even co-direct, something which I had never done. Hamish Turner was an agent whom I met there and he introduced me to the Howard and Wyndham company. In 1955 I joined the company and began a ten year career with them, in pantomime and the *Five-Past Eight* shows.

'What may be remembered most prominently from my time with the show was the creation of Francie and Josie. Although the sketch was first performed in 1958, that as far as I am concerned was not the beginning of its history. It started in 1960 at the King's, Edinburgh, in the *Five-Past Eight* show. Jack Milroy and I brought the sketch together with scripts which had been written before and new material.

'The sketch was created for a reason. The format of the *Five-Past Eight* shows had a definite problem of how to get the audience back in for the second half promptly after the interval. It was decided to open the second half, after the production number, with the stars – namely the two comedians heading the bill and that is how Francie and Josie was born.

'I couldn't have predicted it would be so popular or that it would end up on television which gave it a household name. TV was strong in those days, the early sixties, and theatre was struggling. We didn't initially forsee that it would go on television, that was an accident too. We also didn't predict how popular it would be in the theatre. Jack and I simply billed this new sketch as Francie and Josie and it went on as second item in the second half. It was greeted ecstatically both in Edinburgh and Glasgow.

'It was not following any tradition. The only factor about it was that the characters of Francie and Josie were very recognisable. At that time people were familiar with the daily visit to the Labour Exchange or as I should say, the Broo. It was a very common environment to be associated with. In the same way, work-shy boys, young lads on the fiddle, that type of character, was undeniably recognisable. Francie and Josie were ethnic, they were unmistakably Glaswegian and the audiences simply took them to their hearts. They were truly Glaswegian boys of the time. However, Edinburgh audiences took to them for a very different reason. They found them extremely amusing because they could laugh at two Glaswegian layabouts.

'Francie and Josie was a very different kind of double act. It was a double act but it was composed of two individual comedians. It wasn't a comedian and a stooge, but two comedians in their own right.

'What was never foreseen was that in putting Jack Milroy and me together was the manner in which our own individual personas totally merged. It was like two carefully placed cog wheels. We are totally different comedians on stage, two very different men off stage. We enjoy contrasting lifestyles, have differing outlooks and philosophies. However, in that sketch, there is a oneness, our brains work together, with a telepathic understanding. The best material for Francie and Josie has always been created on stage. It is simply full of ad libbing. I do believe that some very clever stuff has emerged through Francie and Josie, and I do not mind being immodest about what has been created. But it could not have come about without the audience.

'Francie and Josie are classic characters. If you recall the famous double acts, Laurel and Hardy, Abbot and Costello, they were all classic partnerships. One was a know-all, the man who believed he knew everything. His friend believed the other knew everything and looked up to him and was a gullible soul. Francie and Josie have turned out to be a classic partnership although we did not set out to write it as such.

'I love having an ensemble to work with. It is a warmer, friendlier atmosphere working together. I feel nothing can go wrong if there are others in the revue, or a pantomime, as we rely on each other. It is a wonderful feeling when the show goes well and you are all enjoying the company spirit. I feel that is completely lost if you are working on your own. I love working with others. In the *Half-Past Eight* shows Aileen Vernon was the most efficient stage manager and the speed of her mind when she had to make quick decisions was unbelievable. The responsibility and the work she had to do for those shows was incredible. The work we all had to do was unbelievable where we opened the new show every Friday night. On Saturday you were at the piano again, setting keys and rehearsing for the next week. You had no time for nerves, and any stage fright was lost after two or three seasons with Howard and Wyndham. You simply had to get on with the show.'

The unsung heroes of the backstage staff were simply names in the programme to the audience and often went unrecognised. Producers who followed Charles Ross included Heath Joyce, Michael Mills and from 1957, Dick Hurran, who it is said, slowly styled and indeed revolutionised the *Five-Past Eight* show. They soon became spectacular revues featuring the leading comics, singers, and dancers, as well as international cabaret stars, and top class variety acts, with the aim that Scotland should produce a light entertainment show of a standard and setting equal to the London Palladium or the Paris Lido.

AILEEN VERNON

Stage Manager for Howard and Wyndham productions, 1955–1966

'I was involved preparing the *Five-Past Eight* shows from about March but we would only be at the Alhambra Theatre about three weeks beforehand for rehearsals. Even by that time we would be working without any of the star artistes. Eve Boswell knew what she would be going to sing. The comedian, Stanley Baxter, Rikki Fulton or Jimmy Logan, whoever it was, would know what he would be doing in sketches. So ten to one until you got well into rehearsals you didn't really know what was in the show. Only the big production numbers, we rehearsed those until you were sick. The producer, Dick Hurran, was a great man for stage effects. The more mechanical and effective the more he liked it. He would create a Las Vegas set, the Starlight Room, for all the international stars. It was quite something, we had never seen anything like it.

'The set was like a jigsaw puzzle and there were carpenters in here, scenic painters there, and electricians rushing around and God knows who else, and then finally you suddenly saw it finished and lit in all its glory. I remember seeing the Starlight Room from the back of the stalls and just couldn't believe it. The Alhambra was never the same again. We used to have mechanical staircases, everything moved, it was so very very busy. It was thrilling for all that. It hyped you up, and my goodness, it got the adrenalin going. It took a very long time for some of these artistes to wind down at the end of the show, and the orchestra too.

'We had Geraldo's Orchestra although Geraldo himself only appeared on the opening night. There were lavish dancing and musical numbers, and all kinds of speciality acts such as a dog act called Excess Baggage, which was marvellous. Great big shaggy sheep dogs right down to a tiny poodle. The act was run by two ladies, a mother and her daughter and they had six of these dogs. You might wonder how they toured the world, without going into quarantine. They were exercised on the roof of the theatre and they did not touch the streets of Glasgow, that is how they managed it: they had special dispensation and they were allowed to do it. As with all good animal acts, you'll find they are very well cared for, because it is the owner's livelihood. We would also have jugglers, and unicyclists and Dick Hurran would often build an entire circus ring and bring in about five circus acts.

'One of the most spectacular sets that Hurran designed for the show was his swimming pool. It was a real pool with a diving board, and a spring board, half the length of an ordinary swimming pool. It was slightly tilted towards the audience, and there were mirrors up the sides, so that they could see what was happening underneath the water. There were portholes around the side through which they shone lights and illuminated the whole thing.

'We did the Royal Variety show in front of the Queen and the Queen Mother in 1963. It was to be at the Alhambra and Dick Hurran decided to show off this swimming pool. Irene Segala, who designed all the costumes for our shows, decided that the boys' swimming trunks had to be more glitzy and glamorous for the occasion. These were to be arriving for the opening night but they were not to be worn beforehand. So the night of the Royal Performance came and we were into the second half of the show and the Swimming Pool scene.

'All the chorus boys came in at a run and dived into the pool. What we didn't know was that the material Irene Segala had found for these swimming trunks was see-throughable, when wet. It was therefore only when the boys came out of the swimming pool, and stood there like statues, that we could realise what could be seen. Dick Hurran belted through that pass-door like a little tornado, and shouted, ''Get them back in the pool, into the pool'', so all the boys were ordered back in and spent the rest of the act in the pool. I have never seen anything like it. You can't believe things like that can happen. It was just unfortunate and all because of this stylish material which looked so nice when dry. The Queen was very nice about the whole show, and she said the swimming pool was lovely! It certainly looked glorious.

'Dick Hurran went to Las Vegas and the Lido in Paris and was highly influenced by their shows. The sets he devised were thrilling to watch. It is difficult to describe Dick Hurran's work because he was unusual. In the Scottish tradition of backstage staff the response to such ideas for sets went on the lines of, ''Aw, it'll no' work'', ''Aw, ye canny dae that,

Jimmy", "Nae way, the man's stoopid, he's oot o' his mind", "What dis he want me tae dae that fer?", "Dae ye hear what he wants me to dae?" So I just had to say, try it, I think the man knows what he is doing. "Oh, he's an eejit. He canny dae it". Then I'd say, "Do you want the money", "Aye I want the money, alright". And they would do it, and later, very reluctantly, they would say "It looks awfy good frae the front".'

REG ALLEN

Scenic artist, designer, and then production manager, Howard and Wyndham productions, 1949–1979.

'After I had done the first pantomime in 1949, I was invited back to do the *Half-Past Eight* shows but I didn't realise they would be so demanding as they were. We had the producer Charles Ross and his daugher Ilona, the choreographer, doing a show which changed every week. Not only changed every week but transferred from Edinburgh to Glasgow. So we had two shows running concurrently, but also changing over and this used to run all Summer from May to August or September. We did eventually settle down to Glasgow and Edinburgh having their own *Five-Past Eight* show.

'In later years the producer was Dick Hurran who would describe what he wanted on stage and I had to assist with design and make it work. It was technical as well as artistic work where one started with a stage plan grid on which you designed the set. In the planning stage, two inches on the model would become two feet on the cloth itself. Scene changes had to be very fast in some cases so it had to be accurate and the best way was to begin with a thumbnail sketch of the whole thing.

'It wasn't always a simple matter of drawing board design, it was a matter of mechanics. We certainly did go in for elaborate scenes, and often had to use a front cloth for the comedian, Jimmy Logan, or Jack Anthony, who would give us an extra couple of minutes to allow us to make the set changes.

'The Glasgow production of *Five-Past Eight* became known as the *Starlight Room* at the Alhambra Theatre. It became very ambitious and we called it theatre-ama, akin to cinerama. It meant widening the stage, taking out the boxes, and putting in staircases and, rather than a simple revolve stage, we put in three lifts. One sequence for the show involved the orchestra coming up out of the pit, travelling back along the stage to number 3 lift, where it was lifted up at the back of the stage. Following behind was number 2 lift with two pianos on it. There were in total four grand pianos, and finally Rikki Fulton sitting at a piano came up on the front lift. There were then five grand pianos, on different levels, with the full orchestra behind. That was really some staging.'

FAY LENORE

'In 1956 I was invited by the producer, Michael Mills, to join the Howard and Wyndham Company, for pantomime and the *Five-Past Eight* shows. Being Michael, he used to get the most obscure numbers that no one had ever heard of, and never had been put down musically, and poor Pat McCann, the Musical Director, had the job of listening to the records, taking down all the notes, all the words, all the different musical parts, and putting the whole piece together on paper. This was in a week when we had to put on a new show in about five days.

'I worked with Rikki Fulton, Alec Finlay, Kenneth McKellar and Amanda Barrie. We had wonderful dancers and it was Lionel Blair who created and choreographed all the dances. I was a singer, and dancer but also appeared in comedy sketches, ensembles, finales, everything. I never wrote comedy. I am always the one who is given the script and I learn it. It was Stanley Baxter who taught me how to deliver lines because although I was the lead singer, I was also one of his "feeds". With Jimmy Logan I used to feed him too in sketches. "Feeding" teaches you timing and acting. I always say that if you are an actor, you should get on and feed somebody because you have this split second timing that is so essential, knowing how to deliver the line and when. Because if your timing is wrong, you can kill the whole thing, stone dead.

'I always enjoyed working with Jack Milroy. I was in the original Francie and Josie sketch with Rikki Fulton and Jack Milroy in 1960 and in that show particularly I used to feed Jack. We would do a tap dance routine together, he's a great dancer, and he was so good to work with. He would give to you, always standing back and let you have your little bit. He's a real pro like so many in the business. I love my theatre people, they have got a generosity of spirit. There was always a different attitude to what I would find outside. People always help you and if you are feeling ill, they'll say, "I'll fill in for you tonight" or "So and so could do that sketch for you". I've rarely met anyone who was mean in the theatre because you are working together. The show is the thing'.

JIM HASTIE

Dancer, Ballet Master, Howard and Wyndham: 1950–1960s.

'The dancers were always up on the top floor, it didn't matter which show you were in, the hoofers were up above. It's sad that the one luxury which has gone from the variety shows which we see now, are the dancers, because they added such a lot to it. We did the opening number, and whilst the comic did his front cloth warm up with the audience, we would be doing a quick change for another scene. We fled upstairs and rushed down again. These costumes, everything, had to be perfect. The hair style had to go with the period, so they had so many hair pieces and wigs to put on as well as the costume in a quick change and get back on stage.

'I defy, and in fact I would say with absolute certainty, that in the actual theatre of today they could not do those quick costume changes, as well as the scenery, with the cloths flying in and out, with the speed that we seemed to do it. I mean there was black out, change of set, change of cloth, next scene on and you had to get on with it. Nowadays, the technicians and everyone else would freak out and say, oh no, it's not possible, we can't do that. But in those days it all happened. The actual work of the stage staff, and technicians, getting anything from about ten to twenty cloths flying in and out on a night, plus scenery on and off for the different sketches, it was unbelievable.'

'These shows in the initial stages were home-grown products. You had Jimmy Logan, Jack Radcliffe, Helen Norman, wee Johnny Mulvaney and there was Fay Lenore and Stanley Baxter. Michael Mills really concentrated on that kind of Scottish entertainment, but it was a glamorous home-spun show. Eventually, Howard and Wyndham brought in Dick Hurran as producer who changed the whole thing, bringing in the Bluebell Girls, international singers and comics. He would go to Las Vegas and Tokyo to pick up all these wonderful incredible ideas.'

Evening Times, 5th June, 1962

'A showpiece of spectacle and glamour is the Alhambra's Five Past Eight with producer Dick Hurran reaching new heights in his Starlight Room setting. Dickie Henderson tops a talent packed cast with Glasgow's own Lena Martell making a big hit on her own ground.'

The Tiller Girls

Chapter 4

'THE BACKBONE OF THE SHOW'

THE CHORUS LINE

LENA NICOL

'It was hard work in the theatre, with a change of programme each week, rehearsing during the day. We were involved in all kinds of dancing, acrobatic, ballet, tap, Highland, and hornpipes. When we were touring, with all the travelling to theatres and rehearsing, or when we were in between shows, we could not claim unemployment benefit because they believed we were working. We were never paid for rehearsal weeks.

'Out on tour, Sunday was spent trying to find digs, so that the day off was not a day off. Then when we found accommodation there were so many rules and regulations: "Take your shoes off", "No Boyfriends", "No Smoking".

'We were paid about £2 a week. Our digs would be about sixteen shillings for full board which came out of our pay. There was no union to fight for better conditions, until the Variety Club and Equity took up complaints and eventually studied the problem of pay. Chorus girls were regarded as less than nothing. We may not have been principals but we were the backbone of the show. The dancers backed the soprano, did solo turns of ballet and tap, troupe work, company ensembles, opening numbers and finales. There were so many scenes with quick changes at the side of the stage. Monday was the worst day when costumes for the new show had to be sorted out and fitted. It was nothing but sewing and mending, rehearsing and teaching until 3 pm. Then home for a quick meal before returning at about five, to prepare for the first performance.

'During the war I wanted to join the WRENS but as head girl of the troupe, I was asked to stay on in the troupe. I had to train inexperienced girls very quickly, often in the long waits in between the scenes. Entertainment during the war had a tremendous atmosphere when people came at least once a week. Soldiers on leave bringing families together again. There were comics like Donaghue and Ramsay — Jimmy Donaghue and Jimmy Ramsay were great favourites.

'We did not have a supply of tights to wear. Out of our pay we had to buy our stage makeup, and prepare a mixture of leg tan which was red and yellow ochre powder, rosewater and glycerine. We always had bare legs, even on the coldest of days. We were not allowed to wear trousers even in damp, draughty rehearsal rooms. No wonder I have arthritis today. We often had poor health, suffering from muscle cramps and inflamed skin problems on our legs.

'Backstage conditions depended on the theatre. The Metropole in Glasgow was next to the fishmarket and one night a rat came through a drain pipe and into our dressing room. There was an almighty scream as we all ran to the door, so that there was such a crush we couldn't even open the door. However cold it was, or however you felt, you had to go on stage and dance and smile as if you had the most glamorous job in the world.

'I still have nightmares about going on the stage and I am now sixty-eight. I dream I am going to be late for the chorus entrance. Sometimes I'm taking too long in changing and I can't find my shoes, or am wearing the wrong costume when I get down to the wings and everyone is on the stage without me. You just couldn't be late, you daren't miss a cue and this discipline is so drilled into me that I still dream about it forty years later. But once you were on the stage you forgot your troubles and aches and pains. We all did love it and that's why we did it for so little money.'

Edinburgh Evening Despatch, 11th July 1944
'A sparkling programme is presented at the Gaiety Theatre in the second week of the summer show. Tommy Hope keeps the audience in good humour with his cunning antics in numerous sketches, particularly the Lodger. Kay Yourston, crooner, Rita Cadie and Billy Browne, accordionist, are all extremely popular. Adeline Calder with the girls in La Conga, a daring ensemble, and Carr and Vonnie, a dextrous tap dancing team, add to the show's attractions.'

MARGARET BUCKLAND (née Guthrie)

Dancer, Adeline Calder Troupe 1948–1958.

'If you were lucky, and I use that word loosely, you could be doing a twenty week summer season somewhere like North Berwick where the show changed completely twice a week. In the Winter we did pantomime and then it was twice nightly with two matinees as well during the week. As for the theatres themselves, the front of house was always reasonably good but backstage was a different story. The dressing rooms were terrible and not once but many times the girls clubbed together and bought some emulsion to brighten them up. Rats too were a problem and once at the Gaiety in Leith where the dressing rooms were under the stage, I had one run over my foot!

'I remember touring to Aberdeen in the winter of 1953–4 when the weather was atrocious. I think that five of us were sharing a room of average size in the digs. There was a small Victorian fireplace and an allocation of just six pieces of coal a night. We were so cold we used to go to bed with dressing gowns, socks, scarves, gloves and even earmuffs to try and keep warm. If our public could have seen us then, stripped of all our glamour, they would have had a good laugh.

'But through all the hardships and long hours I must say I enjoyed myself as I'm sure the other girls did. There was great camaraderie between us all.'

In January 1937, a month when Edinburgh was hit by a serious 'flu epidemic, with thirty-seven deaths in one week, it was a time to keep particularly warm and healthy. Dressing rooms and digs would have been even more uncomfortable in December 1938, when a snowstorm swept Scotland for days and Edinburgh's tramway service was severely disorganised. At the time, prices for women's clothes were advertised as follows:

'Grey Squirrel coat, £21 guineas; Beaver coat, 5 guineas; Ladies court shoes, 10/–; Afternoon frock, 52/6d; silk stockings, 4/3d; and wool stockings, 2/6d'.
(*Evening News*: 18th January 1937).
In December 1939, C & A were advertising an Astrakhan Cloth coat for 19/11d.

However, these trained, professional dancers, earning about £2, could hardly afford basic winter clothing necessities, let alone luxuries like silk stockings. It was years before tights were readily available and instead the chorus girls had to rely on leg tan which had to be applied nightly.

THE MOXON GIRLS TO THE MOXON LOVELIES
OVER FOUR DECADES

December 30th, 1935:
Metropole Theatre:
Jack and Jill: 5th annual panto. Enormous success with Bert Denver, Charlie Kemble, Peggy Desmond, and The Moxon Girls.

January 1944:
The Empress Theatre:
The Revels of '44 present the pantomime, *The Old Woman who lived in a Shoe*, with Jimmy Nichol, Ken Campbell, Fay Lenore, Bijou Gordon, and The Moxon Ladies.

Winter Season 1956/57:
Metropole Theatre:
Scotland the Brave with Clark and Murray, George Burton, Hugh McIlroy, and sixteen Moxon Ladies.

From April 1st 1963, for four weeks. By public demand: Metropole Theatre: *The Spring Show* with Clark and Murray, Danny Regan, Anne Fields, and the Moxon Ladies.

Pavilion: Summer show: *Lex McLean's super 1971 show*, With Una McLean, Walter Carr, and the May Moxon Lovelies. Opens 16th August, until November 6th.

MAY MOXON

(In 1934, aged twenty-eight, the dancer May Moxon while returning from a touring show in the Highlands, was involved in a car accident, which seriously injured her legs. She was in hospital in Dundee for twenty-eight weeks).

'They first of all said they couldn't do anything for me, that I would be incurable. They even suggested taking my leg off, and I said I'd rather die than have my leg off. I was then taken to the Victoria Hospital in Glasgow and they were good to me. They opened up the leg and found dead bone, which should have been taken away. That was why my leg wouldn't heal. I had to work somehow and dancing and the theatre was all I knew. As time went on I thought I had to do something. Why couldn't I form a troupe of girls and direct them, using all my experience there? I decided to try that. I went to Galt's Agency, and I asked them if they would give me a trial week, and see what I can produce with a troupe. They said they would give a me a week at the Empress Theatre, and if they were up to the standard they would give me work.

'I immediately set to work, asking two girls I had worked with before and four new ones. We rehearsed and rehearsed. I could show them Highland dancing and every kind of step with my fingers, it was all I could do with the iron on my leg. I could direct them fine. With the experienced dancers to help, I was able to train the new dancers one by one, asking them to watch and do what the others did. I didn't have much money but I had to dress them. In those days, a sequin here and there was all we could manage – years later, I used to laugh when we had yards and yards of sequins on the dancers' costumes – but when we started out they were not elaborate but neat wee costumes and I made them myself. I had a sewing machine which I pedalled with my one good leg. Three sets of costumes for each of the six dancers.

'Up we went to the Empress and after the first performance on the Monday, the manager sent for me. I was certain he didn't like us, and I was terrified to go to his office. But when I got there, he said he was very pleased, so much so that he would keep us for another week! Well that meant going away, changing all the costumes and more rehearsal work for a new show the next week. I was even more pleased when a producer, Gordon Inglis, came to me and said he was putting on a show at the Metropole in Stockwell Street for four weeks. 'I'll take you in'', he said, ''but you must give me eight girls''. I was delighted and felt we really have started, we're climbing up from six to eight girls. So away we went to the Metropole and I was there for one hundred weeks. It was the first it was ever known in Scotland for a resident troupe. I had to dress them, with a change of routine every week. So the costumes I made had to be of two pieces; perhaps a little skirt, and a top, all in different colours. Each week I would mix the tops and skirts around. I couldn't think of dozens of different routines, but I could change the music. Alec Frutin who owned the Metropole came to see me and said the costumes were very neat, and that we were doing extremely well. And so we were, for one hundred weeks!

'Then Hamish Dunlop of the Palladium Theatre in Edinburgh said what about giving him a troupe of eight girls. I said how could I, with the Metropole troupe running? He said just find eight new girls. I sent the experienced dancers from the Metropole over to Edinburgh. So, that was the start of it. That meant eight girls at the Palladium and eight at the Metropole. Then he wanted girls for the Gaiety in Leith, and it began to snowball.

'At that time I advertised in the local papers, the *Citizen* for instance. When you put an advert in asking for dancers you would get as many as you wanted, so many girls were wanting to go on the stage. When you think of the girls of years ago, what great wee workers they were. Later on it was the fancy hair-dos, and where before the girls had to put up with leg tan, they could have nice tights showing off the legs and bottoms. At the beginning, girls were covered up much more.

'They would do a line up of high kicks, like the Tillers, tap dancing, and Highland dancing. Maybe the show would have a Scottish, a gypsy or a sailor scene. We would adapt to what was wanted. The producer would tell me what theme he was putting on the next week and I could prepare for that specialised dance routine. I was building up a vast wardrobe over the years so that I could tackle any kind of dance or scene.

'The way my business worked was that I got the contract to supply so many girls. I got the fee and paid the girls, keeping a small amount for myself, and part of that had to buy cheap material for the costumes.

'I was the first person to organise and train a resident troupe of dancers in Scotland. The Moxon Girls were really the Tiller Girls of Scotland. I had some great dancers over the years. Sometimes the odd girl would come to me and say, my boyfriend is going into a particular show at some other theatre. Are you putting girls into that show? I would therefore help them with their love life. I was close to the girls, very close, like a mother.

'I could see the writing was on the wall in the early 1970s so I realised it was time we were packing it in. I retired about fifteen years ago. Looking back I don't know how I had the nerve to go down to the theatre with my walking stick and train those girls, going up to Galt's office with this iron on my leg, and asking for work for dancers. But I had to do it because I needed the money. It was the only work I knew from childhood.'

Sunday Mail, December 5th 1965
Carry on Cranky:

'There wasn't a happier man at the fall of the curtain on the Pavilion's first night than Eric Popplewell. Well might he be proud for he has given the Pavilion pantomime a new dimension. The recipe looks simple: A beautifully dressed show, a terrific pace, glamorous dancing and dancers. Centre it around exuberant Jack Milroy and a happy blend of conventional panto, local humour and you have a show that will run and run. Sally Logan as the very pretty blonde for the principal girl sings delightfully. Long-legged Moxon Girls are seen in spectacular production. Altogether a sparkling success.'

NANCY McILROY (née Dick)

Chorus Line dancer from 1945–1965, first with Adeline Calder troupe, then the Moxon Girls, and finally with The White Heather Club.

'My memories as a Moxon Girl are happy ones as there is nothing quite like the friendship as the girls, and doing something you enjoy. Although dancing twice nightly was hard work there was always laughter in the dressing room. When we occasionally meet now, it all seems just like yesterday.

'The strange thing about most theatres in Scotland was that the dancers' dressing rooms were nearly always on the top floor, especially during pantomime, when there are so many entrances and changes of costume. We spent the entire night running up and down those stairs.

'For the weekly change of programme, the dancers were always in rehearsing during the day from Wednesday to Friday, and sometimes on Saturdays. Monday was an exceptionally busy day when we had Band Call, and it was also the day for getting our costumes ready for the week's show. There was always a queue for the one iron and then we would have to spend the afternoon altering some of the costumes to make them fit us properly. It was nice if you were in a big show where there was a wardrobe mistress as all laundry, ironing and mending of costumes would be done for you.'

PHILIPPA MACKAY (née Saunders)

Tiller Girl in the 1930s.

'At the age of fourteen I began work in pantomime and after a year, I realised I didn't want to teach dance but to perform. I started looking for better jobs and stayed at the Theatre Girls' club in Greek Street, in London, which was run by Fay Compton's mother. It was very sparse. There were no home comforts about it really. We used to look out the window down on to this beautiful restaurant opposite, wondering if we'd ever go to a place like that. And I did eventually! The most important career move was when I joined up with Tillers. I was just sixteen but I was an experienced dancer and had done a lot of professional work. In the following summer, 1936, I came up to Aberdeen. There were four Tiller Girls with the Harry Gordon show and that was super. It was always thought of as one of the best shows to be in for the summertime. Tiller girls were in shows all over the place. Dave Willis used to be in the show in Ayr and that was another which booked Tillers.

'At the Beach Pavilion we changed the show every week, rehearsing every morning for the following week's show. There were stars who would come for a week, or two weeks, while the rest of us made up the resident company. Towards the end of the show they used to have a week where everything was Scottish. Everyone did some act which was Scottish. There was another week where everyone had to take off someone else who had been in the show during the season. For instance I imitated Arthur Askey and another of the Tiller Girls played the piano for me. It was really a family show. You didn't actually know the people in the audience but because they were there every week, in the same seats, it was a nice familiar atmosphere. It was quite likely that you would walk down a street in Aberdeen and say hello to someone you didn't really know. You just knew their faces. On the last night of the show, everyone was showered with gifts from the audience. By the end of the season the company and the audience were one big happy family.

'The Beach Pavilion was right on the sea-front, very tiny with a small stage. There was a resident pianist, Alice Stephenson. No band, just the piano. The theatre held about 750 people and it was always packed out. We Tillers did have our own dressing room as we were there for the whole season and it was a long season too, from May to September.

'The costumes were supplied but the Tiller School also had a wardrobe so that we brought a certain amount of costumes, shoes and accessories with us. We had to do most outlandish things, which you couldn't possibly be prepared for, having thought it up one week to perform the next week. There were always different ideas and themes for our dancing act and Harry Gordon didn't want anything that had been done before. So you were racking your brain all the time for a new act. It could be tap, or a ballet, or musical comedy – all sorts of novel ideas were put in to the show.

'The Tiller training was very hard, because everything you did was done with military precision. There was no point in trying to kick your leg up higher than anyone else because that you mustn't do. You had to be completely in line in everything you did. I didn't think anyone has really been able to copy what the Tiller Girls did. You weren't an individual. You were just part of the sixteen that was in the row, and everything you did was exactly together. It was hard work.

'After the summer season with Harry Gordon in Aberdeen I was on tour with him for a while and then I went into Dave Willis's show in Scotland, which was handy because I had met my future husband in 1936, so the more I worked in Scotland the more I liked it. Not that we were very near to each other, with me being away on tour!

'The Royal Command Performance in November 1938 was very exciting. There were thirty-two Tiller Girls. We rehearsed at the theatre on the day of the performance and watched them decorating the Royal Box all with fresh flowers. It was absolutely beautiful. When the curtain went up, it was just a sea of evening dresses. We were told we mustn't look at the Royal Box but I think everyone had a quick look. It was a lovely show, a very thrilling night. Everyone was on at the end and then you got a good look at the Royal Box. It was certainly the highlight of my career.'

(John Tiller was a prosperous Manchester cotton-merchant who couldn't dance a step but had always been fascinated by the theatre business, and in 1885 he started to train dancers and founded the Tiller Troupe. By the 1920s, their name had become synonomous with professionalism and perfection: these were dancers drilled and disciplined like guardsmen to perform with polish and precision. They were selected for uniform height and weight and could kick as high as their ears. This line-up of respectable young ladies would never be seen to 'drink, smoke or flirt'. They were not ordinary chorus girls, they were The Tillers.)

BUNTY McLEOD (née Gordon)

Daughter of Harry Gordon. Charles Ross Dancer and Tiller Girl.

'I went to dancing school when I was two years old and as theatre was so much a part of my childhood it was always the dancing which took my fancy when I was taken to the Beach Pavilion shows. It wasn't actually so much the dancing but the costumes I was mad on. In those days it was all ostrich feathers, sequins, all very colourful and I thought I could see myself wearing that. I saw the glamour of the Tiller Girls without the hard work that goes into it.

'After dancing school in Aberdeen I joined the chorus of *Half-Past Eight* in Edinburgh and did two summer shows and two pantomimes. This was the early 1940s, when Charles Ross used to produce the *Half-Past Eights* and Ilona Ross arranged the dance scenes. My father was the leading comedian and he was responsible for all the comedy. There would be elaborate opening production scenes and finales, changed once a month. The rest of the programme changed weekly and I suppose we used to learn six or seven brand new routines every week and that was quite a lot. There were often days when you would go up to the dressing room after rehearsals and say to yourself, "What am I doing here?" You really felt you couldn't take any more of that exhausting routine. But it was funny, as soon as you put your makeup on at night, and went down to the stage, you knew what you were doing there, and you did enjoy it.

'Then the head of the Tiller School, Miss Doris, who was with a troupe of Tillers at the Empire in Edinburgh, came down to the King's and before I knew what was happening she had arranged with my father for me to do my audition for the Tillers that night on stage. She would simply watch the *Half-Past Eight* show. Margaret Holden, who was Jack Holden's daughter, was also auditioning and we went into that performance all teeth and smiles, really going to town on it. After the show Miss Doris came back stage and she said, "Alright, Bunty and Margaret, you can start with us in the pantomime season".

'It was a happy time with the Tillers, although the precision dancing, and the rehearsals were very very hard. At the Tiller School the rehearsal room had mirrors all around. You would start with two Tillers dancing together, then three, four, five and gradually build the line up and when you have been used to dancing in your own style for years, it is very difficult to discipline yourself to be as one in a troupe. In a line-up of twenty-four girls, it takes a great deal of control to keep absolutely together. For a long time I had been in troupes of twelve, or fourteen but never twenty-four. For the Opera House, Blackpool I was head girl in a troupe of twenty-four and the costumes were just out of this world. Our big number might open the second half of the show. There would be ten ballet girls on first, then eight showgirls with gorgeous dresses. Then the curtains would open and there we were, twenty-four of us at the back of the stage, starting to kick, very very low. Then we started to move forward and as we did, we began kicking higher and higher. I am not exaggerating when I say that this Tiller line-up was a show stopper. That show went to the London Palladium and we also did the first Royal Command Performance after the war. Once again, you knew that as soon as those curtains opened, the twenty-four of us would start to move, the kicks getting slowly higher and higher, absolutely in unison. It was the tempo of the music which kept us all precisely in step and in time with each other.

We organised a Tiller Reunion and had girls from America, Canada, everywhere; there were over 300 women. One of them arrived and it was Queenie who used to work with my father and another, Ray, was one of the last four at the Beach Pavilion. It was quite an occasion for all of us from the old Beach Pavilion, Harry Gordon days.'

ILONA ROSS

'The *Half-Past Eight* show was not an intimate revue, and it was never Variety; it was an elaborately produced light entertainment company show. We often performed little historical dramas, with music and a song, excerpts from opera and ballets, such as *The Sleeping Beauty*, with comedy sketches in between and tap routines. We used to do about two tap routines, one big ballet and other production scenes all of which I was responsible for arranging. Perhaps a Tyrolean scene or a ship set for a sailors' hornpipe. There were always several routines to learn every week. We didn't have an odd troupe of dancers but a hand-picked group who could do every kind of dancing, Spanish, ballet, tap, anything. We had sixteen girls and four boys, and usually twenty-four in pantomime, which does seem a lot these days. Looking back though, I used to look at this small troupe of sixteen and think what can I do with such few people!

'Ideas simply came to me, perhaps when costumes from a show which had closed in London were rushed up here and I would be called to wardrobe to look at the costumes to see what scenes we could do. Music helped enormously because in those days you had melodies. We had lovely popular songs of the day, which lent themselves to little love scenes. It was the heyday of the light musical comedy and Hollywood films of musicals. People seemed happier and they whistled in the street. I used to lie in bed in the morning trying to identify what song the milkman was whistling because that has got to go in next week. In that way we would always be absolutely topical.

'The company would all rehearse in different corners of the theatre. It must have looked like pandemonium if anyone walked in. I remember a friend popped in to see me and she sat waiting until I had finished the morning rehearsal. She said to me later how could I possibly rehearse the ballet scene with all that racket going on all round me? There had been someone in the orchestra pit, with the iron curtain down, rehearsing a song; there was myself with all the girls on stage, and behind the back tabs, the comics were rehearsing a new sketch. In the foyer there was a couple rehearsing an operatic duo. All the separate rehearsals would go on and then about Wednesday afternoon all these items would begin to coagulate, and people began to come together. We had the dress rehearsal on Friday, starting at nine thirty and continuing until we finished, perhaps not until about five o'clock, just before the first performance that evening.

'We always seemed to be constantly rehearsing. I was always too tired the night before to work out properly what we would do the next morning. I used to get the girls around the piano, and we would listen to the music. Then we got cracking to see what would happen, putting the movements together. It does sound a bit hit and miss, but it did work. I knew my girls and they knew me and things came together fairly quickly. Unless we were doing something fearfully ambitious. We didn't have time to do anything other than straightforward arrangements, varying it with scenery and staircases. I was always rather partial to staircases, everything always looked a lot more spectacular. After many years as ballet mistress, I gradually moved away from that work and was assisting in the production overall. It makes me laugh now because when I became too busy to go on doing the ballet work as well, old Mr Cruikshank engaged *two* people to do my job. One was a ballet mistress to arrange the ballets and another to arrange the tap dances and any national, Spanish dance or whatever!

'I chose my own girls, who had to be trained in ballet, tap and all kinds of dance. Then for the pantomimes, we would have my nucleus of sixteen girls as well as another group of background dancers. In addition we would have another group who were simply showgirls. We used to say if the showgirls can breathe they're alright. They were quite something, especially those Glasgow girls. One had to watch them very carefully or else if one or two were rather intoxicated they would have to be yanked off. But on the whole they were fine and all they had to do was to walk gracefully on and off.'

Evening News, May 31st 1938
Half-Past Eight: King's Theatre, Edinburgh.
'. . . The finely drilled chorus of Charles Ross girls were a strong feature and their team work excellent. Miss Ilona Ross gave some charming speciality dances, the most effective being the ballet in 'Blue Skies'.'

JUNE MURRAY (Stage name, June Don)

Dancer in the Adeline Calder, May Moxon and Ilona Ross troupes touring in Variety shows around Scotland from 1944–1960.

'I was in the Howard and Wyndham pantomime, *Jack and the Beanstalk*, in 1947. Ilona Ross was very strict, there couldn't be a hair out of place, but she was a wonderful ballet mistress and choreographer.

'Touring with the dance troupe always had its amusing incidents. I appeared at the Palace, Dundee for many seasons with the comedians Jack Milroy and also Johnny Victory. Johnny Victory had a yellow Rolls Royce and after the show he would drive back to Edinburgh and quite often he would announce to the chorus girls that if we wanted a lift we had to be at the stage door in five minutes. So about five of us who lived in Edinburgh would cram into his beautiful car and drive home in style, rather than staying over in digs. At North Queensferry at that time we had to catch the ferry over the Forth. It would always be our luck to arrive there and see the ferry just moving off. Missing the last ferry meant we had to drive for miles down the coast to the Kincardine Bridge and we wouldn't get home until about two in the morning. But Johnny Victory in his yellow Rolls Royce was such a familiar figure and of course a popular entertainer and because the ferry company was accustomed to this late arrival, the ferry would actually turn round and come back for all of us. They would only do that if it had just set off from the quay. That really was an amazing sight to watch the ferry swing round and come back to pick us up! They really were great days looking back.'

Robert Wilson

Chapter 5

THE TENORS, SOPRANOS AND MUSICAL DIRECTORS

CAREY WILSON

The following memoir of Robert Wilson was written by Carey Wilson in the form of a letter.

'Talking about my father is, at one and the same time, easy and difficult. Easy, because his story is a relatively simple one, and difficult because of the emotional ties which oddly enough get stronger as the years go by. My father set almost impossible standards for my brother and myself, both professionally and as private individuals. Not in any deliberate way, but simply by being who and what he was. My father was essentially a down-to-earth and ordinary man who considered himself very fortunate to have been able to make something of himself. That his abilities were extraordinary is beyond doubt, but he didn't think so. Even at the height of his fame, had you met him in the street, you would never have guessed what he did for a living.

'In his teens, Robert was already making his mark as a singer. He sang wherever possible with choirs, and local music festivals. He entered the Lanark Festival as both baritone and tenor and won both. By this time Robert was an apprentice engineering draughtsman, working at the Bridge Works, Motherwell, and then with the firm of Potts, Cassells and Williamson. As the depression began, being a junior, he was among the first to be made redundant. At seventeen he went to Eliot Dobie for lessons and I remember him describing their first meeting, and saying how impressed he was by the seventeen year old with "the magnificent voice and air of transparent honesty". Dobie was himself an extraordinary man – an exceptionally fine baritone, and something of a wheeler-dealer who was just the man to foster new talent. He took Robert to the Palette Club at Charing Cross which was then a "shop window" attended by agents. The tenor Herbert Thorpe had been engaged as the star attraction but was indisposed and unable to sing. Dobie looked at Thorpe's programme, persuaded the manager that Robert could perform it, and on he went. He caused quite a stir and from that moment he became a professional.

'After some experience of variety theatre work Robert became principal tenor with the D'Oyly Carte Opera company and toured with them here and in America.

'In his early days, life seemed to be one long train journey. He would sing at the Royal Albert Hall on Tuesday, Perth Music Society on Wednesday, and Lyons Corner House on Thursday. With a Summer season and a Pantomime, the year was filled with engagements, and in fact, while his own wedding reception was in full swing, in the centre of Glasgow, I've heard through family stories that he disappeared for an hour or so singing at a concert, to earn the train fare to take his new bride to London.

'Around 1937 he auditioned for Harry Gordon and was engaged by him for his prestigious Summer shows at the Beach Pavilion, Aberdeen. During the war years he became very popular at the Theatre Royal, Edinburgh, where he shared a dressing room with the young Dickie Henderson; at the Tivoli, Aberdeen and at the Gaiety, in Ayr. He toured with Will Fyffe in ENSA and became a regular in the Will Fyffe-Harry Gordon pantomimes at the Glasgow Alhambra during the war years. The absurdity of a man in a kilt singing "The Road to the Isles", in the middle of *Babes in the Wood*, didn't seem to bother anyone at all!

'I first went on the road with my father in the early fifties, when I was about six. He took a company which included Stanley Baxter on his first venture into Variety, all over Scotland, playing Town Halls or whatever kind of hall was available. Some of the places were so remote that it was said that "only seagulls and Robert Wilson went there". There were many disasters of the kind which usually plague touring companies – car breakdowns and accidents and we even encountered a flood when we couldn't get out of the car in Elgin, because the water was up to the doors. On one occasion we arrived in Inverness to find that none of the publicity material had been put out, so there were no advance bookings. Many people wondered why Robert bothered with all that touring, as he could have taken it easy headlining for Howard and Wyndham, but he really believed in taking entertainment to the people who had no chance of ever seeing the inside of the Glasgow Alhambra. In my teens I appeared in Summer season with him, and was impressed by the casual discipline all good performers have, as they rehearse a change of programme each week.

'I remember the camaraderie and peculiar wit of performers like Jimmy Neil, whose whole act depended on his quick speed of response. The comedian Chic Murray used to come to our home for a business meeting and my brother and I would listen at the door. All you could hear was Chic being himself and my father (and us) roaring with laughter. Business was never mentioned.

'Robert never talked about himself and only occasionally commented on other artistes. He certainly admired Sir Harry Lauder, Will Fyffe, Harry Gordon and Jack Anthony, all comedians, and I mustn't forget his friend Jack Radcliffe. In the singing department he was greatly influenced by the American baritone, Lawrence Tibbett, and by Richard Tauber, but from his early days singing in Glasgow Cathedral, he had the greatest admiration for "Wee" Willie Hamilton. Unknown now, but Robert regarded him as the finest tenor he ever heard.

'My father was a kind man in a very cruel and demanding profession who worked tirelessly for the benefit of others, asked for no thanks and received very little and I am very proud of what he achieved by his own efforts. When his voice gave in to the relentless pressure he had put on it, it says a great deal for his stage presence and personality that his popularity still continued to grow. He was able to use his considerable reputation and influence to help younger performers get started. I well remember him bringing home a test recording of a young tenor and being very excited and enthusiastic about it. The tenor was Kenneth McKellar and while there is no doubt that a singer of that calibre would have made it anyway, it is true that Robert gave him a very firm helping hand. He was very conscious of the talents the artistes he employed possessed and put up with their personal problems to an extraordinary degree, sometimes to the detriment of his own reputation, and certainly to the detriment of his wallet. Among other things, he was a soft touch.

'All my life I have been aware of, and deeply impressed by the great affection and respect he inspired in those who knew and worked with him. He was the most selfless man I have ever known and on countless occasions have had ordinary people try to tell me how moved they felt when they heard him sing in a theatre, church, hospital or village hall.'

Glasgow Empire, 23rd February 1942: *Winter Revels* with Jack Radcliffe and Robert Wilson — 'A sure pack-out in any Scots theatre'.
Glasgow Empire, 7th March 1960: Robert Wilson and the White Heather Group with Andy Stewart, the Joe Gordon Folk 4, Jimmy Neil and Sydney Devine.

EVELYN HENRY

'I think of Robert Wilson as an outstanding person in the profession. He was such a gentleman, and he was never anything less than a gentleman to me. He never went on stage other than in a perfect state of mind for his work, and the ladies in the company were always considered first. Both as an artist, singing duets with him, and just to work in his company, he earned my greatest respect. He would do so many commendable things that went perhaps unrecognised. For instance he would go out to some remote cottage and sing to some old biddy, in his own time, without any publicity. He would give up valuable time to do this. That is real charity work that he must be remembered for.'

GREENIE (Mrs Green)

'Robert Wilson was a proper gentleman. Of all our guests he was one of our favourites . . . He became a very close family friend. The day of his funeral, I'll never forget it. We went into the church with his wife and sat beside the family.

'Robert gave many people a start in the profession. He often had a group of artistes around about him but many made their name through him, like Joe Gordon for example or Sydney Devine. He took Sydney on as a boy when he was only fifteen.

'He was fundamentally a Scottish singer, but his operatic background would enable him to select other songs, "Sylvia, Who is She?", "The Donkey Serenade" and other classic ballads of the time. He had a lovely rendering of the Lord's Prayer, and "My Love is like a Red Red Rose", among other Burns songs. He felt he had to broaden his repertoire, with six week seasons at the Beach Pavilion and eighteen weeks at the Tivoli. With eight to ten songs in every show, he would require a great deal of new material. You couldn't sing the same ten songs every week. Robert would take the Tivoli Theatre over for a season, to present and produce his own Revue. He would choose the other performers for the company, when perhaps Lex McLean would be the comedian.

'I gave Robert Wilson a song, "A Gordon for Me". It used to be a barrack room song and it had never been published. My father used to sing it and he taught it to me. I would get up at Beach Pavilion Company parties and sing it. Robert then said he would set it down to music one day which he did and then sang it in the show. I gave him that song, and then he sold the rights to Lawrence Wright the music publishers and it was a big hit. I could have stepped in there maybe but Robert was good enough to give me a generous backhander.'

CAREY WILSON

'My father rather unwisely sold the rights of ''A Gordon for Me'' to Lawrence Wright and so he didn't make a penny out of it. No doubt it seemed like a good idea at that time. He had a long association with Lawrence Wright and recorded many of the songs published by him.'

The Scottish variety stage in the early days especially, offered an open platform for young talented singers. There were *Go as You Please* contests, rough-and-ready concert parties in many a church hall, which could lead on to the bottom of the bill spot at established theatres. Good billing material and publicity would sometimes help bring in an audience.

Sunday Mail, 21st May 1934
Empress: Joe O'Rourke; and introducing Frank Waters – 'a big discovery, this unemployed Motherwell miner found singing in the streets'.

'Frank Waters is Lauder's double, the same build, features and colouring. He worked in the pits from boyhood, became idle two years ago and went round the countryside with a piece in his pocket and an accordion as his companion. He made £1 a day in coppers. He hit Stirling and collected a crowd, several thousand strong, and attracted the attention of Ian McPherson, the Glasgow vocalist who brought him to the notice of the Empress Theatre'. And later that year:

12th November 1934
Empress, Frank Waters 'Caruso of the Pits'.

23rd July 1934
Metropole: Peggy Toner: 'Scotland's Sophie Tucker'.

As a child Peggy Toner, with her black frizzy hair and a big voice appeared in Florrie Forde pantos during the First World War. On posters of the twenties she was billed as 'The Girl with the Phenomenal Voice', or 'Scotland's Sophie Tucker' which was not always a favourable title:

Sunday Mail: 23rd July 1934
'With due apologies to her excellent act, I think it is a mistake. The only nation that can produce a red hot mamma is America. The wording stamps the act as an imitation, which it is not.'
While she also received excellent notices:
At the Gaiety Theatre: 'The best artistic turn is that of Peg Toner, described as Scotland's Sophie Tucker and who is worthy of the highest praise for a clever performance',

and at the Empress:
'Peggy Toner sings "Some of these Days" à la Sophie Tucker and to judge by the applause she received her impersonation is well nigh perfect'.

October/November 1942
Queen's Theatre: Second House Fridays: *Go as You Please* concerts. £2, £1, and 10/– prizes.

November 30th 1942
Empress: Variety Show – Kardoma, Will Starr, and Vicky Lester, 'Scotland's Judy Garland'.
(It is interesting to note that Betty Melville was also billed as 'Scotland's Judy Garland'.)

JIM FRIEL

'One of my all time favourites is Master Joe Peterson. Her real name was Mary O'Rourke, the sister of Joe O'Rourke who was himself a very big star of the Glasgow Music Hall and a fine singer. She was originally billed as Mary O'Rourke but when I first saw her in the fifties she always dressed as a man and appeared as the Singing Choirboy. She came from an Irish show business family from Melbourne Street in the Gallowgate area. I believe she made her debut at the Queen's. I saw her in several Logan family summer shows at the Metropole and once in the Tommy Morgan show at the Pavilion. She always brought the house down and got several encores and was one of the finest singers I have heard. She sang sentimental songs with such a superb voice. The spotlight would be on her and you would just see her white collar and face. I know she made several records but for tax reasons recorded under several names. She sang songs such as her signature tune, "Sing Choirboy", "My Mother's Birthday", and "Old Pal, Old Gal, Pal o my Cradle Days". One of her last appearances was at the Palace Bingo Hall, next door to the Citizens in the Gorbals. As usual she was given a wonderful ovation. She latterly lived in Hamilton Street, Polmadie, where she died around the mid sixties. Jimmy Logan organised the funeral at St. Peter's cemetery, in the East End.'

Master Joe Peterson has recently had quite a revival of interest in Holland where her records are constantly requested on radio shows and letters have been sent to local Glasgow papers asking for more information on her work and recordings. It seems that thirty years after her death she has been rediscovered.

Evening Times, 29th December 1989
'In Holland there has been an enormous revival of interest in Mary O'Rourke, a woman from Bridgeton who was known on stage in Glasgow as Master Joe Peterson. The Singing Choirboy means a great deal in Holland but until recently nobody there knew she was a woman. Alec Frutin, who used to employ her at the Metropole Theatre remarked "I'm quite certain that she would have been quite a megastar had she been alive today. She had that novel quality people are looking for.'

Mary and Joe O'Rourke were such talented children when they appeared in various talent contests in Glasgow's East End, that Ma Logan used to warn other young hopefuls 'Stay away from the O'Rourkes. They are too good'.

JIM FRIEL

'Edie Haley was another great performer at the Princess and the Metropole and one of the big stars of the Glasgow halls. She also appeared as a male impersonator and her big song was the legendary Glasgow pub ballad "Why did you make me care?". There is a story that she was in love with the manager of the Princess, who jilted her. That was the meaning behind the song. On one occasion in the fifties at the Metropole where she had so many triumphs, some of the audience began throwing coins on to the stage as she struggled to reach the high notes. This was a dreadful sign of insult by the audience, meaning, thank you, that's enough of your act, you can go home now. Mary O'Rourke appearing on the same bill came on and joined her for a few numbers which brought the house down. Edie Haley then walked off saying that she wouldn't take the coins as perhaps those who had thrown them needed them more than she did. I also remember the O'Neill Sisters, Eileen and Annie, a very popular act with songs at the piano and an occasional jig. Songs ranged from the romantic, "Someday", to the comical, "McCarthy's Holiday Camp at Galway Bay". They appeared in several Logan family shows at the Metropole'.

The work and dedicated commitment of the Musical Director is seldom properly recognised. The arrangement of all the music and songs for every soloist, for company ensemble work, interlude music, incidental scene-setting in pantomime, every note played from fanfares to the closing flourish on the drums, was the responsibility of the man in the pit, in charge of the orchestra.

MARJORY DOWDS O'DONNELL

Born 1936. Daughter of Bobby Dowds (1903–1987), Musical Director in Dundee, Edinburgh and Glasgow.

(This memoir of her father was written in the form of a letter from her home in New Jersey, USA).

'I would be disappointed if our late father was not remembered by the theatre profession in Scotland. From his early twenties his life was devoted to the theatre. If the Glasgow Empire had not been closed down and demolished to make room for office buildings, Bobby would have worked there until he dropped. The theatre was his life and his love.

'Showbusiness was a hard life. The ordinary man and woman in the audience saw only the glamour of it, not the hardship, the sacrifices and hard work experienced by people like our father. There was little in the way of family life. Time together hardly existed, as we willingly put up with his unusual hours, no holidays and little money. Very early in my life I learned that in the eyes of some people, ''Showbusiness'' was not quite respectable. Some of our neighbours looked down their noses at us but if it bothered our mother she never let it be known. Our father would explain that he worked hard for his living and he had trained professionally for years for his job and that it was honest work that hurt no-one and brought joy to many.

'We did not have a normal childhood. Before we left for school each morning around 8.45 am we'd have to wake Dad from his sleep and kiss him goodbye and when we returned at lunchtime he'd be hard at work writing music and couldn't be disturbed. Then at the end of the school day, we'd get home around 4.15 pm, and Dad would have already left for the theatre and he'd be gone until past midnight. Of course, most nights we'd be sound asleep at that hour, but no matter, he'd always come into our rooms, wake us up and tell us a story. He felt it was important to talk each night as it could be our last night on earth.

'Bobby Dowds was completely dedicated to his craft. He never once missed a curtain-up. In fact he would set out several trains early travelling from Dumbarton to Glasgow on the old LMS or LNER railway lines in his Empire days, just in case one engine broke down. He was an excellent variety theatre conductor who was able to handle the unexpected and use the music of his orchestra to preserve the illusion of continuity when acts sometimes omitted part of their material.

'One of his special talents which enhanced his value as a musical director was his ability to write band parts and arrange music for every instrument in his orchestra. Many top-of-the-bill singers came to the Empire in Glasgow with only piano music for their numbers. Bobby spent many a weekend transcribing piano music into music parts for all fifteen-plus instruments in the orchestra. He said that he could hear the different instruments in his head, and as he had perfect pitch, he would ask me to sing certain notes while he decided on the best notes to harmonize.

'The transcription work was extra and he should have been paid by the particular performer but often all he would receive would be a thank you, and only sometimes, a five pound note for a whole weekend's work. In that respect he was not a good businessman and never billed anyone for anything. Surprisingly Bobby was asked to prepare band parts for top American performers who brought their own conductors with them. These singers included stars such as Johnny Ray, Dean Martin, Jerry Lewis, Hoagy Carmichael, Guy Mitchell and Frankie Laine.

'My father often worked away from home, and unnecessary stress was added to his life trudging from one address to another seeking decent digs. He would often come back to overcooked, cold sausage or congealed fried egg lying uncovered, which the landlady's cat might have touched. The stories he told his family were a mixture of the pathetic and the outrageously funny. One landlady tried to persuade him to marry her daughter – she just would not believe that he was already married with children.

'Bobby Dowds was committed to the most popular of showbusiness slogans. ''The Show Must Go On''. Like the best of conductors he was able to lead his musicians faultlessly even when a singer missed several notes, or even a full line. The audience would never suspect that the performer had ''fumbled''. He would always be completely alert and flexible. I don't believe he was ever caught by surprise at anything on stage. For example, during an acrobat act, when one girl jumped on the shoulders of her sister, she accidentally dragged off her sister's bra, which then fell to the stage. Although Bobby was just a few feet away, he never faltered. The music continued, he smiled encouragingly at the unfortunate girl and the act continued to the end. The girl quickly picked up her bra and put it back on. She bowed to the audience and left to tumultuous applause. Bobby had trained his orchestra to watch his fingers closely for signals if something had changed such as acts coming on in a different order. The orchestra supplied continuity as well as atmosphere and entertainment to the audience.

'Bobby developed an ability to recognise talent – from his vantage point he had the closest and unobscured view of everything which occurred on stage. He spotted mistakes and ad libs. Many of the beginner performers he pinpointed as having what it takes, actually went on to become stars. Among the artistes he spotted, were a very young Petula Clark, Dick Shawn, Connie Francis, Alma Cogan, Helen Shapiro, Shirley

Bassey. I remember him telling us that he thought the teenage Petula Clark would do very well but she was wearing the wrong style of dress. He must have made some similar comment to her, because she never wore that type of dress again.

'The Deep River Boys singing group were so impressed with Bobby's talents that they wanted him to sign on as their personal musical director. He was tempted to accept the offer but mother was against it. She had already moved a number of times during Bobby's career and did not want to move again, certainly not outside Scotland. Bobby used to contrast his work with other professionals thus: ''Doctors bury their mistakes, bakers eat theirs, but conductors working in the public eye have no place to hide their mistakes''.'

ISABELLE DICK

Younger daughter of Bobby Dowds. Born Dundee, 1940.

'My father had a very high regard for circus performers and in fact had worked in circus himself. He had played for the Bertram Mills Circus for several seasons in his early career. He recognised the work that they put in was really incredible and that they never got the accolade that some stars got. He also admired the chorus line, the high kickers. He said these girls work and work and work and to be a dancer was a tough life. They were there every night and every week.

'My father of course, wore an evening suit. I remember it was a regular thing that he took two or three shirts with him, and he changed at the intermission. The orchestra didn't actually get a long break because they played during the interval, but just before the end, he would come out, wash and change because the work was really quite vigorous physical exercise. I remember my mother having to send his jackets to be relined, because the linings were quickly torn with all the arm movements every evening. It was the days of the starched shirt, so it must have been quite hot and uncomfortable. Latterly he stopped wearing the stiff shirt and tails, and wore a soft shirt and dinner jacket.

'I think everyone was proud, that is the word, proud, of working in the Glasgow Empire, because it was reckoned to be the best. If you made it at the Glasgow Empire, you had made it. It was the most prestigous thing you could do because you either lived or died by what the Empire audience did to you. I don't think my father would have wanted to go to any other theatre after the Empire. He used to say that the Monday nights there were not as quite as bad as the stories told about it, which have become legendary. I do remember him talking about some singers, during whose acts the audience threw pennies onto the stage. This was a definite sign of rejection. There was one woman who went off in tears and he realised then how performing at the Empire was terribly hard when you had to put up with that sort of behaviour.

'And it was, to a certain extent, quite hazardous for the orchestra when the audience reacted in this way. My father's head was badly cut by someone throwing a penny from the balcony and another time he was hit right in the small of the back which almost blacked him out. No-one thought they might kill the orchestra doing this kind of thing, let alone the poor person on the stage.

'The Empire Theatre was certainly a true "Variety theatre". One story he was always telling us was the time he went to the Gents backstage and a chimp calmly walked out. It was appearing in an act of *Educated Apes*, and had actually been taught how to use the lavatory. My father certainly became accustomed to anything and everything happening on stage and off.'

ROSS BOWIE

'Bobby Dowds was the conductor at the Glasgow Empire the night Des O'Connor fainted. He was standing there in the centre stage, centre mike, doing his act, a couple of numbers and one or two gags, at the Glasgow Empire, well known as the graveyard for English comedians. Bobby was in the pit when Des takes a header into the footlights and he coped as professionally as he always did, completely unruffled. The orchestra played on without a hitch, while Des O'Connor was carried off. The MD's job was very difficult, and there was so much to do. Within the two hour show, sixty per cent was music. The only time you might have a break was when it was a comic and you could go and have a smoke.'

JOHN WISHART

Electrician, Empire Theatre, 1955–1963.

'I remember the night Des O'Connor fainted at the Empire. He was very young and inexperienced. He simply froze in the wings and we had to virtually throw him on. He was terrified of that Glasgow Empire audience out there. He got through most of his act, but then sort of staggered and fell down. Empire stage-hands like us were well trained and we were watching the stage and were able to react instantly. When he fell, we just whipped him out under the curtain at the back. It made it look as if it was part of the act. He was so keyed up about going on, that after his spot was finished, I think he was so relieved that he literally collapsed.

'Bobby Dowds was a great wee chap, but he had a hard time of it because if there was one note out at all, he would carry the can for it. It was a fair size orchestra and some of the band were fairly old by the late fifties. One had been there for years, the cellist, and he would have been about seventy. It was quite a hard job, because the MD only had the one dress rehearsal on a Monday. Some of the so-called stars weren't that easy to get on with. They expected the orchestra to be able to cope with all styles of music and new numbers unseen. Bobby Dowds helped so many artistes and if there were any problems with the music he could make alterations and even rearrange it for them. He would sit for hours before a performance writing out the parts. I don't think he was appreciated at the time, but he certainly did a great deal of essential work on behalf of the artistes and the orchestra which perhaps was never recognised.'

PAT McCANN

Musical Arranger, later Musical Director, Howard and Wyndham.

'From 1953 I was music librarian and arranger of music for all the pantomimes and summer seasons, for Howard and Wyndham theatres. It was the job of the producer and the choreographer to come up with the ideas for the music, but my task was to arrange it for the orchestra, and adapt it so that it was suitable for the particular singer, or cast or scene. For instance, the opening routine – that could be three days work in itself, or if you sat up all night you might get it done. Then there was all the listening to music. The choreographer would come here to my home and we would listen to records and tapes and she would say what about that song, and I would say, I can't do that with a ten piece orchestra. For instance a symphony written for a seventy-five piece orchestra, it is not possible to re-score it for ten. I like working with classical music and interpret it as best I can, but it is always authentic. I never take liberties with music.

'The *Half-Past Eight* shows were initially changed once a week, but shortly after I arrived, we went to once a fortnight, which was like having a prison sentence reprieved. It was still very hard work. I had a regular bed time of about three o'clock in the morning, sometimes later and occasionally I would have to work all night to get the music finished for the show. I remember for one short period I had to stay over in Glasgow, and I was staying in digs, and the woman brought me up a cup of tea at eight o'clock in the morning and I was at the desk working. She said, my goodness you've started early, and then she looked at the bed and almost dropped the tray because she could see it hadn't been slept in. That was quite typical.

'In pantomime, music provides a continuity. There can never be a stage wait, there must always be something happening visually, or musically. Music is almost continuous through a pantomime and therefore the role of the Musical Director leading the orchestra is paramount to the pace of the show. In pantomime I generally have about fifty musical cues, and for some it might go up to seventy cues. Now one cue might be a six minute routine or it might be a thirty second fanfare. It can be extremely fast, the music acting as links, as part of the story, supplying sound effects, fight music, fanfares, chase scenes, background music during characters' entrances. It's not by any means all vocal music accompaniment, although we do have many song routines. It does mean that the orchestra, and especially myself, have to be absolutely alert when performing and therefore in control virtually every second of the show.

'With regard to the songs in a pantomime, popular songs of the day are frequently chosen for the principals which fit in with the story. You cannot use songs which are in a musical which is currently running. You normally have to receive permission on every piece of music that is used, but music publishers usually never mind in the least if you use a certain song because they get royalties on it.

'Pantomimes do remain traditional in terms of format and story line, but it is the music which alters to keep it sounding fresh and modern. I sometimes have a fight with the choreographer if we disagree over music selection. So often they want to be right up to date and they will suggest the principal girl singing a number because it is in the charts. That is because they wish to devise a dance routine around it. But they may ignore the fact that the principal girl is perhaps a beautiful soprano with a lovely voice and that a pop number is not her style at all. So there can be arguments. I think we should keep up to date and give the children something to sing or clap along to, music which appeals to them, so we do include something that is in the charts if possible, but we don't go out of our way to do that.

'Nowadays we use click tracks. That is where we have a choir of six people who have recorded a backing track. It gives the choreographer much more flexibility with movement, because beforehand the singers would have to be static around a microphone. The artistes on stage are singing live as well, to back up the tape. They do have to sing for real and this is something I impress on them at rehearsals, that even if they have recorded the backing track, it doesn't mean they can relax. They have got to perform to their tape and the only way to do that properly is to sing out live. Also, people don't come to the theatre to see a recorded show, they want live music, and the backing track is only to assist with the sound level if they are dancing around the stage. The solo artistes always just sing live.

'In the final week, I will have the orchestra to myself for a couple of sessions, then on the Tuesday, arrange band calls with the artistes. Wednesday afternoon we move to the pit, and have the tape recorder in position, with the click track, all the dancers on stage, microphones working and we do a thorough sound check so that we can do a balance with the orchestra against the singers and solo artistes. On the Thursday we do a technical Act 1, which means we don't use the orchestra, just the piano and we run the first half of the show. The pianist would probably spend more time doing crossword puzzles than playing, as the music has been well rehearsed at this stage. This is when the lighting director is making a lighting plot as we go through each scene. In the evening we would have the orchestra in and hope to do a complete dress rehearsal of Act 1.

'Friday would be spent exactly as Thursday but on Act 2. Saturday would be left clear for cleaning up or solving problems. Saturday night is a full dress rehearsal of the whole show. After this it should be ready to put before an audience.'

MAIDIE MURRAY

'In the double act with Chic we used to open together, with a song, never the accordion. Then I would go off and he would do a routine. I would come on again and do another song, probably another gag and a big number for finishing. We usually used to finish with me playing the accordion. When we had to change our act each week we would perhaps do an All Irish week, or a Scottish theme, with the kilts and marching. It was essential to be constantly thinking of new material and new songs, and getting the right keys, and getting them written. This was called "writing your dots". Your music was your dots.

'There were some amazing experiences though. The MD at Greenock used to make faces at me, I remember. Often the small variety theatre orchestra would sound like a piano, hoover and drums, it was so bad. I think it was on a tour called The Balmorals, when our act required the accompaniment of good drumwork, some nice "brushes", so I said to the drummer, could you do this with nice and soft brushes, a nice tempo? Anyway, when we came to that part of the act, and we were singing, "Come to me . . . my Melan-choly Ba-by", instead of what I had said, he was rolling the sticks, even putting them up to his face, regimental style. As well as playing in the orchestra at night, he was also a drummer in a local pipe band!'.

EVELYN HENRY

'I remember being enthralled at my first visit as a child to the Tivoli Theatre, Aberdeen, when the Musical Director, Haydon Halstead, wearing tails with a carnation in his buttonhole, a waxed moustache and white gloves, stood above his twelve piece orchestra. This was when I realised I wanted to go on the stage. Sadly the standard of this type of show diminished. When I sang there, Cliff Jordan still maintained an excellent orchestra, but it was declining and it went down to a band of about six with a piano conductor. Then down to a trio of piano, organ and drums. It was a shame because it just wasn't the same without an orchestra.'

Walter Carr as Tommy Lorne

Chapter 6

THE COMEDIANS

'I love my profession and I think I'll take it up seriously. Mind you it is a serious job trying to make people laugh. Laughter is the sensation of feeling good all over and showing it principally in one spot. And this weary old world of ours needs all the laughs it can get out of life because they help us over the rough places. A ripple of laughter is worth an ocean of tears. To laugh is to be free of worry.'[1]

HARRY GORDON, (1893–1957) the great Scots comedian giving his definition of comedy, from a talk broadcast on BBC Radio in 1949. While he became exceptionally popular in Edinburgh and Glasgow through numerous seasons of the *Half-Past Eight* show, and sixteen years playing Dame in pantomime at the Alhambra, Harry Gordon will always be remembered as The Laird of Inversnecky in his native Aberdeen. With his superb eye and ear for observing speech, mannerism and character, he created an entire village of imaginary people, from gossiping wifies, buxom ladies, to the Inversnecky Football team, doctor's surgery and fire-brigade. From 1924 until the early war years, the Inversnecky Story among other humorous sketches, songs and light entertainment, developed year by year during Harry Gordon's perennially popular summer shows at the Beach Pavilion in Aberdeen.

As the Aberdonian journalist Ruby Turberville has commented: 'Soon Inversnecky was peopled with all sorts of characters who were to become as familiar to all of us as the people next door. The place became so real that visitors would ask to be directed there. Only Harry knew about its whereabouts, and once he revealed all: "Ye gang oot there, pointing towards Deeside, for sixteen miles and ye come to a signpost. On ae side it says, "You are entering Inversnecky," and on the ither, "You are just leaving Inversnecky". It taks an oor by train

frae Aiberdeen and an oor and a half by bus an' if ye wait for a lift it micht tak a lifetime'.
Scots Magazine, December 1987.

The Inversnecky stories would be told through a mixture of song and patter such as The Inversnecky Pub, Inversnecky Art Gallery, or the Bells of Inversnecky:

> The Bells o' Inversnecky ring
> Upon a Sunday morning,
> Eh-my we're awfy late the day,
> Bringing tae the country side
> Encouragement and warnin',
> Hive ye got the pandrops, it's time we were away . . .

and after being advised to take mints to suck during the sermon came the delightful chat: 'But isn't it fine to be wakened up on a Sunday mornin' by the Kirk bells ring, telling ye that the *News of the World* has arrived and then ye ken ye can lie in yer bed until denner-time? It's great, isn't it?'.

BUNTY McLEOD

'It was a chorus girl who first gave my father the idea for Inversnecky. As far as I can remember they were doing some sketch and this girl remarked, "Oh look at them, they're just "snakin'"" along". Dad seemed to catch on to this unusual word and called the girl "Snakey". He then added the name Inver to the front and that was it. This mythical town of Inversnecky, with all the different characters speaking the Doric tongue, simply reflected the people and humour of Aberdeen and the surrounding countryside. Yet people used to write to him from Canada and America, just addressed to Harry Gordon, Inversnecky, Scotland and he would receive a huge amount of mail with that on the envelope.

'The sketches he did with his partner, Jack Holden, were popular and of course he was famous for his quickies. He would have a spot immediately after the opening of the show and he could come on and do about twelve quickies. These were quick gags. Jack would walk on and my father would follow on and say something, and after a few lines of repartee, it would end with a gag. For instance I remember one quickie which began with the sound of a horse passing by and stopping. Then Harry would come on as a coalman with a bucket. There would be a public bar set in the corner and he would walk up and say, "A bucket of whisky for the horse please". "OK Jock, will you have one yourself?". "No thanks, I'm driving".

'They were all like that, fairly short, simple, often stupid jokes but there would be about a dozen or more of them one after the other, bang, bang, bang. As soon as the gag was said, there would be a blackout, then another quickie. He did those in all his shows, even *Half-Past Eights*. Of course he had to find a dozen different gags every single week, and that was just the first item in the show. He had a very good sense of humour. Many people thought he was a very quiet man, which he was, but he had a devilish sense of humour. One of his favourite remarks was when he used to say to people, ''Well I have been pleased to have met you, and next time you're passing this way, just pass''. And people automatically replied, ''Oh thank you Harry, that would be lovely''. They just didn't realise what he had actually said. He simply enjoyed the joke.

'There was nothing he liked better than to sit on a deck chair on the promenade armed with a notebook and watch the world go by. Literally all sorts of people and characters would walk past, in every shape and size. He would come back with his notebook and a bag of French pastries, which he adored, and he would be laughing his head off at some of the people he had seen and what he had overheard. He would often say he had found some winners today. He simply wanted to take a little bit from life, so that whatever character or scene he did, he was believable. I remember being in the audience once when a woman next to me, nudged her friend and whispered, ''That's just like Mary next door''. In that way, he liked his sketches to be identifiable, where people were similar to your neighbour, or your auntie. He felt this was an essence of his style of humour that the audience would relate to and connect in some way to the characters he portrayed.'

RUBY TURBERVILLE

'I loved Harry Gordon. He was clever, he was funny, he was an all round entertainer and he made thousands and thousands of people happy. With his songs, with his records, with his sketches, on radio, on the stage, you name it, he was there. And I still laugh at his jokes. I think Harry Gordon was so popular mainly because it was a very local kind of humour. It was very involved with the North East and Harry was very much dependent on the Doric for his humour, and of course it was a very funny-ha-ha sort of thing that he would be doing.

'He was what Jimmy Logan calls ''a whiplash comedian''. Harry had timing, and he knew his audience. He could tell in the same time, twice as many jokes as any other comedian.

'His wifie sketches were hilarious. He took endless care over make-up and costumes and built up a huge wardrobe. One dress in his collection had belonged to Queen Victoria, and was gifted to him by his fellow-comic,

Jack Radcliffe. And when Harry died most of his wardrobe was bequeathed to Jimmy Logan.'

Aberdeen Press and Journal, 6th May, 1919
HARRY'S LATEST SUCCESS:
'Of Mr Harry Gordon himself it need only be said that he is, as always, the mainspring of the fun that so largely permeates the show. Another tit-bit has been added to his famous Inversnecky series of character studies. This time he is the photographer of that quaint village. The chorus of the song will soon be all the rage, but it would take a nimble mind to recall half the clever jokes that he fires off in patter.'

AILEEN VERNON

'I think it was my first pantomime as stage manager when one of the cast, Harry Gordon's female feed, was ill. Harry said, "She's off. Whit'll we do? Och, I know, the wee lassie can go on". And the wee lassie, me, jumped into the costume, which didn't fit very well and went on. I had been trained as an actress so there was no problem really except that I tried to be funny. I tried to be too funny. So I was given my come-uppance in the nicest possible way. "It is not your job to get the laugh". I was just the wee lassie who had gone on with Harry Gordon, THE Harry Gordon, and I tried to put in gags. Those were in the days when you could slip in the odd one. In between the laughs which Harry got, he told me, "Don't try that again. Don't be too funny. I am the comic, don't forget". He said it with a twinkle in his eye but he was annoyed, and for Harry to get annoyed *on stage* was unusual. But I went on my merry way and again I tried to be too smart. Everything I said, he topped, every time he had a funny line and even if it wasn't in the script, I would come out with another. Afterwards he called me into his room and said, "Now listen lassie, if you want to continue in this business, comic's feed or otherwise, you will let the comics say the funny lines. I don't want that happening again, because you not only did it in that scene, but again and again. I do the funnies, and that is what people come to see and why I am paid hundreds of pounds". I was reduced to shreds but I had learnt my lesson.'

STANLEY BAXTER

Actor and comedian

'I have enjoyed working with almost every co-star and got on with most Scottish comics. Alec Finlay and I got on like a house on fire, and while Harry Gordon was more difficult to get to know, he was always so very nice. He was always very genial but also very reserved and aloof, keeping himself to himself. But he was very friendly towards the rest of the company and he would have ''Harry's Teabreak'', at eleven o'clock in the morning. He would say, ''You'll come in and have a cup o' tea and Minnie will make us all tea and biscuits''. But there was still an arm's length to him, you didn't ever get too close to Harry'.

ALEC FINLAY

(From a BBC archive interview, 1974)[2]

'Harry Gordon and I did twelve years together in pantomime, mostly at the Alhambra Theatre, from the late thirties to early fifties. We had some great times, we were very good friends. We did twelve pantomimes but only fell out once. It was rather unfortunate. We had a callboy, who came to tell us when we were due on stage. His name was Wullie and he was dressed as a page, like Buttons in *Cinderella*. He had tousled hair and a voice like a fog horn. Instead of knocking on your dressing room door, he just breezed in, no matter who was there. He would shout in your ear, ''You're on next'', and nearly deafen you.

'On this particular Saturday night, he came into my room and shouted at me that it was my cue so, as a joke, I said to Wullie, ''I am ready to go on. Harry Gordon is still on so go and tell him he can come off now, I'm ready''. I didn't think anymore about it. Suddenly through the tannoy, I heard this terrible voice shouting, ''Mr Finlay says he's ready to come on so you can come off now'', right in the middle of Harry's act! He was doing 'The Opening of the Kirk Bazaar', a wonderful sketch, and of course he couldn't pick up the threads, while the audience started to laugh, thinking it was all part of the act. Harry just had to go into the last chorus and come off. He was really annoyed with me and I was terribly upset. I tried to explain what had happened but he wouldn't listen. I was worried about this all weekend and didn't sleep at all. On Monday night when I got to the theatre, Harry came to see me in his dressing gown, half made-up. ''You know Alec,'' he said, ''I am a silly ass. I never slept all weekend. I know now it was a joke which went wrong. I just didn't realise. Will you forgive me?''. ''No Harry,'' I said, ''Will you forgive me? It was my fault.'

HARRY GORDON in an extract from
'The Opening of the Kirk Bazaar'

'. . . Now folks if you have been enjoying yourselves up to now, I am definitely going to put a stop to that. This is where I do my wee bit and I'm going to inflict upon you one of my dame characters. I put on my heid, this lady's wig, aroon my neck, a feathery boa, arrange my hat at an angle so, a handbag, brolly, and there ye are, I'm ready for the opening of the Kirk Bazaar'.[3]

JIMMY PARKINSON

Business Manager to Harry Gordon, 1928–1939.

'Harry used all types of comedy. I liked him best in his character roles and some were terrific. Inversnecky was populated by umpteen people, all different characters; there was the postie, the school master, the Provost. They were mostly written by a schools inspector who used to go round the Islands here in the North and while he was travelling, he used to get ideas and wrote many of Harry's comic songs – character numbers we used to call them.

'There was a particular sketch called 'Rough Hands', in which he played the old lady in this, a beautiful old lady, with tears in his eyes. 'Rough Hands' was a delightful sketch, I saw it again and again – a real gem. It was about an old couple and their son is coming home after being away for some time. He's bringing his fiancee with him and much to the surprise of everybody the girl makes an awful fuss of the old lady's hands and the finish of the sketch is when the son and girl friend go away and she sits back in her chair. It was a very moving scene. You really forgot it was a man, it was the actions, just like his mother.

'His humour was very homely stuff, very much down to earth. He seemed to excel in family humour, not a lot of business, mostly jokes but the type of comedy that appealed to everybody. The country person could come in and enjoy it, the same as anybody else. It wasn't sophisticated. It was always clean stuff.'

Evening News, 6th May 1940
Theatre Royal, Edinburgh

'It is no small wonder why Harry Gordon always receives such a rousing welcome when he comes to Edinburgh. Packed with humour, music, song and dance this show is a perfect war-blues antidote. In response to many requests, that domestic classic 'Rough Hands' was put over beautifully by the company, and greatly appreciated.'

JOHNNY WILLIAMSON

'The pantomime in Glasgow in the thirties brought Harry Gordon and Will Fyffe together as two ladies and they called themselves the Sisters

Dalrymple. Their catch phrase emerged as "The Sisters Dalrymple, not a plook, not a pimple". They were marvellous.

'Then we visited the Beach Pavilion in Aberdeen in the summer which was quite a way from the town centre, and we had to take the tram down there. When we came out of the show, there were tram cars waiting to take us back into town. It was all organised by Harry Gordon.

'Inversnecky was a wonderful imaginary village in which Harry Gordon played every character. He was the Inversnecky fireman, and one sketch relates the time someone rings up to say his house is on fire and Harry the fireman replies, "Och, we're awfy busy, can you pit some coal on and we'll see ye in twa hoors time".

'Then he would play the Beadle of the church and did very well in this role, such as a scene when some Americans come into the church and remark "Oh I say, there is a right smell of sanctity in here" and Harry the Beadle would answer, "Och, now awa', it's jist a 'scape of gas". Then he was the road man, "We're gang to pit the milestones closer togither − then ye'll ken much better how far ye have to walk.".'

LETTER FROM THEATREGOER IN ABERDEEN

'With pleasure I recall going to the Beach Pavilion on Friday evenings with my boyfriend. It was the highlight of the week going to see The Laird of Inversnecky. Harry Gordon was wonderful and made his audience respond with peals of laughter. There was always a happy atmosphere and not an empty seat to be seen. Indeed happy memories − it would be wonderful to relive one of those Friday evenings.'

MAY ROSS

Theatregoer; Portlethen, Aberdeen.

'Harry Gordon was a great old-time entertainer and in the 1930s my boyfriend and I enjoyed many of his shows at the Beach. I especially remember his Crazy nights, when he told his pianist Alice and her piano to leave. Harry then brought on a Barrel Organ. It was always a good clean show, and this has brought back many happy memories for me. I am over eighty now, and it's eleven years since I lost my husband but I still have so many memories of those weekly shows to keep me happy. We always said Harry Gordon was a second Harry Lauder whose singing will never be forgotten. He will aye be remembered as The Laird of Inversnecky.'

DAVE WILLIS

Dave Willis, (1895–1973), widely regarded as the Charlie Chaplin of Scotland, was Harry Gordon's contemporary and absolute equal in terms of comic originality and popularity on the variety and pantomime stage. From the early forties, when Harry Gordon left the Beach Pavilion, they shared the star billing in the *Half-Past Eight* shows, one being in Edinburgh and the other in Glasgow. Indeed it was Dave Willis who established these summer shows so successfully, from 1937 onwards, as discussed previously, and who enjoyed the longest running seasons of twenty-eight weeks in 1939 and 1941, rising to thirty-one weeks in 1942.

It is worth noting that these were the early, crucial war years. Entertainment must have provided essential light relief.

Scotsman, 29th December 1938
'Issue of gas masks in Edinburgh. Police to make appeal by loud speakers'.

Evening News, 6th June 1940
'CLYDEBANK HIT AGAIN. Much damage done in new blitz'.

During this period of chaos and worry, there were daily lists of names under the Personal columns in the newspapers entitled, ''Missing on Active Service''.

Evening News, 13th July 1940
'THE SCOTTISH RAIDS: Bombs in three areas caused some casualties. Bombs were dropped on a housing estate in a town in South West Scotland when a lone raider flew over the area. A labourer and his daughter aged seven were killed.'

Evening News, 25th June 1940
The *Half-Past Eight* Show:
'The two hours of lively entertainment at the King's with Dave Willis as the chief funmaker continues to draw large audiences. This week Dave revives by special request his popular A.R.P. number . . . .'

Sunday Mail, 18th November 1940
'Triumphantly the *Half-Past Eight* show at the King's sails into its final week. It began in May and has played in Edinburgh and Glasgow. Dave Willis may well be proud of this record run. Says a lot of both him and his company that they have managed to present a new and sparkling entertainment every week. To Dave, who threw all his boundless vitality into his part, to Nina Devitt who sang and danced with vivacious charm, to lovely singer, Florence Hunter, exotic dancer,

Joan Conley, and the Charles Ross Girls, who added grace and beauty to a delightful revue, I say, we thank you.'

BERYL REID

'I admired many comics, who were really all clowns like Dave Willis, Jacques Tati, and Tony Hancock. They don't need words, just a minimum of words, they are simply funny men.

'I did all sorts of sketches with Dave Willis in the *Half-Past Eight* shows, and touring shows. A scene in India, Dave Willis as Dave Willis Barton, as a send-up of Dick Barton. He used to have a magnifying glass with no glass in it, putting his hand through and saying, "Ah, a footprint!". Or we would have a double act with me pushing him as a chinaman in a wheel-chair. Every single possible subject, character and setting was used.

'Dave and I did a double act at the Empire. We would sing a duet, "You Made Me Love You", with Dave dressed like Charlie Chaplin, playing the fool, and going down to the audience to ask for a light! I was never any good because he would make me laugh. He did the most terrible things, getting under this bench we were sitting on, with this little red nose, and suddenly asking me for a light, when, of course, I was totally unprepared.

'He was a comic with real genius; somebody I could watch night after night and still be totally amazed. It was a great company atmosphere. We worked extremely hard, for no money. I was learning the business at this time and realised that by working with Dave Willis, here was a man who could teach me. And he really did.'

DOROTHY TREWHITT

Dancer in pantomime during the 1930s in Edinburgh and Glasgow.

'Of all the comics I worked with I did like Dave Willis best. He was such a lovely man. The funny thing about Dave was that he never rehearsed anything. He'd say, "We'll do this and say that" and so the cast had to pick it up. He never had a script and yet he was really brilliant – the best of the lot. We worked right through the thirties in pantomime and every year there would be a topical song such as the wonderful skit he did on Ghandi, in a little loin cloth. They even brought on a goat on stage and the things he used to sing about – "Oh Mr Ghandi, wi yer wee dish clout, yer a silly galoot" and so on. He was also renowned for his impersonation of Adolf Hitler, which may seem tasteless now, but at the time, the song "I'm getting more like Hitler every day" went down very well. Then there was his famous comical song, "In My Wee Gas Mask", which was extremely popular in the early war years, and which acted as a real morale booster.

'It was the repetition of such songs and characters that people seemed to love. Favourite catch-phrases were "Way way uppa kye" which he had heard his son Denny say, watching the planes flying over, and the typical cry of Glaswegian housewives, "Wait till ah tell you", as they stand chatting.

'There were songs on every subject such as The Loch Ness Monster, which went something like this:

The Loch Ness Monster,
I don't believe it's anything at all
I've heard folk say,
Och awa, it must be King Kong's mother-in-law
But Ah'm tellin you,
It's no true,
Ah'm tellin you just for once, sir,
It must have been a haddie,
Looking round to see its daddie,
And it's always been the Loch Ness Monster.

'He didn't mimic Charlie Chaplin, he was always his own man, but he did look like him, with a little moustache and bowler hat. A Scottish comic was pawky, rather than slick, and they were homely. You could take your great grandmother to see any of them. I never remember any of those comics being "blue" or offensive. Many of the English ones were, such as Max Miller and others. Another sketch Dave Willis would do was with the goldfish bowl. Except there were no goldfish, only carrots cut up to look like goldfish. And he used to swallow these things, popping them in his mouth and the children, and adults too, used to believe they were real, because they looked as if they were swimming around.

'And then there was the wallpaper sketch. Dave would be the one putting the paper up and his foot would go through the paper. I know it's been done often since, but he was the first. He would finish up sliding on the paste all over the stage when all his hilarious antics were just wonderful. That's going back to about 1931, 1932 when he would be doing that sort of act.'

Sunday Mail, 12th February 1934

'Dave Willis at the Pavilion. Herr Diktator Adolf Hitler is the funniest sketch he has done so far. He also does the Loch Ness Monster. A regular orgy of laughs.'

STANLEY BAXTER

'I loved Dave Willis. He was an idol of mine in the Scottish comedy field and although he repeated himself so much with the same acts, he was always so brilliant, I could always watch him. He was a genius. Far funnier than Chaplin and greatly underestimated. Sadly, he never broke into any area south of the border. The famous impressario Henry Sherek, when I mentioned how much I admired Dave Willis, said, ''So do I''. I was very interested to hear that. He said, ''I used to go and see him and in fact brought him to London, and then used to sit alone in the auditorium because no-one turned up and laughed.'

But in Scotland, in the theatres or at home listening to his broadcasts on the wireless, people would always laugh at the clownish characterisations and quick wit of Dave Willis.

THE SCOTTISH MUSIC HALL

Sketch featuring Dave Willis and Jimmy Plant, recorded in front of an audience, BBC Scottish Home Service. 4th August, 1951.

(Fast double act)

Jimmy	I'll have you know my father had a fish shop in Aberdeen!
Dave	Oh, (pause) had – he? . . . (great burst of laughter)
Jimmy	Hey, what are you doing? Don't poke me in the tummy like that. I've got an awful pain in my tummy.
Dave	You should go to the National Health Insurance. You'll get it fixed for nothing.
Jimmy	I don't know anything about National Health.
Dave	Haven't you seen one of these books telling you all about it?
Jimmy	Is it easy to understand?
Dave	Oh, a child could understand it, – very, (pause) explicit. (laughter)
Jimmy	That's a good word Dave. Will you elucidate?
Dave	(pause) Umm, yes, with the greatest animosity (laughs) . . . Let's look up the book, pain in tummy, – T. Ah, that's Code 3.
Jimmy	Is it?
Dave	*Code* 3, no a fish! – have you filled in form 46a?
Jimmy	No.
Dave	Well you see, there you are! (great hilarity), that's the first thing you should have done is filled in form 46a.
Jimmy	Where do I get the form?

— 99 —

Dave At the Post office. As soon as you felt the pain, you should have got in a taxi and gone to fetch the form . . . .

JACK HOUSE

Theatre critic and authority on the Music Hall.

'W. S. Gilbert once said that "An acknowledged fool only has to say 'Pass the butter' to set the table in a roar". I think that is true because if you analyse what these wonderful comics actually said, you can't understand why people laughed.

'Tommy Lorne had this advantage of appearance. He was very tall and had a long lugubrious face. There is an interesting story about him: it was the custom in those days not to use your full name, but you were called by your initials and surname. That was how Tommy Lorne got his stage name. His name was Hugh Corcoran and he admired immensely an English comic called Tom E. Hughes. So when he started in the comparative big time he was asked for his name for the billing, and he said, Tom E. Lorne, which was misheard and he appeared as Tommy Lorne, and there was nothing he could do about it. Looking back I think the name Tommy Lorne was much better than Tom E. Lorne.

'The great thing about Tommy Lorne was his intelligent use of the Glasgow dialect. One sketch for example involved a Dance Hall. Of course, Glasgow was the greatest dance hall city in Britain at the time. Lorne went to one of the very rough halls and saw a chap come in with his foot all bandaged and they let him in for nothing. He disappeared into a lavatory and he came out with nothing on his foot, except his shoes. Tommy Lorne used that story in a sketch, improving it in various ways, accurately catching the language and atmosphere of the Glasgow dance hall. Tommy Lorne was a wonderful Glasgow speaker, I think it was his natural tongue as well. But among all the great funny men I have seen, he comes very very high.'

WALTER CARR

'I decided once to do an imitation of Tommy Lorne in a comedy sketch because I had often been likened to him, which gave me the idea. I contacted Jack House, who is a great authority on Music Hall, and he told me about his long thin legs, the high voice and the way he held his hands. I put together this act, with some original material of Lorne's and sorted out the costume. I had this large glengarry, the little short kilt, and sporran, the rubber boots, tartan socks with suspenders, the little waistcoat, and the slit hat. Then I made-up with a rather pale face with round eyes. Impersonating Lorne was the most extraordinary experience which I'll never forget. The act was announced, "Here's Wally as Tommy Lorne" and I walked in from the wings. The King's Theatre, Glasgow just erupted with a great round of applause. What hit me immediately was that among the 2,000 people out there, only a fraction could have actually seen Tommy Lorne. I remember walking to the front of the stage, putting one hand on my elbow and the other up to the side of my face, wearing these little white gloves, as Tommy always did, and there was another round of applause. I began with "Oh, in the name of the wee man" which was one of his well known phrases, and before I could get out the material there were five rounds of applause. Honestly my hair stood on end, it was as though a spirit had taken over. I felt cold, and thought there's something funny out here, which frightened me and almost made me dry up. But I pulled myself together and launched into the act. It was an extraordinary experience to hear that incredible reaction. I never ever saw Lorne but I believe he was a funny, funny man.

'There are few comics who can write all their own material. Hector Nicol was only one of the very few who sat down and wrote gags. Rikki Fulton also writes a good deal of original comedy material. The majority of us, including Lex McLean and Jimmy Logan, have to find material and remember gags. I buy lots of books and commission comedy material and bring it all together. But what appeals to one comic doesn't necessarily appeal to another. I can read through masses of gags and then suddenly I laugh and if I laugh, then I think I can tell that joke. If I think it is funny, I know I can make it work to an audience.

'The lovely thing with Lex McLean was he had such a fund of material. When we took our television series to the variety stage, we could have done a hundred shows and never repeated ourselves. He was a wonderfully funny comic and I worked with him so much, but people used to criticise him because he used to do this parody about Rangers/Celtic supporters. I remember he always just dismissed it, although it did worry him greatly. One day he was looking rather down and he said, "Oh Wally, why don't they realise I want them to laugh at the ridiculous situation. When I say these things on stage it's to make both sides laugh at the stupidity of all that rivalry". And that is part of our job. Lex used to knock Rangers every bit as much as he knocked Celtic. This is one of the magical things about comedy, people see that we are all the same'.

Lex McLean had an individual comic talent of his own and could be best described as Glasgow's Max Miller. He was very clever with his double entendres. He never actually 'spilled out' and used coarse language. There was an innocence about him and he would always keep within the borderlines of good taste. There would be no point in offending the family audiences which had been built up over the years at the Empress, and Pavilion, or the Gaiety and Palladium.

ALEC RODGER

'I knew Lex McLean from his early days at the Empress where I was stage manager and used to make all his stage props, his collapsible tables and chairs. Lex McLean was in my opinion the King of comedy in Scotland. He wrote most of his material himself but had a couple of good script writers as well. Wee Jimmy Carr was his stooge and he used to bamboozle him every Monday night. Wee Jimmy would forget his lines and McLean would tease him. "He's forgotten his lines", he'd reveal to the audience, laughing away. Poor Jimmy would stamp his feet.

'Glen Daly was McLean's best straight man. The two of them together made a great double act. Daly was also very funny, not simply a straight man and McLean didn't mind who got the laughs, as long as the act got laughs. He got the credit anyway. He usually had a stooge, but he was good on his own and could do an excellent single act. He would go all over the place on one night stands, when he didn't need to do that, on top of long resident seasons. He just loved working.

'I would drive Lex McLean home to Helensburgh after his show at the Pavilion if he missed his train. He would normally be the first out of the theatre because he had to catch the last train at about half past ten and would often miss it. On my way back to Glasgow on these trips, it would be quite late, and in those days not many people would be out driving. Many a time a police patrol car would stop me and ask what I was doing out at that time of night. Had I been poaching? It took quite a time to convince them that I had quite innocently been driving Scotland's great comic home.'

BARBARA McCALL

'My husband and I used to go every week to the Palladium in Edinburgh where Lex would bring his resident show. He came to our home every Thursday and as theatrical people rarely eat before going into the show, he would just take brown bread and a banana for tea. We would then go up to the theatre, and during the show he would loudly remark, "See these rich people. When you go to their house for tea, all you get is a slice of bread and banana". He used to tease us like this when the house was full, but he was a great friend of ours and we knew how to take it.

'Nowadays you see a comedian once and they do the same things over and over again, whereas Lex did six months with a different show every week and he would be booked out. He wrote different sketches all the time. He used to sit in our flat and write them, having read the newspapers for ideas as topical sketches. By the time he had gone up to the theatre, he was giving out the news scripts to everyone. He had an awfully quick brain. Everyone screamed at Lex and his style of humour, the noise in the theatre was simply terrific. Yet when he was off stage, he was the quietest person on earth. He used to sit here reading the paper and I would say, "Are you not going to talk to me?", and he'd say, "No I'm reading the paper. I have nothing to say". Nobody could believe he was a comic, when he was off stage.'

Evening News, 20th February 1951:
'At the Palladium Lex McLean and a large talented company present the Gay 90s, a bright and tuneful revue. As usual the pawky comedian McLean is the backbone of the show, a clever skit on the food situation being one of the highlights'.

TOMMY MORGAN

Tommy Morgan, (1898–1958) was another very popular comedian who holds the record for nineteen consecutive summer seasons at the Pavilion Theatre, Glasgow. His shows became such an annual institution that he was known as Mr Glasgow. His nickname however was 'Clairty, Clairty', from his catch phrase, derived from 'I declare to Goodness'. He was perhaps admired and respected mainly because of the way he had worked his way up the business, with his partner of forty years, Tommy Yorke, from a poor background in Bridgeton, to top of the bill. After his death in 1958, his ashes were scattered on the roof of the Pavilion Theatre.

ANNE FIELDS

'Tommy Morgan gave me wonderful opportunities when I was still very young and learning the trade. At seventeen I joined his Summer season at the Pavilion. He was the boss and referred to as The Guvnor. I was never a performer who would arrive an hour before the show, or even half an hour. I liked to arrive just in time and this particular evening I arrived five minutes before the half-hour call. I was given a message, "The Guvnor wants to see you". I couldn't think what this was for. What had I done? It turned out that Tommy's great female feed, Maggie Milne had been taken ill with influenza and I was told, "You're on". I was flabbergasted. "What about a rehearsal?". I was simply told to see Tommy Yorke, Tommy Morgan's partner.
    'Fortunately I had been brought up by my father to stand at the side of the stage and watch other acts so that I would learn from them. I had

watched sketches with Tommy and Maggie and knew what she did, although I didn't know the lines at all well. On stage, Tommy seemed to forget that I wasn't Maggie and whispered, "What's next?" while I stood there floundering. I decided that the only thing to do was to put the ball back in his court. "Well you're the one who knows what we're doing", and the audience absolutely loved that, seeing Tommy's face, because they knew very well that he usually worked with Maggie. It all went down very well in the end.

'Now at that time I was earning about £15 a week. But that night, Tommy must have sent out for the largest box of chocolates he could find and he left them for me, with £5, which was a lot of money to me in those days, tucked into the top, with a thank you card. He also took me out to lunch to Guys Restaurant for a treat. He asked me if I had ever had smoked salmon and when I said no, he said, you must have some. I never had the heart to tell him how much I disliked it!'

Extract from *7 o'Clock Special*, BBC Scottish Home Service, recorded in front of an audience, 14th July 1952:

Musical overture: introducing Tommy Morgan
'What a lovely crowd of people . . . and so young, (laughter) and so beeyootiful . . . (burst of laughter) . . . I don't think there's one of yous . . . (pause) . . . over twenty-one years of age. (great hilarity). God forgive me for telling lies, but I need the money . . . (laughter). Well, now that Dave Willis has retired with a million pounds, there's not many of us left noo. There's Harry Gordon, he's 98 . . . (laughter) and Jack Anthony (pause) . . . 82, (laughter) and Jack Radcliffe, (pause) he's . . . 79 . . . (pause.) And Ah'm just the wean . . . (applause and laughter).'

JOHNNY BEATTIE

'Scots comics were great in doing sketches. Tommy Morgan, Lex McLean, Jack Anthony, and Jack Radcliffe. They were all great sketch comedians. Tommy Morgan's Big Beanie, the GI bride is a classic. Tommy Morgan would come on in drag and looked like a cross between a Christmas Tree and some way-out transvestite, it was unbelievable. I always remember him doing that marvellous gag about Big Beanie, the GI bride. He had this gruff voice, because he'd worked in the shipyards, having had to shout above all the riveters, and Tommy as Big Beanie would say, "I married Elmer and oh, he went away back to America, and he sent for me six months later, and I went across in a big boat, and I'm coming doon the gangway in New York and there's Elmer stonding there on the pier, oh, you couldna see him for flooers, och, flooers everywhere. I says och, look at all those flooers, you shouldna have bothered. He said "Bothered nothing. Get yer jaiket off, you're selling them". That was a typical Big Beanie story.

'He had this round face, or to use a wonderful Glasgow expression, a ba' face. He had such a marvellous rapport with a Glasgow audience, because he was one of them. I remember him saying one night, "Oh, you're in late," to all these women, maybe it was a Church Guild or something. "Oh, you're late, whit happened, did the bus break doon? I bet you've all still got yer pinnies on inder yer coats". He would enjoy just chatting away to them.

'Another thing he'd say, "Oh, they were right toffs. They had fruit in the hoose, when naebody was seeck". That summed up a toff. The working class only got an apple at Halloween. They never had fruit. But that kind of Glasgow language summed him up beautifully, like "We were at a rare party last night, mixed bathing in the jaw box". Now the mind boggles. The jaw box was the kitchen sink, called that by virtue of the wifie pushing the window up and chatting to the wife next door, that was the jaw box. And "toasting the breid on the stairheid gas" that was another thing he would say! That's real poverty, the gas cut off. He was a wonderful comic.

'Then there were all those Glasgow songs. Tommy Morgan used to sing a parody of "Cruising down the River", as "Strolling round the Barras on a Sunday afternoon". I wish I could get a copy of that, but I've never been able to get it. It would be very interesting.

'Jack Anthony was marvellous with his song "I Canny come oot the noo", that was another one:

'I'm courting a nice wee lassie by the name of Jeannie Mackay
A nicer lass than Jeannie, you could never ever spy,
I told her I would take her to a Music Hall you see
And dressed up very nicely she came dancing round for me.
And when I heard her at the door, I was awfy sorry I had to roar,
Oh I canny come oot the noo, the noo, I canny come oot the noo
I'm awfy sorry Jeannie, hen, for disappointing you,
But my mother's taken my claes to the pawn, so whit am I to do,
I've only a muffler round my neck, so I canna come oot the noo.

Wee daft songs like that, they were lovely songs. Then there was Alec Finlay doing his wee Kirk Elder, and Jack Radcliffe doing his drunk. Tommy Morgan would also sing "No-one loves a Fairy when she's forty". He would actually come on dressed as a Christmas fairy. He always had his body covered up wearing Long Johns, and a vest with the tutu sticking out, this outrageous wig, a hand, stockings and boots. And in his deep gruff voice, sang, "Nobody loves a Fairy when she's forty". You can imagine, it was very funny.'

15th May to 28th October, 1944
Pavilion: The Tommy Morgan Show – Summer Symphony – the 6th
resident season.

2nd July, 1956
Pavilion: The Tommy Morgan Show, with Jimmy Neil, Tommy Yorke
and Sally Logan.

JIM FRIEL

'There were dozens of talented comics appearing in the smaller Glasgow
theatres, who never actually became star names but who were superb
entertainers. I remember Jimmy Neil, a very funny man, a stand-up comic
from the Townhead district of Glasgow – he never quite made it and
emigrated to Canada. Sydney Devine used to play a much requested
monologue of Jimmy Neil's.

'There was a very popular Jewish comic, Ike Freedman, who I saw once
at the Empress in an old time show. His songs were ''Hang me by the
Gooseberry Tree'' and ''Only a Jew'':

Why do they say,
That I'm only a Jew,
And despise me because of my breed?
Gentile or Jew
They're both just the same
Though may have a different creed.
I've got a Dad with a heart pure as gold,
And a Mamma we all think divine,
So why do they say that I'm only a Jew,
When I'm one of God's own mankind.

It is hard to believe there was such a song, but his Jewish wit was very
popular in Glasgow.'

Daily Record, 10th September 1935
Empress Theatre:
'That yiddish wizard of humour, Ike Freedman, walks on the stage by
himself, and without feed or foil, keeps the entire audience in
convulsions, with his Hebraic stories and songs. He is a greater favourite
than ever and there will be few people who cannot appreciate this act.'

JIM FRIEL

'Many comics had their own regular ''feeds'' and it was often these straight
men or women who really made the act. Tommy Morgan had Margaret

— 106 —

Milne, Betty Melville and the superb Tommy Yorke. It was originally Yorke who was the funny man when they began and called themselves Yorke and Morgan. Lex McLean had Glen Daly and Carr and Vonnie. When Lex split with Daly he often had the superb Walter Carr. Jack Anthony had Bond Rowell, and Bertha Riccardo.'

JIM HASTIE

'It has not just been the top comic who has been fabulous in Scotland, but you have the comedy feed men. Jimmy Logan had wee John Mulvaney, with the big pop eyes, "Oh, see see me!". I just died when he came on and couldn't stop laughing. Hector Nicol was with Johnny Beattie for many years before he made it on his own in the clubs. With Hector I would have to walk on stage for a sketch but I could never deliver the line; tears would just stream down my face. He had a look, an attitude and a wee quick word and he would steal it all from everyone else. Hector Nicol for me should have been a big, big star.

'Scotland has produced so many of these second string comics. For me they were often better than the first string. Helen Norman, she was a fabulous comic feed to Jack Radcliffe. Then there were the great double acts, the fabulous Chic Murray and Maidie; Mr and Mrs Glasgow – Gracie Clark and Colin Murray, who were wonderful. Anne Fields too is another great comedy feed. In one particular sketch she was dressed in this knitted dress, all coloured stripes like a honey bee, from head to toe, very tight, with a wee balaclava hat of the same knitted material and glasses with no rims, perched on the end of her nose and her teeth blacked out. Every time someone wanted to light a cigarette, this figure would come on, with a soda syphon, saying, "Ah smell smoke", in a husky nasal voice. "Oh there is a stoatin smell of smoke" and then she would chase the person smoking and they would get the soda syphon on them or the cigarette, and she would run to the front of the stage and say "Smoke's away" and run off to terrific applause. It became so funny that this character started coming in all the time. Even in a dance number if we had dry ice, suddenly she would come on and the audience would shriek, "Ah smell smoke", before she could say it.

'People like that just make a show. It is not the individual star names, it is to do with being a company show with everyone there doing it together. It is important to remember that the comedy feeds, the people who do the back-up, are the ones who have made the comic who he or she is.'

JOHN ROBERTSON
Comedy-script writer.

'The very successful and exceptionally popular double act, Clark and Murray began way back in 1926. They later married in 1931. Grace Clark was a pianist and Colin Murray a singer. They were in the same show and that is how they met. Freddie Luca said to Grace one day, we've got a new young baritone coming into the show and she thought immediately that she didn't want any handsome young baritone taking away any of her glory. But it transpired that this young baritone was Colin Murray. When they first worked together it was a straightforward musical double act, but people began laughing at amusing things they said and did to each other, which slowly developed into the wonderful domestic sketches which they perfected together.

'Grace and Colin were regular church-goers and on their first date they went to church together. They moved along the pew when others arrived. Grace, not realising, moved up and promptly sat on Colin's bowler hat, and spent the entire service trying to straighten it out again. She said that maybe that was the reason that she stuck by him, because she didn't want to offend him. The bowler hat became quite a symbol of theirs. It was often a prop in the Bus Stop sketches. The Bus Stop sketch always started with the tune of "Dear Old Glasgow Town", and they strolled on to that. This couple they played would be standing at the bus stop, after a funeral, a wedding, or a family gathering, which would have started an argument, and he would be ripping her family apart something terrible. A famous line I remember was when he says to her "I'll have you know Gracie, that there was a Murray at the Battle of Bannockburn". And she replies, "It was probably a Murray that started it". This was the type of humour. The success of it was their unique timing and they worked brilliantly together. Sometimes they couldn't continue, the hilarity was so tremendous, they couldn't speak for a few moments. Then they would ad lib and keep going with nothing scripted. It was a gift they had, this great rapport with the audience, and a natural ability to see humour in life; it's something you can't script.

'It was all about presentation. Grace would send-up her own dresses, if they were expensive. She would come out wearing a chiffon train on her dress, and she would say to the audience, "D'ya like my wee Cairry-on?" then she would play with the frill and say, "I got this today, it was a very good buy" and continue a great patter about it.

'It is intrinsic in Grace's nature, just in everyday speech. A few months ago my wife sent her a sultana cake and she wrote back to say thank you. "I do like your sultana cakes dear" she said, "You have all the currants in the right place''. And that's a woman now of about eighty-five.

'Grace always looked nice on stage, with very graceful hands and very graceful movements. She would often play the ordinary housewife in sketches, but she could also play the Lady. You've got to have the right balance; you can't come down and be too coarse because many people won't like it. Clark and Murray would never use bad language. They just kept themselves on a level where the audience could see they were very nice people, who could put across the comedy about the natural things that we all see in family life.'

Sunday Mail, July 1958
Metropole: Booking now for Winter show: *Thistle of Scotland* with Clark and Murray — Last year's ran 20 weeks — "The Longest twice nightly run in Britain''.

Sunday Mail, 6th January 1963
Metropole: Clark and Murray in *Scotland Calling*. 120,000 Scots have seen this show. New record for Metropole.

JOHNNY WILLIAMSON

'The sketch I remember well was when Grace Clark came on in an old fashioned hat, a handbag made of beads, a square basket with her mother-in-law's china in it. For years we saw Clark and Murray at the Perth Theatre, and she always kept special costumes for each particular sketch, all beautifully cleaned and spick and span. We used to see them regularly in the summer at Dunoon and they were always top notchers. Sketches would always be about his mother: "Your mother!" Grace would say, "If I could tell her . . .''. This used to go on all the time. They used to have sketches where they stood at a bus stop, when she would have this basket of china, for some family gathering. She never failed to complain about his mother.'

ROSS BOWIE

'The greatest character I have ever met in my life, was Chic Murray. He was so unique, so unusual, although when he came out of the army and started in the late forties; he was terrible, because he had this unique form of comedy that no-one really understood. He was so far ahead of his time that nobody understood him. I remember my father's remark in Falkirk at the Roxy, when he was running a series of Friday and Saturday evening shows, which Chic and Maidie were to be in. This was in the early days of their double act. After seeing Chic he said that he would take Maidie, provided that her husband didn't go on the stage. Poor Chic was relegated to stage manager, opening and shutting curtains.

'Then of course he developed, standing behind Maidie, and he began his kind of patter and people began to understand this different type of comedy, this thinking-man's comedy. But he was the type of man you couldn't use in production scenes. I remember George Clarkson producing a show in Dundee and it was the usual sort of scene set in a gypsy encampment, the company dressed as gypsies. There was Chic, as Chic, and he used to stand there shaking his head, really sending it up. So much so that George Clarkson would tell him off and tell him just to sit there, fill the stage but don't be obvious. But he couldn't help himself. Chic was Chic. So business wasn't all that great in the early part of the week, and the producer was demented by Thursday. Friday night, full house, Chic's in his dressing room getting into his Gypsy costume when George sneaked up and locked the door. Chic shouted to be let out but he shouted back, "I'm bloody sure I won't, you're not going to ruin my gypsy scene tonight!". He kept him locked in the dressing room.

'However Chic Murray went on to be tremendous as a comic. I remember going to see him at the Prince of Wales Theatre in London and he had that sophisticated London audience in raptures. He was such a funny man, and such an original comedian. All the other comics were stealing each other's material, but no-one could pinch off Chic because his stuff was original, nobody else could do it. It was a sad loss when he died. He used to come about this office a lot, when he was in Glasgow and we used to talk about the old days. He was an hysterically funny man, when he started to talk, with a tremendous sense of humour. Chic had to educate audiences to what he was doing, he was so far ahead of his time. Once you got a grip of what he was on about, it was terribly funny and nobody else could do it. It was just *him*. I remember on tours you would see them together. Maidie would have her own big accordion case as well as the suitcase with all the props in it. She's staggering down the road to the van to go on tour, carrying all these cases and Chic's walking behind her just carrying a plastic bag. That was him, sauntering along with his bonnet on.'

Daily Record, 3rd May 1955

'*The Spring Show*: Every week in every way, we're getting better and better. If that's the Spring Show company slogan for their season at the Pavilion, they're certainly living up to it. Jack Anthony, and Chic Murray and Maidie are tops in this week's better than ever edition. Chic Murray enhances his growing reputation with his novel form of comedy.'

MAIDIE MURRAY

'He obviously had this humour which is difficult to describe. I almost think that he was like a storyteller, from the days long before radio, because he was more of storyteller basically, than a comedian. It wasn't even the punchline, but really the bits in between. He would fabricate on things, he couldn't help it, he must have got it from some relative from way back. He had a good voice, a great yodelling voice. He used to yodel to harmony. I would be singing a song and he would take the harmony to that. With his comedy, he just had this way of talking. First he had to make the audience understand his humour, which was difficult, until the timing was there. He worked at the timing and I could see this developing. I took a back seat but I had to be there. He just couldn't work at first without me there, I don't know why, but just to get him launched.

'Once he had the confidence in doing his act, he would go over ten minutes and he was forever getting into trouble for overrunning his time, but if he had the audience in the palm of his hand, naturally enough he would just keep going. The managers used to get mad at him because getting the first house down used to be a shambles on a Monday night, because it used to overrun, which meant your second house was going to be late, which meant the manager would go daft because at half-time he had to get them in the bars, because the bars had to close at ten o'clock, and if he didn't get them into the bars, he used to get very angry at the performers and come round and say, you'll have to cut. After Monday night you found your act was cut by so many minutes. It was always hectic on a Monday. Also getting the last bus was a problem, because if it was a late curtain-down, the buses would be off.

'In a double act, two personalities have simply got to gel together. Perhaps it happened with Chic and I. I was probably bright and peppy while he was sombre, so I think we just fitted each other fine. Different wee items would creep in like I would be standing in front of him and he would be making gestures and signs that a man would make to his wife, and it was a natural thing. We had a thing when the tabs, the curtains, would slowly close and he would have this lovely wee look. He used to have a joke with the two stage hands, and as the tabs closed he would just look and try and catch them, and get a laugh out of that. I didn't see it because I was getting on with the job, doing what I should be doing, selling the song, or whatever, but comic behaviour just crept in. I think it was a natural thing, double acts have got to be like that. You have got to know each other so well, and then you can blow your top when you come off stage if something wasn't right, if the music wasn't right. There was that famous pair, George Burns and Gracie Allen, something just gelled with them.'

JOHN NELSON

Theatregoer in Edinburgh during the 1950s and 1960s.

'Chic Murray was known as the "Lang Dreich" north of Dundee and Aberdeen. Perhaps his sense of humour didn't go down very well in Harry Gordon country. As far as I am concerned, Chic Murray was the finest comedian Scotland has produced. His cracks such as his story of walking down the Waverley steps one day and he meets a friend carrying a dog. "Where are you going with the dog?" Chic asks. "I'm going to have it put down" he replies. "Is it mad?" asks Chic. "Well, he's not exactly pleased with the prospect" '.

'An old gag, but put over with such skill and timing, that you had to admire it. Another popular story was the one about the man who had purposely fallen over on the pavement. "What did you do that for?" his friend asks. "I'm trying to break a piece of chocolate in my back pocket".

'The Palladium theatre would have different shows each week or seasons of about six weeks with Chic Murray, Lex McLean or Johnny Victory. Johnny Victory was the son of an Edinburgh taxi driver. He had a superb character, "Pierre, ze great lovair" when he would come on wearing a long black cape, and all you saw were his eyes. These Pierre sketches were very amusing, with an amazing French accent. Victory would also do fifteen minute monologues, which were often serious commentaries on topical events. Rather than laughing at these you would more often be drying your eyes at the emotional impact he was able to put across. He was extremely clever and versatile because the next moment he would be impersonating Bing Crosby, because he was a Crosby fanatic! Even his dog was called Bing.'

STANLEY BAXTER

'Script and gag writing was always a difficult team effort for the radio series *It's All Yours*. There were no full-time professional comedy writers in Scotland and we had Jack McLeod who was a car salesman in Stirling and Andrew McIntyre a school teacher in Edinburgh and they had to do a lot of work by phone. We would meet up on Sunday and a lot of the script was changed and partly re-written around the piano. We would suggest things and we would all have a hand in partially re-writing, so that the script would be covered in dozens of bows and arrows, and bits written in ink, where we had written in a gag ourselves. But all credit to the boys who had to turn out twenty-six pages of comedy per week.

'It was amazing how simple ideas would develop into great little sketches. I was telling the writers about a female dresser I had in the pantomime *The Happy Hap'ny* at the Citizens' Theatre, and she kept calling me thingme, thingmyjig, as she could never remember names. Very cleverly they thought about this and later said to me that they had written a sketch based on that dresser. It was absolutely marvellous. As soon as I read it, I knew it would go down well. That was the character Bella Vague, who could never remember anybody's name, or the name of any object which she would refer to as Whirlymagerries or thingmajigs, with phrases like Hello Thingme, and she always ended up by saying, in a very nasal voice: ''Well don't forget, my name's in the book, so if you want me, thingme, ring me.''

JANET CRAIG

Theatregoer, Leith and Edinburgh, 1940s.

'I used to go to the Gaiety in Leith in the late forties and it had a wonderful intimate atmosphere. It was here that Denny Willis made a great impression on me. He was very handsome and tall, and extremely funny. There would be about three other men, including his stooge, Johnny Mack, but my favourite was Denny Willis. His timing was just so good. It was knockabout comedy, where Denny was always the one who would be knocked over, or slapped in the face or end up in the wrong place, when they were marching up and down. He had the most wonderful catch-phrase when he fell over. He would turn to the audience, with a pathetic expression and sigh, ''It's the shoes, it's the shoes'', to explain why he kept falling down. It wasn't all slapstick, there were sketches as well, such as 'The Four Hunstman' and 'Four Chelsea Pensioners'.

'At the Gaiety, the boxes were very close to the stage, and Denny would lean over and ask the unlucky patrons who were sitting there if he could have a sweetie. However it was usually ''regulars'', some older women who sat in the boxes and they would know what was coming, and probably loved it.'

ALEC RODGERS

'Denny Willis used to do a good act at the Empress several times. He didn't copy his father, he was a great juggler with ping-pong balls. He would call them Wee Waterfalls, and he would always catch these balls and really got the house going'.

DENNY WILLIS

'I wasn't influenced at all by my father's style of comedy. I was too tall. He said I would never make a comic because I was too tall. He thought all comedians should be small. He had a Charlie Chaplin figure himself. But that was until Danny Kaye came along and messed his theory up, because he was a tall man who was also very funny. My father had to give in after that.

'I didn't really create my own style of comedy, it was just something that happened. When I first started singing, apparently people couldn't hear me past the front row, as I was singing "A Room with a View", in a wee quiet voice. So I had to work on the voice production side of it and it grew from that, but I had to struggle. I didn't know why I was struggling, I just knew I wasn't good enough then. I never aimed to be a name. I always had the advice of my father who said, you just keep in the middle of the road, and you'll go on for years and years. Never you mind about this star business. He was right.

'You need a feed, you have to have a feed. I had a fellow called Johnny Mack and we were together for about thirty years, and he was very reliable, especially since we went to so many different countries. I went to play in twenty different countries and you needed someone who would travel with you all the time. The good thing was that I didn't have to adapt our act, The Hunting Choir Quartet, which became very famous. This was just four men singing, with comedy in it; so whether they understood it or not, they still laughed. The last four or five minutes was just me knocking about, falling about, dodging about. So I could go anywhere in the world. It went down very well in Kuala Lumpur too!

'I am not a Scottish comic, I am a comedian with a Scottish accent. There is a big difference. The comics and of course the audiences here have a wonderful sense of humour. When I go on with Andy Cameron, the gags he comes out with I have never heard before, and which you wouldn't hear down south. It is such a pawky type of humour no-one else has. Like the line he had in pantomime the other day, "I was six before I knew my name wasnae Shut Up". That's Glasgow humour.'

HARRY GORDON

From *Why I am a Comedian*, BBC Archive talk, 1949.

'There is no doubt that the richest humour is to be found in Scotland. And many a time only a Scot can appreciate its depth of character or see the point of a particular joke. Over the border some of our native stories fall flat, not on account of the dialect, but because of the pithiness, pawkiness and subtlety, which usually form the ingredients of the Scotch joke.

'Outside Scotland, the Scots joke always looked for is the one concerning the mythical meanness of oorselves. They love to hear about the fire in an Aberdeen tobacconist shop where the police had trouble dispersing the crowd which had gathered to inhale the free smoke. Or the one about the Fife billiard player who died and left his son two snookers. One thing about Scotsmen is that they have a sense of humour and they can always appreciate a joke against themselves.

'The majority of Scottish comedians have had the sense and ability to keep the party clean. My own personal opinion has always been that when a comic has had to fall back on a risqué joke in order to obtain a cheap laugh, then he has ceased to be an asset to our entertainment world. We Scots comedians should always play follow my leader, and that leader is of course Harry Lauder, whose clean and healthy humour enabled him to reach the highest pinnacle and become the greatest Variety star the world has ever known.'

Stanley Baxter

Chapter 7

THE PANTOMIME

'The National Theatre of Scotland is Pantomime'.[1]
Sir Lewis Casson, Actor/Manager, and husband of Dame Sybil
Thorndyke, after a visit to a Metropole Theatre Pantomime.

'On March 2nd 1717, the *London Daily Courant* carried an advertisement
announcing that at the Theatre Royal, Drury Lane, that evening, would
be presented "A Play called *The Maid's Tragedy*, together with a new
Dramatic Entertainment of Dancing after the manner of the Ancient
Pantomimes, called *The Loves of Mars and Venus*."[2]

This was the first time the word pantomime had been used in the
billing of a British theatrical entertainment. It was John Weaver, the
theatre's dancing master who introduced the term, having studied and
written about Greek and Roman dance. He was keen to initiate a
renaissance in the art of classic dance and in doing so, followed the
traditions of the "pantomimi", the performers of Ancient Rome, who
put on stories by way of masks, clowning, dumb-show, dance and music.
It is Weaver who has thus provided us with the name for the theatrical
form in which music and tumbling acrobats play a large part.

The development of our contemporary pantomime entertainment also
owes its legacy to the Commedia Dell'Arte Theatre tradition of sixteenth
century Italy. Commedia actors, provided with no scripts, learnt how to
improvise with wit and speed given a set story line and stock characters.
These included the rustic dolt, Arlecchino (the Harlequin); the miserly
merchant, Pantalone, (the Pantaloon); the dashing soldier, Scarramuchia
(the Scaramouche) and the cruel hunch-back Pulcinella, who lives
on today at the seaside as Mister Punch. The plots were generally
amorous intrigues of low farce and sentiment, involving a chase scene

between wicked masters, comic servants, and the young lovers. As early as 1677 comedies after the Italian manner were being staged in London. By the early 18th century, any kind of theatrical entertainment which involved familiar stock story line, recognisable characters, acrobats, tumbling, clowning and singing came to be known by the public as a pantomime.

Pantomime was never intended as a Christmas entertainment and neither was it directed primarily at children. Pantomimes were staged at holiday times, at Easter or during the summer. It was the Victorians who first appropriated pantomime at Christmas, when moral tales of good triumphing over evil, based on traditional fairy tales, such as *Cinderella*, *Aladdin*, and *Jack and the Beanstalk*, provided ideal shows for children. The part of Principal Boy emerged from the tradition of the "breeches" part of woman dressed as man in 18th century drama, when the actress Peg Woffington popularised the role in the early knockabout comedies at Drury Lane. It was during the late 19th century that a new kind of performer found his way into the pantomime. This was the music hall artiste who brought a bright, jovial Victorian burlesque style to the show when long legged girls became the 'brave, busty champion of faith, hope and chastity' and Dan Leno became the archetypical pantomime dame. Yet it wasn't until the 1920s that the comic George Lacey began the practice of wearing outrageous costumes, so that this 'tradition' is less than seventy years old.

Pantomime today is thus a hotchpotch of performance styles, derived from Greek dancing and dumb shows, Italian comic characters, the world of circus and clowning, with a touch of the ribald buffoonary of Victorian music hall. There are still to be found elements of ancient theatrical forms and conventions such as good entering from the right, evil from the left, and a Fairy singing rhyming couplets. In Scotland particularly, the perennial popularity of old fashioned pantomime ensures that we cling on securely to many of these traditions. And thus it offers the comic, singer and dancer of the Scottish variety stage the vital role in continuing, and handing on to the next generation, this delightful performance art.

Sunday Mail, 23rd December 1934
'Inverness has its first panto because Tommy Lorne bet Alec B. King he wouldn't put on a panto so far north. When Lorne appeared at Inverness Empire, the audience came from Wick, Thurso, Ross-shire and Caithness. A crofter from one of the Outer Hebridean islands brought his two children to the show. They travelled for twelve hours by boat and train and slept overnight in Inverness and went home tickled to death'.

Sunday Mail, 15th December 1940

'Wartime entertainment remains unchanged this Christmas as far as Glasgow is concerned, for no fewer than seven first class pantos are being presented. Glasgow is probably the only town in Britain with an unaltered Christmas entertainment season. Three of the pantos are already running and have proved themselves successes; *Babes in the Wood*, with Dave Willis at the Royal, *Bonnie Prince Charlie*, with Tommy Morgan at the Metropole, and *Humpty Dumpty* at the Queen's'.

Evening News, 19th December 1950
Robinson Crusoe: Gaiety Theatre, Edinburgh:

'Tommy Morgan was given a rousing welcome last night when *Robinson Crusoe* started a Christmas Season. The children took him to their hearts and shouted with great gusto when asked to co-operate in guarding his goods from the evil spirits . . . and the company includes Duncan's obedient Scottish collies, and a spectacular high wire act by Swan and Leigh'.

JACK HOUSE

'Scotland seems to have this special feeling for pantomime. It is partly because that with a few startling exceptions, it is not the scenery that counts. First of all there's the comedy, and then the sentimental bits, because the Scots are a very sentimental nation, the Glaswegians most of all. The pantomimes I enjoyed most were at the Queen's Theatre. The Queen's Theatre was rather a good building just off Glasgow Cross, and the pantomime there was run by a chap called Harry Hall, and he had the same cast every year; Sammy Murray and Frank and Doris Droy. Frank Droy wrote the script and he wrote it on a F2 jotter, in pencil. Wee Sammy Murray, he is more or less forgotten now, but he was one of the best Scots comics I have ever seen. He had a natural gift for it. He was a wee man and for example I saw him once come on the stage, at the Pavilion, and all he did was to sing "Horsey, keep your tail up". The audience were rolling about. Just an innate gift for making anything funny.

'The great pantomimes really were at the Queen's Theatre, and there it was very, very vulgar, in fact that is putting it mildly. One year, it was discovered that the script had not been licenced by the Lord Chamberlain. At that time all scripts had to be passed by the censor. So Frank Droy's F2 jotter was produced, and sent down to St James's Palace. Goodness knows what they made of it. Probably they couldn't understand any of it, but they gave it permission and so it went on. It became quite the thing for young men about Glasgow to arrange to go out for dinner but to go to the first house of the pantomime and they would, at that time of course, be in dinner jackets. The management of the Queen's Theatre disapproved of this very much and they were always marshalled by the two biggest bouncers in the theatre who watched them all the time in case they stepped out of line and then they would throw them out.'

Queen's Theatre, Winter 1941–42
Hi Diddle Diddle; with Doris Droy and Sam Murray. 6.30 and 8.40 with matinees on Saturday. From 6d to 2 shillings.

Sunday Mail, 30th November 1941
'Hold everything, here's old man pantomime with us already. It's called *Hi Diddle Diddle* but that doesn't mean a thing. When you get Doris ''Suicide Sal'' Droy, and Sammy Murray roaming about the stage, ''It's a rare pant'', as Sammy would say – and ''a rare Panto''. A cheery gang in support. There are some Glasgow folk who have never seen a Queen's Panto – and I'm one of them. The reason? I couldn't get a blinking seat.'

MAIDIE MURRAY

'I played principal girl at the Queen's Theatre when I was fourteen. Ivy Val was Colin, the principal boy – the Principal Boy was always called Colin regardless of the panto – and then I went back the following year. It was a famous place, the Queen's. So much colour there, the Droys, Sammy Murray. He lived in Soho Street, just off the Gallowgate and was ''Parliamo Glasgow'' as a person. It was an absolutely fantastic pantomime and a beautifully dressed show.

'The material was risqué. The things Sammy Murray and Doris Droy said were absolutely outrageous then, not so much now. They got into trouble sometimes. I mean we think nothing of swearing now but they did it then and had to submit scripts to the Lord Chamberlain for the censors to vet. If you changed it you could be in trouble, but many people did, I expect.

'Sammy Murray was a complete and absolute nutter as a person. He was very loud, very ribald. He would say, ''How are you doing China?'' He used the word china all the time. He was lovely, and he would say to me, when I was fourteen, ''See you, hen, you are far too good for this place''. He said that because everyone else was so rough but it really was a beautiful show. The Jackson Sisters, their gowns were just gorgeous and it was all in this tatty theatre'.

GEORGE CLARKSON

'I worked for fourteen years for Harry Hall at the old Queen's Theatre at Glasgow Cross. We had all the celebrities there; Frank and Doris Droy, Sammy Murray and the Jackson Sisters. I was choreographer for twelve pantomimes at the Queen's with Frank Droy producing, and then I produced two of the pantomimes myself.

'Sammy Murray was a character; he was more than a character, he was a definite worthy. I remember one particular sketch I was appearing in at the Queen's and because it had a small stage we hadn't much room to work and had to stand on one spot otherwise the cloth would come down on the top of you. In this sketch I had a big oversize coat and I was supposed to be coming out of the dentist. At the end of the scene, just at the blackout, Doris had to say, "it's not the dentist you want, it's the infirmary", then I spat out a mouthful of beans – as if all my teeth had fallen out.

'Then I don't know what happened, whether it was the men in the flies to blame or myself for not standing in the right spot but the cloth came flying down and hit me on the head. I was knocked out and as I fell Doris picked up my feet and Frank got hold of my shoulders and dragged me off. Coming onto the dark stage Sammy Murray saw me being carried off, and apparently my head had gone right inside this oversized coat I was wearing. Sammy got such a fright that he shouted, "Oh my god, big yin, you've beheaded my china!"'[3]

Extract from *The Glasgow Story* by Colm Brogan:
'The most completely liberated Glasgow comic is a woman, Doris Droy, Queen of the Queen's, that small and profoundly prolific Music Hall behind Glasgow Cross. Her approach is direct and dynamic and her voice would make a pneumatic road drill or an electric riveting machine sound like the soft purring of a contented cat. If it may be said that Lorne and Morgan sprung directly from Glasgow earth, then Doris hasn't even sprung. She is a completely authentic interpreter of Glasgow life on the basement level. It is weak to say that she belongs to Glasgow, Glasgow belongs to her.

All come into their own in the pantomime season. Glasgow's passion for pantomime is even greater than its passion for musical comedy. Year after year the Princess Theatre ran a panto which would brook no rivalry in the whole of Britain. Starting before Christmas it would show no signs of flagging until Easter. Comics who first found fame in the Princess, might graduate to more profitable theatres, but they never did better work, and they sometimes deteriorated. The Princess was not the essence of Glasgow comedy, for the fine distilled methylated spirit of Glasgow is to be found only in the Queen's Theatre pantomimes.

It may be objected that pantomime comics are hardly culture, as the word is understood by the architects of The *Third Programme*, but they are "culture", in the wider and more tolerable sense. They come much nearer the truth of the Gorbals, than any dialectical exposure has ever done.'[4]

WALTER CARR

'I never was very keen on dressing up in female clothes, and never really thought of playing Dame, but there was a producer at Perth Theatre, Jimmy Montgomery, who said to me "Wally, I want you to do Dame in pantomime". This was at Perth, in 1950 something and I went up there and he was the first person who put on me as Dame. What I discovered with Dame was that when you put on a curious wig, funny clothes and if you are tall and skinny like I am, you're half way there, comedy-wise. Then you just needed to be a wee bit funny as well, have some material and you had got it. So I did three pantomimes there and since then have just gone on and on. And one earns a reputation for doing it and I've done it all over the country. I think this year is my thirty-first Dame. The really great thing about it are the extraordinary clothes you wear, and so it's all much more funny than a comic walking on in a dinner suit. He has to start from scratch.

'Scotland certainly still has a very traditional approach to pantomime. For a long time that had died out in England – they still do a lot of pantomime, but when the pop scene started they brought in pop singers and tradition and storyline seemed to go by the board. But Scotland thankfully, with Jack Radcliffe, Tommy Morgan, Will Fyffe, and then Stanley Baxter, Jimmy Logan, Rikki Fulton and Johnny Beattie, we've always held onto the storyline. Freddie Carpenter, one of the directors of the big Howard and Wyndham shows in Edinburgh and Glasgow from the early fifties, was a great believer in a good strong storyline and then get your comedy into it. And we have found that that format still works for us in Scotland.

'Certainly in the number one pantomimes in Edinburgh, Glasgow and places like Perth and Ayr Gaiety, there is a very high standard of costuming, of settings, and musically they're good. We have perhaps not so many chorus boys and girls as we used to have, because that is a very expensive item now, but the beautiful clothes, the principal boy with lovely legs and the principal girl being vulnerable, your goodie and your baddie, and your witches are well dressed. Thousands of pounds are spent nowadays on these pantomimes but they do go on tour for about five years. You must put all these ingredients in, because people see such lavish things on television now that you've got to do it; they're very spectacular, and wonderful and they work.

'I like to put as much comedy into what we call the straight book. The book is the progression of the story. You have the fairy and the witch on, then your principals, then your plot with the squire and that sort of thing, so your whole story is developed there. Rikki Fulton and Jimmy Logan and I like to pepper the book with a lot of comedy. There is the comedy which will already be in the kitchen scene, the schoolroom scene and our opening spot, which is the real hard comedy but the salvation of the book is to pepper that with as much comedy and colour as possible.

'It has to keep fresh, but the great art of all comedy, of all acting, is to make it look spontaneous, as if it's only happening at that moment. But there is a danger if you ad lib too much. You might do an ad lib one night and it gets a roar, you can do it again the next night, and no-one can tell you why, but it will get nothing. If you ad lib too much sometimes the structure gets lost and you'll suddenly find that instead of a two and a half hour show, you're now three hours. You've got to watch the time, there are so many technical things that you've got to watch. Ad libbing does happen; it's not greatly encouraged, but if a comic feels like doing something, and the audience are in on it, and it gets a laugh, then by all means do it. But as a general rule, walking onto the stage and hoping that your ad libbing will make an audience laugh, no, that doesn't work, even Lex McLean never ad libbed. It was the same every night, yet it sounded so spontaneous, but that is the art of doing it, to make it sound as if you have just thought of it that second. That is the art of it. But if you do it too much, you can upset the balance of things.'

CHRIS POTTER

Director of fifteen pantomimes in Kirkcaldy and Edinburgh, from 1973–1990, of which he has written the book and lyrics for twelve.

'There is a big difference between today's spectacular King's Theatre pantomimes in Glasgow and Edinburgh, and some of the big English ones. They have the big star and it's the star who draws them in and the money is all spent on that. I saw *Cinderella* at the Dominion, London, last year and it was appalling, literally thrown together. There wasn't a designer mentioned in the programme, and they had just cobbled together the sets. In my opinion they even got the first-half finale wrong, in which you normally can't fail. There's the coach scene and everything else which you build up to. It's usually a winner but they didn't do it properly.

'That show was a much smaller affair than our pantomimes, where we have eighteen in the chorus, twelve dancers and six singers. You wouldn't get that anywhere in England, but Scotland has kept that tradition, very similar to the Howard and Wyndham pantomimes which I was brought up on.

'On the whole the script, the "book", doesn't change a great deal. Obviously any comic worth his salt will slip in a topical joke, but on the whole it doesn't happen much. I have written the book many times but last year co-wrote it with Walter Carr. I'm used to pantomimes where the Dame and other comics in the show arrive with their own material. Well, not necessarily their own, but material gleaned through the years. Otherwise I need to bring in a professional script writer, such as Russell Lane because while I write the story line, the basic dialogue, I am not a joke writer.

'As far as the traditions and customs which must be included, you must have your Principal Boy and Girl, who are two girls. I do think that is important. And your Dame obviously should normally be a man. The traditional witch and fairy have got to come on from the proper side of the stage; the witch from the left, "sinister" in Latin, and the fairy from the right side. So you have to have that correctly staged. There's another tradition in that it must always be the Principal Boy and Girl who walk down last at the finale, even if they are not the stars. So even Rikki Fulton wouldn't be the last in the walk down. I've known people try and change that but you actually can't. And of course the story is traditional and you can't depart too far from that.'

ILONA ROSS

'I like tradition in pantomime to a certain extent although both my father and I were always agitating for a male Principal Boy. He always said that pantomime was for children so that the story had to be first consideration. Even the comedy had to be second to that. Alright you can have a female Principal Boy but one always felt that the children would have been even more convinced if the principal boy had been a man. Not every pantomime has a demon king, not all have a fairy godmother, they all vary, so that I don't know if all pantomime can be seen as "traditional" and have a set format.

'The pantomime script or book was a commotion every year we had a new pantomime. Generally, the script was reverentially taken from head office and brought down to us and usually it was totally unworkable, as it was so out-of-date. Then there was the matter of fitting in the comedy, whoever was going to be dame, or comic, like Buttons in *Cinderella*. It had to be worked into the story so that it wasn't just somebody's turn to come on and say a few jokes. Generally speaking my father rewrote quite a number and later on I wrote quite a few myself. The first time I did *Babes in the Wood* I knew that the finding of the babes scene was usually a desolate sort of thing, where you would have six little girls dressed as birds fluttering around before Robin Hood comes on and finds them. That had to be rewritten and I decided to use all the dancers as nymphs, with the little ones as birds. We had them flying down from above, and then we gradually brought the lights down, until there was just one spot light pointing at the babes under the tree. There were lanterns bobbing about, as the searchers slowly made a circle around the babes. Finally the lights faded for the end of scene as they were found. It was a most successful scene that one. That was story, everything had to be part of the story, the dancers, the ballets, everything.

'Rehearsals for pantomimes were two weeks, that was it. We had to fit in band calls, scenery calls, lighting calls, and everything. When I was producing the dances for pantomime, we didn't use the theatre for the first week as we were in rehearsal rooms so that left the theatre clear to get the scenery hung, to set the lights and to get the traps working. The traps were really something to see. We used them in ballets, we used them in many scenes. The obvious use of the trap is by the Genie in *Aladdin*, who springs out from the trap in a puff of smoke. They were used many times in my day. The comics used them a lot. The grave trap opened up in a clever way, so that comics could roll into it and disappear. We sometimes used it in ballets for the demon king who would enter with a red light coming up from below. I was trained how to use one when I was young, my father taught me, but he would never let me use a star trap. There had been an occasion when someone broke their neck. Acrobats and others who had learned how to use it, would be sprung up in the air, and by the time they landed, the trap had snapped shut. For that you had to adopt a suitable pose, with your head down. This poor fellow can't have settled his head properly and it broke his neck. It was called a star trap because the wood was shaped and fitted together like a star, which would trap your neck if you weren't careful. In those days we used trap doors a great deal and I am furious they are taking them out of theatres nowadays. That is the magic for children.'

Scotsman, 23rd December 1940
Aladdin: Alhambra Theatre

'Harry Gordon leads the cast as Widow Twankey and has ample opportunity to indulge his pawky humour. He has numerous stories to tell and manages to sing a song about Inversnecky Museum as well as councillors, taxes and Aberdeen. There is a happy blending of drama and comedy while knockabout acrobatics and tap dance are introduced without detracting from the original Chinese setting.'

JACK HOUSE

'The most realistic Dame was Harry Gordon who would appear in various odd Dame's outfits, and always made one appearance as a very, very good looking up-to-date well dressed woman in a blue rinse wig. It was actually said that when he was appearing as Dame, certain ladies in the audience would especially come to see this scene so that they could see his latest outfit and then go and buy one like it.'

JOHNNY BEATTIE

'I am a traditionalist in pantomime, I must say. I don't like to mess around with it too much. They mess about down South, they bring in a big television star, and they will chop and change the show just to tailor it to this particular singer or comedian. Scotland still has the strongest tradition of pantomime in the United Kingdom, and that is generally acknowledged by everyone concerned. And I think it's because we have maintained standards and kept to the traditional pantomime, which I think is the way it should be, I really do. It's all great fun, I love pantomime. I'd say it's my favourite form of theatre, marvellous.

'I decided a long time ago, in 1962 or so, that Dame was the thing to do; you gotta fly, you gotta do pantomime, get the high heeled shoes on. I was working with big Duncan Macrae at the time, in *Aladdin* at the Glasgow Empire. I was playing Wishy Washy, but I don't look like a Buttons type or Wishy Washy type. I looked like a smart Alec, while Buttons is a sympathetic, poor wee soul. I don't look like a poor wee soul. Maybe I am, but I don't look it. I thought I must get into the old frocks if I am going to do more pantomime. And from that day I've never played anything other than Dame. Pantomime is like a game, it's like a big party. If you think of the pantomime audience, they psyche themselves up. You sit in the theatre at a pantomime, as soon as the curtain goes up, everyone cheers, yet nothing's happened. We haven't even said Hello, and they are cheering because they have been looking forward to it for weeks. Invariably they have come in groups, and parties. The children are there, their wee faces all shining and they've got their sweeties. You sit in your dressing room in the theatre during a pantomime, and the tannoy is nearly crackling off the wall with the buzz in the auditorium. Then that curtain goes up, ''Hurray!!!'' – so you're home and dry before you start. Great fun, I love pantomime.

'Sir Lewis Casson said that pantomime is the national theatre of Scotland and I'll second that motion. I'd say of all the theatre forms in Scotland, that is the strongest, consistently the strongest. I honestly can't see that it will ever die. There will always be pantomime. I'm sure there will so I won't throw my bra away yet.'

Opening on 15th March 1920
Olympia: Fred Collins all Scotch panto, *Mother Goose* concludes a 16 week tour in Glasgow. Kitty Evelyn is Principal Girl.

For the Christmas season 1935
Princess Theatre: *Tammie Toddles* with George West. (The Princess pantomimes traditionally had thirteen letters in the title, because the owner, Harry McKelvie had thirteen letters in his own name.)

Sunday Mail, 18th January 1942
Pavilion: *Aladdin*; This panto with the effervescent Jack Anthony and G. H. Elliot has worked its way into the hearts of theatre goers. Anthony's a scream, each performance proving his nimble wit, and a word for Bond Rowell, surely the most patient, friendly feed in the business. (This pantomime ran until 11th April 1942).

STANLEY BAXTER

'My move from straight acting to comedy happened in a show at the Citizens' Theatre in 1949, called *The Tintock Cup*. It was James Bridie's idea to restore the tradition of the old Princess Theatre pantomime, with titles of thirteen letters, most of which I had seen all through my childhood, so I knew what they were talking about. So John Casson, son of Sir Lewis, who was working at the Citizens' at the time, invited me in as assistant producer while Bridie wrote the book. With the confidence of youth, when I saw the script, I said "No, that's no use, that scene's no good, that's not light entertainment enough, that won't work", and I had the impertinence to take out most of Bridie's book and seek out people who could write more light entertainment stuff.

'I was introduced to Alec Mitchell by Duncan Macrae and he started writing for me. As a kind of hotch potch the whole thing was put together. The opening night was quite incredible. The audience went mad, they almost went mad before the curtain went up. It was as if they knew there was a great, strange, new thing happening. It was a huge success, and it resulted in Duncan Maccrae being whipped over by Tom Arnold to the Alhambra Theatre and I was left to take over from him as Dame in the pantomimes which inevitably succeeded *The Tintock Cup*. Of course, everyone was asking what was going to be the follow up? We followed it up with *Red Riding Hood*, and then followed that with *The Happy Hap'ny*.

'These shows and my radio work then led to a contract with Howard and Wyndham and the first pantomime role I played was Buttons, in 1952, followed by 1953, and 1954, as Wishy Washy, and when they realised I had enough experience I was promoted to Dame. It is a very different technique and is a lot more difficult to do than other roles, and my first dame for Howard and Wyndham was appearing with Alec Finlay. This was how they were clever, because they buttressed me. Instead of shoving me in at the deep end as a solo dame, they had me work as an Ugly Sister beside a very experienced Scottish comedian so there were the two of us, with him seeing the youngster through, and then they felt that I could do this very well. That is how I started playing Dame, all those years ago.

'I don't ad lib a great deal. I'll introduce the odd topicality, but most of the topicality and stuff has been thought out before you begin. Things that are going to last, and that is why Christmas and New Year jokes are no good because you are going on until February, when Christmas is a distant memory. I even avoided having dresses like a Christmas Tree, because by February it begins to look a bit daft.

'The whole process of pantomime as you put the thing together, is like piecing together a mosaic, until you finally finish the fresco, the finished job. It is never truly finished because there is always the odd line you want to put in, and the odd few lines that are there that you wish you had never thought of, but you can't get rid of because you can't think of anything better! There will always be something like that. There is no such thing as perfection even in a very good show.

'I have usually always ignored some pantomime traditions, in favour of practicalities. If the witch finds it easier to enter from the *right* side near her dressing room I would allow that. That is a tradition which I've broken many times but not had any complaints. It is fascinating what can work in pantomime, such as a woman coming on who is supposed to be the mother of Aladdin, a Chinese boy, and she comes on talking about Sauchiehall Street! That kind of surrealism is absolutely alright. However, one thing you can never do is to have a woman wear modern dress. Let a woman appear in a tweed jacket and skirt and you have suddenly violated something. Pantomime has rules of its own, but you know it when you see it, and you say, Ah ha, no no, that you mustn't do. It is important that the thing is played for real to see and hear a pained voice: ''Uncle! Uncle!'', as if it really mattered, otherwise how are the children going to suspend disbelief. I don't like Principal Boys being played by males either, I like the tradition of Principal Boy played by a woman. A Prince Charming played by a boy merely looks camp, it doesn't work. It is too effete a part to be played by a male. And Dame should be played by a man. Let us hope it continues'.

After an absence of several years away from the pantomime stage, Stanley Baxter returned to play Dame in *Cinderella* at the Edinburgh King's, for the 1990–91 season, produced by Chris Potter.

The popularity of the annual Christmas pantomime, with the seasons often running three or four months and the vast choice of shows around the country, clearly earned its accolade as Scotland's national theatre. The selection of excellent top cast pantomimes seemed to increase and improve year by year. Dave Willis starred at the Theatre Royal, Glasgow from 1937 until 1941. Jewel and Warris had joined him in the cast for the 1939 show and made such an impression they were invited to take over as lead comics in Edinburgh the following year.

Evening News, 21st December 1940
Robinson Crusoe

'It is indeed probably the most brilliant pantomime Howard and Wyndham have presented in the Scottish capital. Edinburgh will long remember the team calling themselves Jewel and Warris. As Billy Crusoe and Private A. Harris, these comics have a great triumph. The audience would hardly let them go at the finish. Clean and smart humour, fantastic wise crackin' and clever dancing were their attributes. Undoubtedly a first class show.'

The 1956/57 choice of pantomimes in Glasgow included:

Pavilion	*Puss in Boots* with Jack Milroy.
Empire	*We're Joking*, with Chic Murray, Duncan Macrae, Jack Anthony and Robert Wilson.
Theatre Royal	*Robinson Crusoe*, with Harry Gordon and Jack Radcliffe.
Metropole	*Scotland the Brave* with Clark and Murray.
Alhambra	*Babes in the Wood*, with Jimmy Logan, Rikki Fulton and Kenneth McKellar.

while the exceptionally cold winter of 1962/63 offered a warming selection:

Pavilion 6.20, 8.35pm.	*Dick Whittington* with Alec Finlay
Gaiety, Ayr 6.30, 8.40pm.	*Victory Vanities* with Johnny Victory

Glasgow Empire   *Cinderella*: with Johnny Beattie and Callum
7pm daily.   Kennedy. 'City's best panto', *Scottish Daily Mail*.
Sat. 1.30, 4.45
and 8pm

And at Jimmy Logan's Metropole Theatre during the winter, 1971/72:

Clark and Murray star as The Ugly Sisters in *Cinderella* with Joe Gordon, and Sally Logan, Pete Martin and Jan Wilson. 50p Mon–Thurs; 60p Fri/Sat; Children, 25p.

BARBARA McCALL

Worked during the 1940s in the office of Mutries, theatrical costumiers, Edinburgh.

'What a lot of work pantomimes were. Fraser Neil, head of Mutries, where I worked, also produced a great many pantomimes. He put on *Jeannie Deans* at the Palladium and it was a tremendous success. He also produced a magnificent show, *Rob Roy* at the Braidburn Valley, the outdoor theatre on the southside of Edinburgh. It started at 9 pm at night, and it was a wonderful sight to see everyone with torches.

'I typed all the pantomime scripts for the Gaiety and the Palladium, twenty-three copies, at home, with papers spread all over our dining room table. My husband got fed up stapling them all together!

Such an enterprising fellow was Fraser Neil. He and his wife would invite a large group of people to their home on a Sunday night and we would all be sitting there chatting, when everyone would be handed a large hat, great big bonnets and then we all had to sew sequins on the hats for his pantomimes! It was the funniest thing on earth to see us all beavering away. He would invite performers from the Theatre Royal, Jeannette Adie and Ivy Troy, and other acts from the Gaiety and then ask us to help with the sewing of pantomime costumes. He would simply say, "We can't just sit around chatting all night. I have to get on with my pantomime".'

AILEEN VERNON

'I worked in pantomime for eleven years for Freddie Carpenter doing *Cinderella* with Stanley Baxter and Ronnie Corbett, then *Mother Goose*, with Stanley Baxter and Fay Lenore. I also did *Goldilocks* with Rikki Fulton. There are comics and comic actors, and everyone's style is different. Harry Gordon was always called Maggie, no matter what show it was. He always had size 2 to 3 shoes, very small feet, very small gloves.

He was always a bright, chipper little fellow, and he played Dame for years and years. I think playing Dame is an art, and one of the most important elements of pantomime. Rikki Fulton was another who was superb. I think some of his sketches were a dream. He did one called The Bathroom, which was a set just like an ordinary real bathroom. It had a bath, a shower and a loo with real water plumbed in. Rikki went in there to take a bath, perfectly dressed in a negligée thing. That was one of the funniest things I have ever seen. He got soaked in it. The water had to be a certain temperature for health safety. It wasn't easy to do something like that twice daily, matinee and evening. After working with Rikki for so long and even at the end of all that I can still say he was the best. He never repeated things, it was always fresh material even with his characters, the scouts, girl guide or the nurse coming out with her trolley.

'The situation with Howard and Wyndham pantomimes was that I went in as stage director. When there was a new show, such as *Goldilocks* at the Alhambra, I stayed with that show, and the producer guided it, nursed it and built that show putting his own ideas into it. The next year and the year after that, the producer would do the same with another new pantomime, but I would move to Edinburgh or elsewhere with the first pantomime. The producer would turn up for the first rehearsal, the read through and then would leave me to be in his boots. I was in charge to build that pantomime as he had built it. He came back for the dress rehearsal so the responsibility of getting lights, electric scenery, special effects, everything was yours. You are doing the same pantomime but it is not easy in a strange theatre, with a new crew. A woman in charge was not the usual thing, not at all.

'Standard pantomimes were usually rather predictable and Stewart Cruikshank, our Managing Director, had always had a dream and kept talking about the day he was going to have a typically Scottish pantomime, by Scots for Scots. Many people said this can't work because the Scots don't like to be tartanised, and it is for tourists. He didn't think of that and finally he said he was going to do it. There were then all the questions of story, casting and the Jamie pantomime just fell into place.

'*A Wish for Jamie* was the title and Freddie Carpenter was called in to produce it. He wasn't called the Pantomime King for nothing. He knew children and the reaction of children. They want a good script, good music, and he didn't want a *Brigadoon* type show but it had to have an eeriness, that feyness. He cast Kenneth McKellar as Jamie, Rikki Fulton as Dame and Fay Lenore as Principal Boy. Reg Varney was the English sidekick, and Russell Hunter as the King of the Frogs. We slogged away, all a bit in the dark. Was it going to work? Tartan was in multitude together with a pipe band on the first night. It was an amazing experience because no-one knew what had happened because the audience suddenly started applauding when the curtain came down and the actors came back on the set and they continued applauding. Normally the producer came through the pass door at this point to let us know how it had gone out front. But no-one came through. Instead of decreasing, the applause was increasing. They started cheering, and the curtain was down. Suddenly Freddie Carpenter tore through the pass door, shouting, ''We made it!'' It was unbelievable, that first night. That was pantomime history in Scotland, December 9th, 1960. John Law wrote it and the Musical Director was Jack Bolesworth. It was all beautifully done and I was very proud of those years.'

FAY LENORE

'The Jamie pantomime was certainly a new thing for Howard and Wyndham. It was at the Alhambra Theatre directed by Freddie Carpenter with Kenneth McKellar and Rikki Fulton with myself, playing the part of Donald. Everyone thought it would be good, it was a fairy story, as well as a Scots show, but would it take as a pantomime? On the preview night we were greeted with deadly silence and we all went off stage thinking, ''Oh my god, this is not going to go down well, after all''. But the following night we nearly took the roof off. We did so well the season was booked out in the first two weeks practically, and they had to bring it back the following year which was unknown. It had never happened before to bring the same pantomime back the following year to the same theatre. Again we played to packed houses. Because *A Wish for Jamie* was so popular and we had done it for two years, John Law was asked to write a sequel, *The Love for Jamie*. Then there was another one *The World of Jamie*, while meantime *A Wish for Jamie* was playing in Edinburgh and other theatres.

'I started at seventeen playing my first boy part and I played Prince Charming for about four seasons, and *A Wish for Jamie* for four seasons. I did *Mother Goose* with Stanley Baxter for two or three seasons, and then there was *Robin Hood*, *Goody Two Shoes*, and *Jack and the Beanstalk*. I must have done about twenty five years as Principal Boy. Then a few years ago, Joan Knight at Perth Theatre said, ''Fay, I want you to play Fairy''. ''Oh good'', I said, ''Comedy''. ''Oh no, dear, I want you to play it straight''. ''What, at my age?'', ''Oh yes, you'll have the gold wig, and the gold lamé dress and everything''. But that's the only time I have ever played anything else but Principal Boy.

'To be a good Principal Boy you have to be sincere about it. If you are not sincere and believe in everything you are doing and saying, your audience won't believe in it either. If you believe implicitly that you are a boy, a tom-boy, but a lovable tom-boy, and you are full of fun, then they'll believe it. If not, you'll never be a boy. You've got to think of yourself as a boy and act like one. Tough, rough and positive, without losing your femininity and being sexy at the same time. You've got to have sex appeal, and you've got to make it believable or it won't come off.'

STEWART CRUIKSHANK

A Wish for Jamie programme, December 1961.

'*A Wish for Jamie* was an experiment. It was an attempt to get away from some of the standard pantos which I thought you, the public, were beginning to tire of. I introduced the new show last year by saying, "I don't want to say that *A Wish for Jamie* will be better than all your *Cinderellas* and *Aladdins*, but I'm hoping it will". This hope was much more than fulfilled. Our experiment was a great success. The critical press called it, "The greatest show at the Alhambra for a long, long time". I hope it will continue to live up to that praise and that it will again enjoy a wonderfully successful run.'

Evening News, 15th December 1962
A Wish for Jamie: King's Theatre, Edinburgh.
SCOTTISH PANTO IS A BOMBSHELL:
'With the first act finale having all the appearance of a miniature military tattoo, *A Wish for Jamie* burst on the capital last night like a tartan bombshell, sending bagpipes, heather and haggis showering in all directions. The audience whistled, they clapped, they sang and they cheered. A puff of smoke brought Aggie Goose, a Scottish fairy played by Marilyn Gray, sweeping across the stage, astride a Scottish version of a broomstick, a set of bagpipes in MacLeod tartan. There is much humour and a good deal to help one forget the cares of the day in this show. In fact it has all the ingredients one expects of festive season entertainment. Need more be said?'

JIM HASTIE

'I remember the first night of *A Wish for Jamie* where we had a wonderful set with this big staircase. Rikki Fulton was meant to come down the staircase for the finale, in a dress in the shape of a thistle. It was absolutely enormous with a big headdress. But then something happened to the machinery in the staircase and he couldn't get down them. There was just a huge gap like the Khyber Pass which he couldn't possibly cross as he hobbled down in that dress.

'This panto was pure magic, it was like a wonderful, colourful *Brigadoon*, with loads of comedy, like Aggie Goose the Fairy who flew in and out, with Kenneth McKellar, Fay Lenore, Rikki Fulton. They were wonderful pantomimes, those three Jamie shows. By the time they got to the third one *The World of Jamie*, I was Freddie Carpenter's assistant. We had just opened, and I was understudy to Johnny Hackett the comic as well as principal dancer.

'In the first week, it would be about the fourth night, I arrived in the theatre, went to my dressing room and was then told that my costumes were down in Number 2. I said, "You're jesting, why are they down in Number 2?" And they said, "Because you are on tonight. Johnny Hackett hasn't come. We don't know what has happened to him". So I had to flee downstairs, and sure enough there was Johnny Hackett's dresser with my costumes, my dance costumes as well, because I would have to go on and dance, come off and change for the comic's part. There was a space at the side of the stage for a quick change. So I said, "But I don't know it, I really haven't learnt the part". I was told, "You will have to do something". So I had to go out there.

'I did the Opening dance number, came off and was thrown into this costume for Johnny Hackett's first entrance. So I hurtled out there, and I was going daft, trying to remember what I had heard in the rehearsals. What I didn't remember I made up, and after a bit, I heard the audience laughing and I thought maybe it isn't as bad after all. I was beginning to enter into this with great relish, because I thought, well there is nothing else I can do. We're out here and having to get on with it. Next thing, the orchestra starts up and I see Kenneth McKellar starting to walk towards me. And I remember thinking, Oh my God, I have got to sing a duet, but which key is it in? The orchestra said to me afterwards, "Jim, we've never heard anyone change key four times in one bar of music". I said, "Oh that can't be true!" But anyway I thought I must hit the right key or Kenneth will be all wrong. However, I got through that.

'The other thing in that show was that we did a Scottish Music Hall finale, and Johnny Hackett was doing the part of Will Fyffe, the "I Belong to Glasgow" song. By that time I had done the dance numbers, I had got through the show and I am thinking we are nearly there, and this is a piece of cake. At least I know "I Belong to Glasgow". Luckily I had said to one of the stage hands, get me a beer bottle. So I took this beer bottle, and had painted on my red nose of the drunk, and put the bonnet on, and I was wheeled out on a truck and stepped onto the stage. The orchestra were playing the opening, and I suddenly thought, I don't know this at all. What do you do in a situation like that? I then began acting up, staggering about the stage, more and more drunk. All I could do was say, "Now, Ladies and Gentlemen, I'm sure you all know the words of 'I

Belong to Glasgow' " and I finally got away with it by getting the audience to sing the entire song. Eventually I began to remember the lines, but it was sheer terror.

'In Scotland I think we have been fortunate to have had, and to have, so many wonderful comedians, who have been terrific at playing Dame, a role which is supposed to be the tradition of the English pantomime. But in the south, I almost feel the Dame becomes a drag act. They are all too glamorous, whereas in Scotland the tradition goes back so many years, when you get people like Stanley Baxter, Jimmy Logan, Walter Carr, Rikki Fulton, and beyond that, with Harry Gordon — the Scots comic as Dame captures the audience right away. To me, the pantomime in Scotland becomes a fabulous family show, and you can feel the warmth coming across the footlights onto the stage. Pantomime is something which is very special to the Scots. They seem to have the right approach, and it still goes on today because they can bring in something topical without destroying the traditional story. For the Scots it really is a special annual event and to be in a pantomime over Christmas, it is fabulous. You don't mind missing your Christmas dinner doing two shows a day, because something is coming back at you that you know is worthwhile. It is for all the family and that is the important thing.'

The Three Aberdonians

Chapter 8

THE SPECIALITY ACT

The relationship between circus acts and clowning as an element within pantomime also developed as part of the true 'Variety' theatre, as distinct from the Music Hall. Acrobats and sea-lion trainers found insufficient work in the circus during the winter months and were invited to show off their talents inside proscenium arch theatres when the circus ring was packed away after the summer. It was also the case that many circuses toured to the smaller seaside towns and villages in rural areas, and it became more difficult to set up the circus ground within a built-up urban environment, with few green sites. The inclusion of animals, circus performers, and speciality acts in the Variety theatre in Scotland offered an extraordinarily wide range of skills, tricks and acts:

Escape artistes; plate spinners; fire eaters; jugglers; trapeze artistes; contortionists; trick cyclists; one-man bands; speciality dancers – apache, sand, Highland, Irish, harem, and belly dancers; ventriloquists; yodellers; balloon sculptors; cartoonists; knife throwers; whip experts; rope handlers; roller skaters; paper cutters and marksmen; instrumentalists who played bells, tubes, xylophones, harps, banjos, ukeleles, zither, spoons, glass bottles, and the Jews harp.

There were many different trained animal and bird acts including dogs, seals, cockatoos, parrots, doves, pigeons, rabbits, horses, ponies, elephants, snakes, organ grinder monkeys; also wonderful entertainers such as clowns, puppeteers, marionettes and male and female impersonators. There were daring circus performers on a tight-rope which stretched from the front row of the balcony to the centre of the stage where a girl equipped with a pretty parasol would slide down all the way from the balcony to the stage.

One of the most eccentric speciality acts of the turn of the century and through the twenties and thirties, was 'The One and Only, Dr Walford

Bodie, the Electric Wizard'. He was a Scottish doctor of dubious qualification, and his act was described as being an electrical conjurer, hypnotist, cartoonist and ventriloquist. With his wife as his partner, they would have long four-month tours around Scotland, to nearly every theatre and hall, where he exploited the wonders of bloodless surgery, telepathy, and electricity with superb showmanship.

The *Sunday Mail* on 12th February 1934, reviews his Cage of Death act, where 'a hushed audience in Edinburgh watched as Bodie enters the cage where he claims he can stand up to 30,000 volts of electricity without ill effects'.

JACK HOUSE

'Variety was a better name than music hall because they did give you the most amazing variety of performers. I remember shows where you got everything bar the kitchen sink. It always started with a dancing troupe, or sometimes a couple of dancers, then you went on through animals of all kinds and conjurors, I liked them very much. In fact I was quite good at magic myself, until my hands let me down because you can't do magic without having very supple hands.

'I remember David Devant, and while they say that Jasper Maskelyne was the greatest conjurer, I don't see how anyone could have beaten David Devant. I saw him at the Empire many years ago, and by this time he was an old man, but still appearing. I was in the stalls, quite near the front, and I could actually see his hands and watch how he worked very clearly. He was the first man I think who produced eggs from a bowler hat, and he had two assistants on the stage, a small boy and girl. David Devant could even produce eggs from the empty air; he held out his hand and there was an egg. He would put it into the basket held by the boy or girl and occasionally an egg would fall and smash on the floor, which of course was probably done intentionally to show that they were real eggs. Where he kept the eggs, I cannot imagine.

'He did one particular trick when he invited someone from the audience onto the stage, and he had a big magic mirror, which seemed to be a real mirror, because you could see the auditorium in it. He would take the volunteer round the back of the mirror, and the chap would then appear coming round the other side. David Devant himself would then make a miraculous appearance through the mirror. I have seen some very good conjurors, but he was undoubtedly the best. Variety shows would always have an acrobatic turn. Some were absolutely remarkable, and you wondered whether they had actually overcome the forces of nature.'

SEAN PATCHELL

Circus performer, fire-eater, animal trainer.

'I originally got involved in the circus when I was a child in Ireland. I was quite young, about twelve, and just ran away to join the circus. In Ireland in the early fifties there were many Freak shows, such as a half man-half woman, a Leopard boy and side show exhibitions showing two headed children and mermaids. If the manager couldn't find sufficient freaks, he invented them and this is where illusion came in. I myself played the part of the Leopard boy. The story went that Dr Johnstone while travelling in Africa found this creature, the child of a poor woman who had a tremendous fright by a leopard while pregnant and this was the result. I was covered in ''spots'', using a potassium solution, dabbed on with a cork.

'I remember coming to Kirkpatrick, in Scotland when I was about sixteen. There were two shows daily, one in the afternoon geared to the grannies and children, and one more adult show in the evening. The hall is still much the same today. There was a change of programme daily for six weeks. We rehearsed in the morning and went on at night. Unbelievable.

'Many years later I was invited to play a seven week season at the Glasgow Pavilion by the singer and producer, Callum Kennedy. I was a speciality act, with a bed of nails, fire-eating, lying and walking on broken glass. I had dogs, ponies, and foxes, I had all sorts of skills. Therefore, I was able to offer something a wee bit different. It was a novelty. When I was told there would be a change of programme weekly I wondered how I could change an act with a bed of nails. Callum insisted that I kept the dog, Mr Plod, and the bed of nails, and the fire-eating. Other performers just needed to change their music or their jokes, but it is not so easy changing my act. But we did it.

'One of those weeks I introduced a snake to the act. I borrowed it from a friend. This particular snake was coming towards the end of its life as it hadn't eaten for about three years, which is not unusual, that is what happens. We had it at the Pavilion and one of the backstage boys must have poked it or something, because when I went to the basket to pick it up for my act, it bit me. Two wee bites. The result was that we got a bit of publicity out of it because I had to stay in the hospital overnight. By then there were huge stories in the *Daily Record*, about ''This Mad Irishman'', and we got national coverage on television news. People were ringing up and booking seats, and the bloody snake is now deid!

By this time Callum was getting worried. What are we going to do? All these people are coming to see the man who was bitten by this snake.

We eventually got a fridge, threw out the icecream, froze the snake curled up in its appropriate coils, and kept the thing frozen until Saturday night.

'But it was away from the conventional theatres that I enjoyed touring and performing. I actually began the smallest travelling circus in the world. The idea came to me because in the winter, the traditional circus stopped after forty two weeks on the road. When I was younger, you could make enough money during the eight month touring season to live for four months in winter quarters. But as we came into the sixties, there was inflation and everything became very different. It wasn't so easy to live then. I conceived the idea for a one man circus, with a little tent, 150 seats, all packed on a lorry, a couple of caravans, a couple of boys to put up the tent, a chap who would do the clowning, and myself. We toured and nothing stood in our way, because we were unique. We could go anywhere with this little show. We became quite popular, and got good bookings. We played with people like Ken Dodd. We were never a top act, but a different novelty act. We were quite popular and did many of the big shows down south, indoors, outdoors, anywhere under the sun.

'I toured Scotland with my own little show during the late fifties, sixties, early seventies. This was the latter end of the variety show era, just before the television and video age really got to the parts up in the Highlands that were still a wee bit remote. There were beautiful church and school halls in the villages. We played Kirkcudbright once and the sign outside the village hall said, Public Toilet. During the day it was the public convenience and at night it was the village hall. There were daft things like that.

'The first show I produced and directed, I had Gunga Din and Sapphire, Europe's strongest man act. Genuinely this man was, he could lift sixteen men. In the circus he lifted two elephants, but on the stage, he lifted sixteen men. He could bend iron bars with his throat, and take nails out with his teeth. He was really a crowd puller. We had a dog act, called Rough the Wonder dog, a wee scruffy thing but a very good act. We had goats, we had a magician in the show, and I had two donkeys, two shetland ponies, three goats, and a collection of dogs. You could certainly earn a good living touring around to the smaller halls, with a rough and ready, portable fit-up show. In 1959 we were touring the Highlands and I could make nearly £100 a night, charging 1/6d or 9d on the door. Shows like ours would do very well and you could charge various prices if the hall was big enough, right down to 6d at the back and 2d for standing room only.

'I did all the traditional circus acts, and the clown came on and threw water all over the place. Then I would go off and change my costume. I would do the dog act first of all. I had dogs, birds, ponies, foxes, and

I had a lion at one point. I was the first person in Scotland to be registered as a wild animal trainer; No. 1 in the register. I would go and put on the top hat, or feathers, and the clown would hold the arena, until the next introduction. And then it was me back out again for a totally different act. It used to be quite comical because children would come up to you at the interval and ask to see the man in the black suit, or the man with the dogs, and it was the same man all the time, *me.*

'Theatres were alright in the winter time. When it was snowy, cold and wet, it was nice to come inside and be static somewhere, and do a pantomime perhaps. It was nice to do a theatre show after being out on the road. You had band calls, music, lighting plots, and stage management to look after you. It was like a holiday in comparison. This was sheer luxury because it was three or four weeks in the one place. As soon as the summer came I would get fed up with that kind of life, and it was back to the one night stands. I have gone touring round the halls, three or four times, and I think I have played every single village hall in Scotland. There is hardly one I haven't been too.

'Callum Kennedy was the King of the one night stands. He played every blessed place in Scotland. On one occasion he had arranged for his company to perform two shows on the one night. One started in Brora, at seven-thirty, and the other, five miles away at Golspie, started at eight. I played the second half in Golspie, after playing the first half in Brora. During the interval, there was just enough time to swap the cast and show around. That was a real combination of two shows in the one night.

'It was always interesting being out on tour, meeting the likes of Elliot Williams, the last of the barnstormers. He literally went around on a bicycle and took his props and costumes with him. He had done things like bits from *School for Scandal* and *Sweeney Todd, the Demon Barber*, a one man show of dramatic extracts. A good little entertainment. He went all round the borders. There was another old act called A. J. Matheson and Nelly McNab, who came from the Dumfries area. They were an old act, and toured extensively in the South West of Scotland and Ayrshire, every six months or so. They were a Clark and Murray of the South of Scotland. They did more farewell tours than anyone I have ever come across. Every time you came across a poster, it would state, A. J. Matheson and Nelly McNab, Farewell Tour, but they kept these farewell tours going for years and years.

'Hans Vogelbein, the Dutchman and his bears were a variety and circus act, who travelled theatres everywhere – Uncle Hans Vogelbein's Circus. Kripps Canine Wonders, that was a dog act which had travelled for decades, derived from an ancient circus family, the Winnships. This was a very slow moving dog act which always seemed to be appearing somewhere.

'There are not many speciality acts around now. They go to the continent and get good money in the circus. The variety show always had one or two novelty acts. Knife throwers, jugglers, strong men, or contortionists were popular. Men and women did double acts, such as a trampoline act. You hardly see them today on the stage. I suppose the people are not there to be trained, but at the same time there are few people about to pass on the secrets of the acts'.

ROZA LOUISE THOMPSON

One of The Three Aberdonians (Contortionists).

'I began my career at the age of thirteen, in 1929, starting in a small concert party on a pitch on the sands at Burnham on Sea. It was called *Freddie Fay's Frolics*, and I was one of four girls, called The Dinky Dots. After school I would do part of the afternoon show, then a show early evening. That was tough going. We lived in a caravan and I was paid five shillings a week and my keep. In the winter we toured what was called the Fit Ups, in little village halls. This was when we travelled in an open top lorry, with all the props, scenery and costumes. In the village hall there would be some kind of platform, on which we would build our own stage, and erect lighting, scenery and curtains. We would perform in that hall for a few days, as long as we had an audience, otherwise we took down our stage and moved onto the next village. I then had to go to a different school each week.

'My mother was a wonderful dancer, and it was said she was England's highest kicker. She was also a dancing teacher and ran a dancing troupe. She had a hard life as my father left her when I was only nine months old. She had to work hard to keep me. You could say I was almost born in the business as I used to spend all my school holidays with her, always training with her girls and I loved it. She never wanted me to go in any of her troupes but always said she wanted me to go into an act in order to learn the business. I was therefore very lucky that one time in Bristol, she was appearing in a show with a contortionist act called The Barr Brothers. They had asked her if she knew of a young girl who did acrobatics, as they wanted a girl for their act. She mentioned me, and brought Charlie Barr along to see me. After the show Charlie asked me if I'd like to join their act. I was thrilled to accept their offer.

'We started off by being called The Barr Brothers and Roza, then changed our name a little later, after a visit to His Majesties, Aberdeen, to The Three Aberdonians. My first date with them was in Londonderry, Ireland and from then on I never looked back. We were together from 1930 for nearly twenty years with hardly a cross word. We all got on very well.

'When I joined the Barr Brothers we were on about £12 a week for the three of us, so as I wasn't a partner at fourteen years old, I think the boys gave me about £3 a week. We toured all the dumps, as we called them, for years on a very low salary. Digs were twenty-five shillings, all in. I had that for years, going up gradually until the age of twenty-one when I became a partner. That was just before we did the Royal Command Performance, because after that our money went right up from around £30 to £60 a week for the three of us, to £100. So I became a partner at the right time!

'We always looked forward to playing the Empire Theatres, as we always did very well and usually had a good position on the bill. The dressing rooms were nice and the stage spacious and clean which I liked because I had to lie on the floor doing my acrobatics. We always loved the Edinburgh and Glasgow Empires because with the boys being Scottish their jokes went down very well, and we used to put in a good deal of humourous chat all the way through our act.

'Our act used to last between ten and fifteen minutes, according to how many minutes we were allocated. One of the tricks I did I have never seen anyone else do, in the twenty years I was in the business or since I've retired. I used to do twenty or twenty five "overs" with one hand on the spot. The boys used to count them. I wore a long flowing skirt so it looked like a catherine wheel going round and round. I also did three lots of splits. Starting off lying on the stage on my tummy, facing the audience, and bringing my legs right round to the front – that always got a round of applause. Then I'd throw myself up and over into the splits. I'd never seen that before as my mother taught me that. We were sometimes asked to alter our act, so my partners did a double act and I would do a solo act, but we normally worked together as a threesome all doing our various acrobatic displays. We never used ropes, boxes or springboards, we didn't need to.

'I remember the Gaiety Ayr, a very nice theatre and a most appreciative audience. Once again they loved the boys' patter and jokes. We played the Pavilion, Glasgow and also had five months in pantomime with Harry Gordon at the Alhambra which I enjoyed very much. The dressing rooms were comfortable and the audience was terrific. We played most seaside theatres including Blackpool Circus. This was something very different and I didn't enjoy working there as we would follow an animal act and because I had to lie down on the floor for my tricks, that wasn't very pleasant at times as you can imagine!'

Reviews of the Royal Command Performance, 9th November 1938:
'The Three Aberdonians at once made a fine impression with their quietly clever conversational acrobatics, keeping up a flow of verbal

comment with almost every trick, and working everything with a neat ability. The development of Roza's work is amazing since last we saw her, and her acrobatics are fast and gracefully accomplished'.

'. . . The two male partners perform their acrobatics with an ease and assurance that only skill and practice can give. Roza, the attractive young lady, who is the third member of the team did some very surprising things in the way of hand springs and bending and came up smiling every time. A fine act and received accordingly.'

Royal Honour for Comedy Balancers:
Success for 'The Three Aberdonians'.

'. . . they go about their task in a good humoured manner, devoid of haste or apparent effort. Roza displays amazing vitality with her rapid somersaults and high kicking. She does the splits, and in that attitude, is lifted by the feet. Later, she lies flat on her chest and after bringing her legs to the splits position, propels herself like that across the stage for her exit. The brothers balance a chair by one leg on the forehead and then by its back on the chin. They kneel and prostrate themselves in acknowledgement of the applause.'

BETTY BARR

Tap dancer and juggler. Widow of Charlie Barr, of 'The Three Aberdonians'.

'I started as a Terry Juvenile in 1934 at twelve years of age. My mother paid a guinea an hour for me to learn extra special tap dancing. Eventually I became part of a tap dancing trio. We toured the country and then eventually through variety circuits as we moved about, we joined a show which included Kitty and Jerry who were straw hat jugglers called The Buckley's. Being ambidextrous, I used to practice down on the stage with them. Jerry soon asked me if I'd like to tour with them and join the act. I decided to do so and after I learnt the tricks, his wife stepped out and then eventually I went into the full act and we became Jerome and Frances. I would begin the act with a tap dance, as an introduction, perhaps playing the song, "Where did you get that hat?" and then we would go into the juggling act.

'Learning to juggle was six months hard labour, that was for starters, just to get the bare necessities. But it was really super, and the straw hats were light, made in Puerto Rica, moulded over a pudding bowl when wet, and lined with bias binding of different colours. They were always set out around the stage in groups so that you knew which you were going to use for such and such a trick. It was a very good speciality act. We toured around the number ones, the Moss Empires, or the number twos, the smaller theatres, to Mansfield, or the City of Varieties, Leeds. I toured during the war years, and by now I was eighteen, and eventually I went to Luton where I met my future husband Charlie Barr, who was one of the Three Aberdonians. I was twenty, he was forty four, but when love happens, it goes, ping, and you can do nothing about it. I married him and then I had a son, Douglas who, from ten months to five years of age, toured with us.

'The Three Aberdonians had come about when Tom Barr, who was a weight lifter, persuaded his brother Charlie, a miner, to leave the pits and train as an acrobat. They were extremely lucky to find work with Duffy's Circus in Ireland, where they gained great experience. Tom was two inches taller than Charlie and extremely strong and the bearer in the group. Roza was tall, over five foot seven, and slim, not the small contortionist you usually see. She was an exceptionally good contortionist and the three of them together simply looked good on stage. It was a marvellous act.

'We went to the Empire, Glasgow and Edinburgh, as well as the Metropole, the Empress, the Opera House, Dunfermline, any theatre like that which we would call the number two, we played. Aldershot, Eastbourne, Morecambe, and the Garrick, Southport, where we worked with Max Wall. He was lovely and he had a brilliant act. His parents actually came from Glasgow. When he was young he had a solo act and then married Marion Polo, and she had three sons, and they all had the initial M. They were a great family together, the five M's. Max Wall was a wonderful acrobat, and we had good fun together. His sons were ages with my son Douglas.

'It wasn't all fun, especially travelling by train in war time, with the soldiers and airmen going on leave, coming off leave and you couldn't move in corridors, and you can imagine with a young baby, and because the poor thing was being breast fed, I couldn't feed him properly for hours. When you reached the destination, in the blackout, you would be searching for digs with a torch and everyone shouting, "Put that light out!"

'Most of the digs we knew, because we had been there many times before. I remember once Charlie, the baby and I had to share a large bed sitting room. There was a fire, but coal was rationed during the war. We even had to go to the Ex-Army Store and buy blankets for the bed and if we saw any old bits of wood in the theatre we used to bring it back for the fire. This night the landlady, who had a cat, came into the room and after a chat, she went to the door, turned round and said, "Come on Puss, come out of here, it's far too cold for you". I couldn't believe her logic in that it was too cold for the cat, but alright for our baby!

'In variety they had the likes of Ben Warris and Jimmy Jewel, who were brilliant. Douglas, our son, loved to stand at the side of the stage and got to know all the performers so that he knew which act he wanted to go down to the theatre and see. *Jewel and Warris* was one act he loved. At that time they had a great act at the end of which they sang a number called Timber. "Timber, everybody crying for Timber". And from the flies, a net opened and a whole load of timber, firewood fell down on them and my young son thought that was super.

'There was also Wilson, Keppel and Betty, the wonderfully eccentric sand-dancers and the many other marvellous, original entertainers. I must have seen all the famous speciality acts of the day because I toured around all the theatres across Britain for many years. There was such tremendous hard-working talent around; everyone, I expect, trying to offer something unusual. Finding work on the variety circuit was a very competitive business and theatre managers would always be on the look-out for first-rate entertainment which was a little different, something special, or even quite bizarre and gave the audience a bit of a thrill.'

The Daily Record, 30th July 1935
'The re-decorated Pavilion which opened last night after a summer vacation, started off with a fine show. Arthur Prince and "Jim" in a new ventriloquist act, were quite up to their best; Hetty King, the well known male impersonator was given a well merited reception for her clever work. Mystifying card tricks were put across in fine style by Billy O'Connor, who completely bewildered the audience. Don, Honey and Bea Ray did clever work with ropes, while the Three Bulvonas showed some really fine acrobatic work.'

The Empire Theatre, Glasgow
Copyright Strathclyde Regional Archives

The Panopticon Theatre, Trongate, Glasgow, 1936
Copyright Strathclyde Regional Archives

The Empire Theatre, Edinburgh, 1948
Copyright Edinburgh Room, Edinburgh Central Library

Jack Anthony

Dave Willis

Dave Willis (centre) and his son Denny Willis (right).

Clark and Murray – Grace Clark and Colin Murray

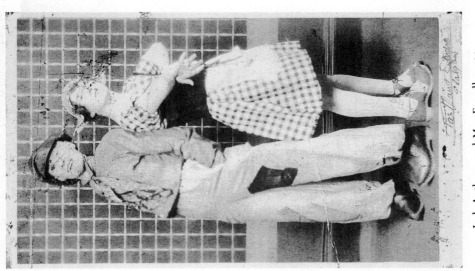

Jack Anthony and Mae Farrell, 1922

Letta's Entertainers at Portobello, 1926.

Letta's Entertainers at Portobello, 1926. Dave Willis is fourth from right.

Alec Finlay

Chic Murray and Maidie

Programme for *Finlay Frolics*, 1947

Programme for *Finlay Frolics*, The Pavilion, Glasgow, 1948.

"SAMMY TAKES THE CAKE"

FRED COLLINS' BEACH PAVILION ENTERTAINERS
BURNTISLAND --- SEASON, 1915

Beach Pavilion, Burntisland, Fife, 1915. Harry Gordon is third from left.

Francie and Josie
Copyright: Glasgow Herald (George Outram Picture Library)

Ilona Ross

Charles Ross

Programme for *Five-Past Eight* Show

The Palladium Theatre, Fountainbridge, Edinburgh.
Copyright Edinburgh Room, Edinburgh Central Library

Johnny Victory

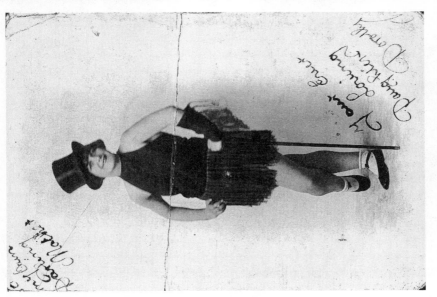

Dorothy Trewhitt as a young girl in 1924.

The Tiller Girls at the Beach Pavilion, Aberdeen, 1936.

Harry Gordon and the Tiller Girls, Beach Pavilion, 1936.

Bobby Dowds

TWICE NIGHTLY

PALACE
DUNDEE

THEATRE
OF VARIETIES

| 6.25 | Proprietors............Dundee Varieties Ltd.
 Managing Director......J. J. F. Lockhart
 Resident Manager and
 Licensee............................Leo A. Lion | 8.30 |

PLEASE SEE
THIS SEAL IS
INTACT

"Where the Best People
See the Best Shows"

Programme, Price 2d   *Please see that Seal is intact*

GUINNESS
is good for you

Programme for show at the Palace, Dundee, 1949.

The Palace Theatre, Dundee.
Copyright D.C. Thomson (*Dundee Courier*)

Harry Gordon

Johnny Beattie

Tommy Lorne

The Queen's Theatre, Watson Street, Glasgow.
(Originally the People's Palace)
Copyright: Strathclyde Regional Archives

Lex McLean

Tommy Morgan

Theatre Royal

Edinburgh

Programme for *Babes in the Wood*, Theatre Royal, Edinburgh, 1945.

Leaflet for the *Gaiety Whirl*, Diamond Jubilee, 1990.

Evening News

EDINBURGH KING'S THEATRE

THE CITY OF EDINBURGH DISTRICT COUNCIL
EDINBURGH
IMPROVING SERVICES · CREATING JOBS

TUESDAY 4 DECEMBER 1990 · SATURDAY 16 FEBRUARY 1991

STANLEY
Baxter
IN

The new lavish Spectacular Pantomime

CINDERELLA
WITH
Angus Lennie
and Alyson McInnes as Cinderella

KALMAN GLASS
as the Baroness

LUCKEN'S
Shetland Ponies

and

BARNABY

as

b u t t o n s

*Choreography
and Staging by*
SHERIDAN NICOL

Musical Director
PATRICK MCCANN

Lighting
FRANCIS REID

Designed by
TERRY PARSONS

Written and Directed by
STANLEY
Baxter

EDITH MACARTHUR · CLAIR MASSIE · DIANE BARRIMORE · BRUCE GREEN

Flyer for *Cinderella*, Kings Theatre, Edinburgh, Christmas 1990.

The Three Aberdonians

Wilson, Keppel and Betty.

PALACE THEATRE, DUNDEE

WEEK COMM. 28-10-39   Week Commencing 28th. Oct. 19

TIME SHEET   FIRST HOUSE   SECOND HOUSE

approximate times.

	ON	OFF	TIME	ON	OFF	TIME
OVERTURE	5.50	5.51	1			
TEMPLE & HOLMES	5.51	5.58	7			
LUCILLE BENSTEAD	5.58	6. 8	10			
4. BRANSBY WILLIAMS	6. 8	6.20	12			
LILY MORRIS	6.20	6.32	12			
INTERMISSION	6.32	6.38	6			
7. GORDON STEPHEN	6.38	6.45	7			
8. HARRY TATE	6.45	6.57	12			
9. TALBOT O'FARRELL	6.57	7. 9	12			
10.ALBERT WHELAN	7. 9	7.21	12			
11.REX HARTE & JUNE	7.21	7.28	7			
12.FINALE	7.28	7.30	2			

(6 minutes Compere)

| | | 7.36 | | | | |

Leo a Lion ....Resident Manager.

.............Stage Manager

Time sheet at Palace Theatre, Dundee, signed by Leo Lion.

2.

TWICE NIGHTLY
Tivoli
Theatre of Varieties

6·30	Proprietors, Aberdeen Varieties Ltd Licensee and General Manager, G. W. Bolton Telephones— Manager and Booking Office, 884/885	8·35

PRESENTS ALL THE YEAR ROUND—

The Very Best in Variety

Gramophone records by the courtesy of Paterson, Sons, & Marr Wood

PROGRAMME - - - - - PRICE 2d.

Chapter 9

PRODUCTION, STAGE MANAGEMENT AND THE BACKSTAGE CREW

AILEEN VERNON

'While the theatre business all sounds wonderful and glitzy and great, it is not. Theatre is a hard slog, and pantomime and *Five-Past Eight* was a back crippler. I couldn't relax for one minute because it was my responsibility and mine alone to put any problem right. I came out absolutely shaking some nights, thinking did I do the right thing?

'I was in control of everything and I was literally the boss while the producer was not there. His job was to come up with the ideas for the pantomime or show, while I was there to carry them out. I was called the Stage Director until Freddie Carpenter, the producer said we will have to call you something else, because part my job was also to take over and re-direct revivals of his previous productions where he would only arrive at the last moment for the dress rehearsal. So I became Assistant Producer as well. In all areas of stage management and production, I cannot emphasise enough how homework is essential. If you arrive on stage and do not know what the hell you are doing, you might as well go home. The production is a combination of your ideas, and the producer's. He may have the majority of ideas and plans, the show is his baby, but you assist and ensure that these ideas work on stage.

'When the show was running, I would be overall in charge. The wardrobe mistress would tell me if there was a problem; you obviously don't go round every member of the cast to see if they all have their costumes. Before every performance of the *Five-Past Eight* shows, half an hour before the curtain, I would go round the principals' dressing rooms, paying a courtesy call to check that everyone was alright. Before any show, or pantomime, I would spend a few minutes with say, Rikki Fulton or Kenneth McKellar, because it is worth your while. It puts them in a good mood, and it is your job to see that they are alright. Perhaps someone has had a distressing day, or even some good news which may affect their performance. Another may complain of a sore throat, which alerts you to a possible understudy replacement, or at least you would tell the Musical Director about the voice problem. You have to be aware of everything that could happen in the show. "I've lost my tights," they cry. "Well find them, or see Wardrobe".

'The stage crew start coming in, your stage manager is setting up for you, so that when you walk down ready to start, all you do is call the orchestra. There are so many things to check, ensuring that all the departments are there, and in control, and that the orchestra is in the band room. I would also pop into wardrobe for a quick Hello and Goodbye. The choreographer doesn't stay after opening night so I liaise with the head-girl of the troupe and if there are any problems with costumes, makeup, dance steps, or if anyone was absent, it was up to her to tell me. She might say we are altering a scene because we have a girl short. I would say, "Does it interfere with the principals at all?" She might say, "No, it is just a straight dance," or "Yes, it does interefere but I've seen Rikki and cleared it up". It was up to me to know exactly what was happening on stage at any moment.

'The company trust you to see the show through, trust that the scenery will come in on time every night, at that time, and no other time, because the stage hands have to do x number of things behind the curtains within only six bars of music from the orchestra. Unless that is done and everything is ready and actors come on last, as the lights come up, then you have a scene change. Unless you can do it properly night after night, you are not worth the salt. If you panic, if you flutter about, it is no good. That is not good stage management.

'The people who worked the limes, the three spotlights, are encased in a box and they are the people you never see. The stage manager is the only person who sees them when they come down to check the lights and cues. They follow the artistes in the spotlight and it is hot, sticky and very noisy in there. During my time at the Alhambra not many realised that the chief lighting electrician was a women, Greta Cullen. There was nothing you could tell Greta about electrics. Her husband was the resident stage manager. This was all pre-computer lighting when it was all done by hand. I have never worked a computer in the theatre and it is a totally different ball game now, where every lighting cue is pre-set rather like a video. Now it is the feeding-in of the information which is so crucial. But in those days it was all manual, absolutely everything.

'We worked long hours, spending a great deal of time standing around on concrete or lino, but I don't think we ever complained. You simply said, "Oh goodness, I could do with a cup of tea". There was always a cup of tea handy. One of the accolades was to be asked to join the crew in the staff room under the stage. Once you had proved your worth, and that you were not a Charlie and shown that you knew what you were doing, they accepted you. I was often asked to have tea with the producer, Freddie Carpenter, who was brought a silver tea tray and china cups in the stalls, but I preferred to go down under with the boys because socially it was a good thing. It meant that you had won your spurs really.

'When the performance is about to begin, you know, because you have double-checked everyone, that you have your crew beside you: "Right is everybody ready?" Nothing happens for that moment before you prepare to press the red button which will alert the orchestra pit, because they can't start until you tell them. This signal of buttons was the system we used in my day, but I don't think they have that now. You press the red stand-by button meaning, "I am ready to start but have not said go yet". The MD is poised with his baton, and it is at that moment you can be as sick as a dog, because you are as hyped up as you ever can be. You know that as you press that green button, everything will happen. The orchestra strikes up, the villagers enter, laughing and dancing and the pantomime has begun. You start it all off by pressing a green button.'

REG ALLEN

'Howard and Wyndham had a yearly contract of five pantomimes to be produced in various cities in Scotland and England. Also *Five-Past Eight* shows, so one had to plan the year. When pantomime finished, we started touching up or designing the summer show scenery. I began a library system of storing the vast amounts of scenery. All the flats were numbered and placed in "bays". We had two hundred cloths to look after. It was an enormous amount of work but we got it down to a fine art by cataloguing everything. Scenery was all wrapped in sail cloths to keep the damp out and it was all racked and numbered. One worked as hard as possible to get the thing as streamlined as you could. Sometimes you slipped up but on the whole it worked out very well.

'The heaviest year was 1954. We had to arrange the schedule of eight pantomimes very carefully with all the get-outs and get-ins. A get-out means that you are loading up three vans with scenery, costumes and props, to be transported to another theatre, for the next get-in. My job, although I was basically a designer and painter, was production manager, which meant that I could synchronise the whole thing. The responsibility was on my shoulders for the scenery, the costumes, wardrobe, electrics and props, all of which I had to supervise. Once the first get-in was arranged, it was a tight schedule, while I moved on to the next one, and in reverse it was the get-outs, putting the sets back into store.

'I put the full production on and then handed it over to the stage manager. In those days we had a stage director, a stage manager, and an assistant stage manager. There were so many things to watch and if you got a good stage director, you felt fine. Sometimes I was called back to rearrange things, but very seldom. I usually moved on to the next project.

'When I first started designing for pantomime, everything was very realistically painted such as a brick wall that you could hit your head against and not hurt yourself. But I tried to bring a little bit of colour and using a pen and ink drawing, a wash, making it sort of decorative, more than realistic. After all it is fantasy. If you allow the realism to go too far, it goes outwith the realms of fantasy, which to me is pantomime.

'In pantomime sets we have a series of vamp doors which the cast roll under and run through. A vamp is a door with a double hinge. When you come through it, it stops automatically, so that you cannot see where it is against the painted backcloth. They are used to good effect in a chase scene. Another design we've done is a haunted bedroom scene for Stanley Baxter and Ronnie Corbett, as the Ugly Sisters. When they went to sleep, there was a tassle which used to come down over the top of the bed and tickle one of the sister's head in turn and go up again. And they would each blame the other which started the process of a chase sequence again. There would be a huge wardrobe concealing a large number of people and also a trick staircase. As people started to come down, the stairs disappeared and it became a steep slope, a skid. These are really all typical pantomime gags.

'We would work on designing and building a new pantomime set over a period of three months, but that is interspersed with other things. We didn't go at a pantomime non-stop but it was part of our work schedule. Fortunately I had quite a large staff. We had very good costume designers and twenty-four wardrobe mistresses so I didn't have to worry too much about that side of things. I had chief electricians who looked after all the equipment, keeping the electrics up-to-date and repairing where necessary. I had very good scenic artists working for me, four painters, and eight carpenters; between us we built the whole thing up. It was based on good organisation.'

DOROTHY TREWHITT

Wardrobe Assistant, early 1930s; theatrical landlady, and widow of Jack
Trewhitt, Stage Manager, 1928–1946, at the Theatre Royal, Edinburgh.

'In 1931 when I first came to live in Edinburgh, I worked for six months
in the Wardrobe Department at the Theatre Royal, after my marriage to
Jack Trewhitt, the stage manager at the Theatre Royal. The Wardrobe
Mistress for a few years at that time was Madame Clark, and I was one
of about two or three of her assistants. While the Wardrobe Mistress was
directly in charge of making and caring for the main costumes, I would
help to sew sequins, machine trimmings on dresses, do the washing and
ironing and the repairing of torn costumes. At the beginning of the
pantomime season, all the garments were professionally cleaned and
during the run of the show only washable items, like sashes, blouses and
shirts would be washed regularly. The principals normally would have
their own dresser who would care for the wigs and many costumes they
wore. We were busy enough looking after the chorus girls' clothes,
which could be up to ten changes of costume each performance. They
were always tearing them too, and Madame Clark would get so annoyed.
She always blamed the girls for torn dresses always putting it down to
carelessness, never an accident. So there was always something to mend,
or buttons to sew on. The Theatre Royal had a vast wardrobe of clothes,
built up over many many years, to be used for all the variety and
pantomime seasons.

'Bumper Wark (A. J. Wark) was manager at the Theatre Royal from
the mid twenties to 1946, when the theatre burnt down. He always wore
a top hat, tails, a bow tie and was immaculately dressed. There he would
stand each night, front of house and no one was better known in the
Scottish theatre world than Bumper. He was a character. I think he must
have been the only manager who dressed like that.

'Horace Collins became the proprietor of the Theatre Royal, as part
of a chain of five theatres in Britain, after his father, Fred Collins died
in the early thirties. Horace Collins was a very stout man for his young
age. Very strict with his staff, he wanted his pound of flesh, but if you
played well he played his part in return. He was well liked and was always
a very fair man.

'We also ran theatrical digs at our home in London Street, from the
early thirties to the late sixties. Even when the theatres closed, we took
in club performers. I always cooked a late supper, and in fact they had
four meals a day. It didn't bother me, because I had always had to prepare
a late meal for my husband, who worked long hours in the theatre all our
married life. I charged one pound twelve and sixpence, for full board for

a week. That was in the thirties. I remember going out on tour in my young days, and paid eighteen and sixpence for full board. I still used to send ten shillings home to my mother. And the most I ever earned was two pounds five shillings.

'My husband Jack Trewhitt was stage director for Fred Collins in touring revues for many years and then for Horace Collins' productions at the Theatre Royal, Edinburgh. During the war years he couldn't get staff for the pantomime matinees because men were all away at the war. Evening staff had day jobs and couldn't come in during the afternoon. Therefore, I became a jack-of-all-trades and would work back stage, scene shifting. I could brace a flat as good as any man, I'm not kidding. I loved it because I was helping my hubby. The electrician's wife, she came in too to help him because he couldn't get any men either. It was a help for us, being paid four shillings for a matinee which made us believe we were millionaires.

'Part of my husband's job was to ensure that each act kept to their time allowance. Every Monday morning he would give so many minutes to each act and then he had to ensure that this was adhered to. If they went over he sometimes used to drop the curtain on them. There was a well known comic piano act, Herschel Henlere, who was a Frenchman or he was supposed to be French – he had a foreign look about him – and he would never come off on time. My husband dreaded him being on the bill. He was supposed to do about six minutes but sometimes he would carry on for nearly twenty minutes which was unfair to the next act because that would be cut short. When he became known for this behaviour, Jack would just close the curtain, when he was still at the piano. Yet Henlere would run down under the stage and finish his piece at the piano in the pit. That is true!

'Jack Trewhitt was a very experienced stage manager and there was nothing he couldn't do. For a scene with Will Fyffe singing "Sailing up the Clyde", my husband built a big liner, crossing the back stage, all lit up with electric lights. It looked just like a ship sailing by and was a wonderful setting for that song.

'After the Theatre Royal burnt down in 1946, our lives folded. We weren't in the least bit interested in moving to another theatre. We still went on as theatrical digs, looking after the pros, until my husband died fourteen years ago. Then I became very involved in the campaign to open up the Playhouse Theatre in Edinburgh which had been a cinema but had been closed for many years. After a great deal of time and effort raising financial support, the Playhouse reopened in the late 1970s, as a large scale theatre for musicals, opera, ballet and pop concerts. I was now seventy years old, but began working as resident wardrobe mistress and enjoyed every minute of it, being paid the kind of wages I had never had in my life. I had a lovely job, looking after performers like Lena Zavaroni, and the Second Generation Dancers. The twenty dancers all wore white stretch jersey suits for the opening number and they all had to be washed every night and kept in good repair. But we had an excellent boiler room so that they would dry quickly.

'I would also assist when Scottish Opera came for a session at the Playhouse, although with so many exquisite costumes, they brought their own specialised staff to look after certain clothes and wigs. But I helped with all the continual washing and ironing.

'Then after a few months the Playhouse Theatre management discovered that I wasn't in Equity. In my day there was no such thing as Equity. There was the Variety Artistes Federation but only the stars would join that, those who could afford the money. Once they found out I wasn't a member of Equity, I had to leave. I didn't exactly get the sack, but I wasn't phoned for anymore. I knew that was why. After all who wants to employ me, an elderly lady? But I really loved the work and I knew what was wanting doing. I had toured all round the country as a dancer since I was a child, I had been wardrobe mistress, scene shifter, stage hand, and assisted my husband as stage manager of the Theatre Royal for years. I might not have been a member of Equity but I probably had more experience of the theatre, both on stage and back stage, than any of them put together.'

DAVID SMITH

Stage-hand, Pavilion Theatre and then the Empire, Glasgow.

'I began working in the Pavilion Theatre when I was twelve, in 1937. I helped out with the dressing and the costumes. I was quite small at the time and just ran around doing jobs for "the dragons" — the wardrobe mistresses. By the time I was fourteen I was quite an expert sewing on hooks and eyes. The year I was fifteen I grew about eight inches and when I appeared back for the pantomime season I was barred from the dressing rooms. I had to work backstage now as I was old enough and tall enough to do the heavier work there. The Pavilion stage manager, George Daly was really famous in Glasgow, and I worked for him for many years with my brother until we thought we would try for higher things, that is the Empire. When we said we were leaving, George Daly said we were a bunch of traitors, jumping over the road as it were, from the Piv, the Pavilion, to the Empire. This was in 1953.

'I was a scene shifter, running the flies, get-ins, get-outs, we did the lot. It was really very interesting work because the Empire was the place to be. The show changed every week and it was true Variety theatre. All the American acts used to start their European tour at the Glasgow Empire because if they went down well at the Empire, that was them made. Everyone who was anyone in showbusiness came there. It was said that we were the best stage staff in the world; we had to be. The Empire Stage Manager was called Laurie Whitson, and at the first house on Monday we were perhaps allowed to make one slight mistake. By second house you had to be perfect and that's no joke. If there were six folds in the curtain on the prompt side, there would be six folds on the opposite prompt side. It had to be identical. Laurie was a perfectionist and all the stage staff had to be too.

'We always worked to a script, so that you knew when to move at the end of a scene or act. When Laurel and Hardy came to the Empire, there was no script and even Laurie Whitson didn't know what our cues were. After Tuesday's second house, he said, alright lads, you are completely exonerated now for this act. Just follow them, play it by ear. So we just watched them for our cues. They were brilliant, too good to be true.

'There were other *Thanks for the Memory* Farewell Tours, such as Marie Lloyd Junior, Marie Lloyd's daughter, and Gertie Gitana. They were able to give a superb performance including the splits, although goodness know how old they were. The audience weren't aware of this, but we had to go and help pick them up when the curtain came down!

'There was also Frank Carroll, the stage door manager, who was a tyrant, George Hughes, the chief electrician, and also a great Empire character, our tea lady, Mary. She sat up on the ninth floor, running her little canteen with a vast pot of tea always on the go for staff and performers. No matter what kind of star came, they would go up to see Mary for a chat, when they came back year after year. She had hundreds of signed photographs. She had been in the business all her life, and started in the wardrobe when she was a girl. Then she became tea lady and would receive birthday cards, Christmas cards from entertainers all over the world, literally sacks of mail.

'Liberace came to the Empire, but with the eighteen inch rake on the stage, Tommy, another stage hand, and I had to sit behind holding the piano while he was performing so that it didn't roll forward and land in the band pit, or the front stalls. Because we were appearing on stage during his act, he should have paid us forty-eight shillings, but he never paid us. He scooted off afterwards. His suit used to light up, as well all his rings, the candelabra, and the piano. His finale would be "I'll be seeing you". The lights would go down and he would walk to the front of the stage, when the sequins of his suit would be sparkling, and he asked if anyone wanted to touch it. He was really first class, simply a brilliant showman.

'Then we would have animals on stage which was nerve-wracking at times. I remember Vogelbein's Bears. Now Vogelbein's own father had been mauled by a bear and here were these bears on the stage. At the end of this act one night, Tommy and I moved out as usual for the change of scene and found ourselves in the centre of the stage staring at this big brown bear. "Don't move" said Vogelbein. We certainly didn't move an inch, we were so rigid with fear. Volgelbein later gave up training bears and moved over to chimps which would be kept in the animal house at the top of the theatre.

When Adam Faith came to the Empire, that was an episode to remember. Being of the older generation, and having been in the business a long time, Tommy and I had never seen any artiste turning up in denim jeans. Jeans and overalls were for working in. This guy turns up in tatty old jeans at the stage door so we threw him out. This was Adam Faith. As he was trying to explain that he was in the show, we replied that there was no way he was getting into the theatre. "This is the Empire, get out". He had to get an escort to get him back in. We just didn't recognise him, and we really didn't know who he was.

'There was a certain mime act, when this chap would impersonate Jimmy Durante. He was a miserable fellow when he came the first time. He therefore got his card marked so that if he came back we would know how he had treated us. This character came back and it was really fatal for a mimer not to pay you. There he was attempting to mime to Jimmy Durante, and we put on a recording of Maria Callas! He was shattered. But he did not co-operate with stage staff, and so we nobbled him in return. Officially he should have paid us about twenty-four bob, to assist with his props, set and everything, but we would never go up to artistes and ask for a tip. It should have been given out of courtesy.

'The Americans were very generous and would give you fifteen pounds. Max Bygraves and Andy Stewart would give everyone an envelope with a gratuity. You couldn't depend on the wages you got, because that was only about three or four pounds a week, for all the hours you put in too. That would be from 6 pm to 11 pm Monday to Saturday or perhaps even one in the morning after a Saturday night get-out of a show. But the theatre was in your blood and you did it because you loved the atmosphere. You wanted to help put that show on.'

JOHN WISHART

'I started working in the Empire theatre when I was about fourteen until it closed in March 1963. I was one of the electricians and also worked the limes, the carbon limelights up in the balcony. The scene shifters at the Empire were excellent. They could do a set change in thirty seconds, they were experts, being able to lassoo the flats of high scenery in seconds, and in the blackout. I used to crack up with worry sometimes because they would always be running over my cables. It was a dangerous manoeuvre because someone could have been electrocuted.

'On stage, when the lights went down at the end of an act, the stage hands had to get the scene changed very quickly. I was always concerned about walking over these cables in the dark, so one night I grabbed these two light cables and nearly electrocuted *myself*, during the Max Bygraves show. I conked out and had to be whipped up to the hospital. They kept me in overnight for observation.

'There were two electricians usually, one on each side. I would also be up in the limes, working the spotlights. There were two performances a night, 6.25 and 8.25. Pantomimes were twice a night and three on a Saturday, a killer. On the first house on Monday, we wrote down a plot of all the lighting effects that were wanted for every act, such as different colours, spots, fading, and black out cues. By the second house you were expected to know it. By the third night you could do it without a plot, and just carried on.

'One of my other jobs, when we had some of the rock and roll acts appearing in the early sixties, was to stand at the door at Sauchiehall Street, waiting for the car to collect the artistes. The teenagers would be waiting at the door in West Nile Street. Then I would open the door and throw the singers into the car. All worked well until this particular night when it was Joe Brown and it was an ordinary taxi which came for him. I opened the door, pushed him in, but the teenagers had arrived and opened the other door, and were holding on to him. I tried to pull him back from my side but he turned round and hit me, not realising who I was. So we were caught out that night, and had to go back into the theatre. His clothes were all torn but once he heard what had happened and who I was, we got on famously.

'I really did like to offer every service to the artistes who were good to work for. If the wardrobe mistress was very busy and couldn't attend to all the laundry at once, I would take home shirts for my mother to wash. She would find it a hard job because of the make-up engrained into the white collars. She would be scrubbing away all day at these performers' shirts, warning me not to bring any more home!'

ALEC RODGER

'I worked at the Metropole, Stockwell Street on the limes, the spotlights, and all sorts of backstage jobs, scene shifting and the switch-board, from the age of eleven right through the war years. I was eighteen and probably the youngest stage manager that a Glasgow theatre has ever had. The wages were a measly sum of £4.16.4d a week, that was in 1947. I may have been young but I was very experienced and had learned the job for seven years. I did make changes and it didn't take long to get the place into shipshape order. The theatre needed modernised a bit with fancy drapes and a good stage set.

'There were so many acts I remember, Renee Houston, and Donald Stewart. Wee Alec Munro died a death at the Empress. A real death. He said to me, ''Alec, have the doors opened yet?'' No wonder he was worried, because nobody had come in! I remember George Cormack and Irene Sharp, the best vocal act in Great Britain; Irish entertainers, like Billy Stutt, a comic, he was very funny, and Sammy Short, another Irishman. They were both front cloth stand-up comics. Frank Harvey from Possilpark, he was a good front cloth comic.

'It was certainly variety in those days. I had circus acts in the theatre many a time. Great bears and lions would appear at the Metropole and once I took a tigress for a walk along Howard Street and around St Enoch Square. It was just a big cat but I had to take it for a walk. Fenella its name was and it stayed in the dressing room. Anyway, it got the show some great publicity, ''Mad Man takes Tiger for a Walk''.

'When it was a variety bill, there was a change every week, which suited me: that way I could rely on getting good tips. Wages were rubbish and you had to depend on a travelling show, different acts every week, so that you would earn a little extra by helping with the get-in and the get-out.'

ROBERT A. AITKEN

Duty Fireman at various Glasgow theatres, 1948–1951.

'I was a fireman in the North Fire station in Glasgow and one of my duties was that of fireman in Glasgow's theatres. We would normally have two theatre duty nights every month. From my station we covered the Glasgow Empire, the Empress, the Lyric and the Pavilion.

'I would arrive an hour before the performance and check that no-one was smoking on the stage or causing a fire hazard in any way. There was a fire alarm on the prompt side of the stage, which rang directly in the fire station, so that there would be no delay in raising the alarm by trying to telephone. A theatre fire was a major incident and had a predetermined number of fire engines which would attend. Therefore before the show this alarm to the station would be tested. The fireman's real job began after the show ended and the audience and cast had left. Then every dressing room and backstage store was checked for smouldering cigarettes, electrical lights and appliances, and waste paper baskets. Then every row of seats in the theatre was checked carefully for any burning cigarette stub.

'It was interesting work as theatre fireman, because you were able to watch the show from the wings. But it was also very responsible work because you were constantly checking that no-one was smoking. At the Empire I saw an American singer smoking a cigar and told the stage manager who went up to him and simply shook his hand. The cigar which was being concealed in his palm would have been stubbed out into his hand! He couldn't complain because he knew he shouldn't have been smoking backstage.

'Another thing we had to check was that the exit fire doors had not been padlocked and bolted. This was often something the back stage staff would do to ensure they got a quick getaway after the show.

'Despite stringent precautions like this, there were a number of theatre fires yet these could never be blamed on the duty fireman. I attended two theatre fires, the Queen's in 1952, and the Empress in 1956. The Queen's theatre fire began at about four in the morning and therefore was long after the duty fireman had finished his rounds. The Empress Theatre fire started about midnight, about an hour after the fireman would have left. In both cases it was probably some electrical fault which couldn't have been detected earlier.

'When short of stage staff at the Pavilion, the stage manager would contact the fire-station for some off-duty fireman since we were used to working at heights and could work up at the top of the fly tower. This ''moonlighting'' work, for which we would be paid about two shillings a night, was without the Firemaster's permission I might say. We would assist on the fly grid high above the stage and drop in back cloths and fly off the one used in the previous scene. One Christmas Eve I was one of the five firemen manning the grid and Tommy Morgan was on stage giving his usual patter with a back cloth of George Square and the City Chambers. Our cue sheet showed that Tommy would finish his patter with a black-out on stage and we had to fly off the George Square back cloth. We would then drop in a tropical island cloth complete with palm trees while the chorus girls would come on doing a Pacific dance.

'Just before Tommy finished his act we noticed one of the senior fire officers coming across the fly grid, obviously doing a theatre inspection with the duty fireman, and since we were not supposed to be there, we would probably be put on a charge. We made a hasty retreat from the platform and into the upper circle of the auditorium, via an exit door. We were just in time to see Tommy finish his act. The stage blacked out but with no one to fly the Glasgow back-cloth, the chorus came dancing on complete with hula skirts, right across George Square, much to the delight of the audience. Tommy Morgan was not amused!'

DOROTHY TREWHITT

'One year in pantomime, 1936 I believe, we had an act with the song, "All the world is waiting for the sunrise and the air is heavy with dew", with the dancers out in front. Some of the girls wore silver dresses, others wore blue ones, so that together it gave a sky and stars effect. Some of the girls were holding sparklers. It was just one of those unexpected accidents — the dresses had been at the cleaners and because the girls were waving these sparklers, perhaps some inflammable substance caught a spark and one girl's dress just went up in flames. They wrapped a blanket around her and eventually they put the flames out. She survived thankfully, but she never danced again because her legs were so badly scarred.

'On another occasion at the Pavilion in the pantomime *Sinbad the Sailor*, starring Dave Willis, the chorus girls were in the dressing room. As I was head girl, I didn't change with the chorus, but was sharing a room with the Wardrobe Mistress. It was 16th January, 1937, I will always remember the date. The girls were getting dressed for the finale scene with beautiful headdresses and crinolines which came out from the hips. One girl, Phyllis Herbert, was getting ready, fixing her headdress, when her crinoline swayed on to an open electric fire which was under the table. Again she was up in flames in a second and I heard those screams, but of course didn't know what had happened. I ran in to give them a row, because they were creating such a noise. The girls were screaming, and running out, shouting, "Phyllis is on fire". Girls are noted for playing pranks but the girl was literally on fire. By this time various members of the company had arrived to help and we all tried to lift the carpet off the floor but these filthy dirty carpets were nailed down. We brought her into the corridor and eventually got her to hospital.

'The pantomime of course was still going on, with this fire backstage. Dave Willis was doing his act, on the front cloth, before the finale. The dancers then followed him on but the first one fainted and then another was in hysterics, while the Fire Brigade had arrived, clanging its bells outside.

I went to the hospital with Phyllis, but she died the next day. It was such a tragic accident, just one of those things. The problem was that there wasn't sufficient water backstage to put the fire out. But next day there were hydrants everywhere, down the staircases, all over the theatre. Never again was there an open electric fire allowed. The whole dressing room had been on fire in minutes, because all the straw skirts hanging around the room were a mass of flames. And that is a scene I will never, ever forget, even if I live to be a thousand. Never.'

Sunday Mail: 17th January 1937

'Dancing Girl's Dress on Fire. Backstage heroism in Glasgow Theatre. Audience unaware of outbreak.

'. . . the screams of the girl attracted the John Silver Trio, three male acrobats, one of whom has only one leg. Despite this infirmity, he dashed into the dressing room and assisted the other chorus girls to extinguish the flames. Unfortunately the crinoline frocks are supported by wire hoops and the metal got red hot and became entangled with her legs. Mr George Daly, Pavilion stage manager, and Jack Trewhitt, stage manager for the pantomime, were also immediately on the scene'.

Daily Record: 18th January 1937

'. . . The dressing room was on the top floor of the building, remote from the auditorium and the audience were completely unaware of what was happening, and were roaring with laughter while Dave Willis was putting over one of his funniest scenes. Later it was stated that had it not been for the presence of mind of the Call Boy, the dressing room itself would have been gutted. When someone shouted fire, the call boy dashed upstairs and helped to pull the burning frock off the injured girl, and ran into the dressing room. There he saw several dresses hanging against the wall, ablaze. Without fear of injuring himself, the boy tore the frocks from the pegs, ran into the corridor with them and stamped the flames out with his feet.'

Scottish theatres have had an unfortunate share of ill-luck concerning fires. In Edinburgh, it was the fire of 1946 which destroyed the beloved Theatre Royal, at the top of Leith Walk. Dorothy Trewhitt, whose late husband was stage manager there, recalls the tragedy.

'This particular night was the final night of Tommy Morgan's show which had been running for a few weeks. We ran theatrical digs at the time and had theatre people from the Palladium staying with us. We were sitting in our dining room in our flat in London Street. I could see flickering out the window and thought what a lovely sky there was. But it became brighter and bigger and I said, it must be a fire somewhere. This was about one o'clock in the morning. I ran downstairs to the corner of the street, and people were running up the road, up Broughton Street, shouting, "It's the theatre, the Theatre Royal is burning down".

'How I got back up those stairs, I can't imagine as my legs were like jelly. The Theatre Royal was my life. Absolutely, there was no other theatre in Scotland like the Theatre Royal, Edinburgh. It was our theatre. I still allude to it as "our" theatre. I loved it. Jack and I rushed away back to the theatre and the two artistes staying with us came up too. By this time, the Police, and the Fire Brigade were there. The trouble was that they couldn't find a hydrant to get water. The damage mightn't have been so bad if they had managed to get water straight away. The Fireman were flummoxed trying to find hydrants in the street.

'In the gallery in those days we had arc lamps, using charcoal. They used to be in the first row in the corner of the circle and balcony, so that the spotlights shone down on the stage. These lights used to get red hot and little bits would fall off and normally do no damage. It was thus assumed but never proved that a piece of this hot charcoal started the fire. It did start in the gallery and of course it was an old theatre and with all the wooden seating and panelling, it went up like a tinder box. The iron curtain was down and the row of sprinklers along the top of the curtain started so the fire never got passed the curtain. The auditorium was absolutely gutted and the roof. The two pass doors were all buckled, but the fire never reached back stage.

'There is a story that on the night of the Theatre Royal blaze Dan Campbell, the manager of the Palladium at Fountainbridge in Edinburgh, went down to the Theatre Royal, after hearing the news of the catastrophe. On his way home later he had a strange premonition and decided to go back to the Palladium to check that everything was alright. He walked all round the auditorium and suddenly found a burning cigarette, and thus saved the theatre from a disastrous fire.'

JOAN NICHOLS

Box Office assistant, Palace Theatre, Dundee 1938–40

'I was just eighteen, and I really was supposed to have gone to the School of Art, after I left school but I wasn't at all keen on it. So that didn't happen and I started working at the theatre, and loved it. The booking office opened at ten in the morning until nine at night officially, but after nine you had so much to do checking tickets and all the rest of it that it was always far later than nine when you finished. You didn't work all that time. The first shift began at ten, finished at two and then you came back at five and you worked from five until about ten. Another week you would work from two in the afternoon and work right through with an hour's break for tea. At that time you used to get a very good tea at the Crystal Bell in Union Street; something like a pot of tea, and fish and chips for one shilling! So those were the hours we worked, not Sunday of course, but Saturday so that was six days a week. The hours were long looking back on it, but I never thought of it as hard work.

'If you worked in the theatre you were given cinema permits, so that when you were off in the afternoon, you were able to see free cinema shows. I was mad about the pictures too, and I went to all of them. It was a great perk, the La Scala, the Kinnaird, the King's and in those days films were so much better. The King's had a marvellous tea room, the Rose Room.

'I considered I was very well paid; I had one pound five shillings a week and that was very good because my sister worked in the Courier newspaper office, and when she started she only got ten shillings a week. It was amazing what you could buy with a pound a week, and in those days you always helped with household expenses, not like nowadays when so many youngsters think their parents can keep them.

'There were four of us in the booking office, working two at a time, but there was also a woman who came in at night, Mrs Thomas, and we all thought she was a bit of a mystery lady. At the time I thought she was pretty old, but I don't suppose she was much over fifty. We were told that at one time she had been a chorus girl, and she wore the most shocking makeup. Even at that time I thought it was bad: dead white powder and very, very bright lipstick. She only worked in the evenings, in the booking office which issued tickets for that evening only. On a Monday night the house was always "dressed", that is, padded out to make it look full. This was only on a Monday night. Then the word went about, "Oh, yes, it was packed". These were complimentary tickets, and sometimes we were given tickets to give to friends.

Then we had permanent bookings, where people came every week, and there were some characters. There was one man, Mr Hay, and his family who had an antique shop in Dundee. He used to bring us the most extraordinary gifts. Not a box of chocolates, but fresh carrots out of his garden, this kind of thing. If he liked you he brought a present, but if he didn't like you he was a very abrupt man. He always wore leggings, it didn't matter the weather, or where he was going. I always remember the carrots, which my mother was always pleased with when I took them home, because of the food shortages during the war.

'Some people would say they would like a permanent booking for Monday, second house, or Friday first house, whatever day it was they wanted to come each week. Their name would be entered in a book and instead of them having to phone up every week, we looked in the permanent bookings register, and those tickets were automatically reserved. They didn't have to do anything until they came in and collected their tickets on the evening. Normally tickets would have to be collected by four o'clock but if we knew they were regular customers, they could just arrive for the performance. A lot of children would come to the first house which was out by eight thirty, older children these were. Also the matinees and at Christmas they were brought for a treat. We didn't often have pantomime and it was still variety at Christmas.

'It was a difficult job in lots of ways. You might for example, be all prepared to leave, and everything was all tallied up and then the Customs and Excise inspector would come in. All the tickets were checked against the stubs you had in your book. It all had to be just so and if there was one out, or any discrepancy, you would have to stay until the mistake was found. This was so that people wouldn't sell tickets and pocket the money, and that is why when you stamped a complimentary ticket, you had to be sure that it was marked up properly.

'In those days all the usherettes wore uniforms, brown with a yellow gold trim. The door keeper, he was a tall Englishman, a charming man, very tall, very thin, called Arthur. There was a little bellboy, called David Martin, who at that time would have been fifteen. He was tiny and he wore the round pill box cap. In the evening, before the first show, all the usherettes were lined up in the foyer, and the head usher inspected them all first, then the Manager came and inspected them. The Manager always wore evening dress, never an ordinary lounge suit. The manager's name was Mr Walker and when he left his successor was a man called Leo Lion, surprisingly enough. He was quite small, and he looked like Punch, the same big hooked nose. He was a very hard man, but who was popular with customers because he would offer people a drink at the bar. He was a Londoner, and he was very Hail Fellow, Well Met, on the surface. But that was his name, Leo Lion.

'Two of the directors of the Palace Theatre were Jock Lochart, who had a business in town to do with car repairs, and the other was a Mr Crerar, who was involved in boats, so they had money. They used to come into the booking office asking how takings were going and what returns they were making. Mr Lochart was a big man while Mr Crerar was short and very fat and smoked cigars, which impressed me no end at my young age. Then Horace Collins, who owned the Palace, would occasionally visit, always wearing a camel coat.

Some of the advance booking agents for the artistes, were a very smooth lot. They would come about a fortnight beforehand just to see how the bookings were going for the show, and perhaps if they thought a little more publicity was needed, they would get on to the manager.

'As I sit here, fifty years later, I can still remember everyone so clearly. The doorman was always very smart, in his uniform. Everyone took a pride in dressing well. The manager was always there in the foyer every evening, saying hello to people, to make them feel welcome. There was an old man at the stage door who was always so avuncular with the young girls. I mean in a nice way, helping them. I think he had been gassed in the First World War. He kept things going, as best he could, with problems and complaints, but the dressing rooms they had were not great, always cold, as the theatre was an old, draughty, building.

'*Jock's Box* was a charity show which we had in 1940 to raise funds for sending comforts to the troops. They did it in theatres all over Scotland and it started at midnight, after the evening show when everyone gave their services free. Harry Lauder was top of the bill on this occasion at the Palace Theatre. And a very ill-natured Harry Lauder he was at that time. I remember he had the pianist in tears, because he had said she wasn't keeping proper time. But the place was packed out. I couldn't honestly tell you how much they made but it was a lot of money. The prices were higher than normal.

'Florrie Forde came, and this was a whole show made up of a group of "older", perhaps semi-retired performers, of the early days. She was still a big, handsome woman and she sang one of her famous songs, "Anyone here seen Kelly, KELLY from the Isle of Man". That was a favourite and people always asked her to sing that. But she was a very nice person too, because you got to know them, when they came for their post. You could always tell if people were genuinely nice, as opposed to others who ignored you.

'It was a funny thing but before the performance, even though I only worked in the box office, I always had this feel of excitement, this buzz as if I was part of the show. I was always wondering how it would go each night.'

Dundee Courier 21st August 1978
Letter from Ernest Massie:

'Although the Palace Theatre in the Nethergate no longer exists, it has left many happy memories and enriched countless lives. Dundonians loved their weekly visit to the Palace whether it was variety or revue. Audiences rocked with laughter as they lapped up the humour and antics of stars like Johnny Victory, Lex McLean and Jack Anthony. One important member of the staff was stage manager, Matt Brown, who was responsible for everything going smoothly back-stage. It was all in a day's work for Matt whether he had to supervise arrangements for a mini circus, the fitting of a trapeze for acrobats, or catering for a performing sea lion.

'One of the strangest acts I ever saw at the Palace was a huge Frenchman who was billed as The Human Aquarium. A large tank of water containing assorted types and sizes of fish was placed on the stage. He proceeded to scoop up these fish with a jug and swallow them. He would then take a stance several yards away and with one glorious belch, his "prisoners" would be released. It was uncanny to see all these fish travelling in mid air, and being cascaded back into the tank.'

CATHIE MACDONALD

Barmaid, Theatre Royal, Edinburgh, 1940s.

'At the Theatre Royal we had a great manager, A. J. "Bumper" Wark, who was always immaculately dressed. He used to polish the soles of his shoes, wore a large cummerband, and he always held himself so straight. I was working up in the dress circle this night and Bumper said, "Miss McHale? Please leave the bar for a moment. I have to prove something to this gentleman here, Tommy Morgan". So I left the room. When I came back in he said, "It's alright. It's proved now". Tommy Morgan wanted Bumper to prove to him that he did not wear a corset. He held himself so straight that Tommy Morgan was convinced that he wore a corset to keep himself looking so trim. So he proved he did not wear one.

'Working in the bar at the Theatre Royal was great, you met all the stars when they were rehearsing and they treated you like their friends. My boss was Margaret Millar, a lovely girl. Life was strict though, and Bumper checked that we were well presented when you came in so that we were all dressed the same. We worked in the morning, and then you went back at night and Sunday was our only day off.

'There were regular bookings and there was a particularly good crowd who came every Thursday night. One year, I think it was 1944, the "Thursday Nighters" wanted to show their appreciation to the entertainers, and actually crowned Jack Anthony the Laughter King of Scotland. They came down the aisle one Thursday night with a lovely crown on a red velvet cushion and they crowned Jack Anthony. One of the group was a great character, old Walter Duncan of Duncan's Chocolates; he used to come every Thursday, and you could count on him being there.'

ARCHIE FOLEY

Son of the late Andrew Foley, Bar and theatre manager.

'My father was bar manager at the Palladium Theatre, Edinburgh before the Second World War. This theatre had a wonderful history as a site for entertainment. From 1886 it had been Cooke's Circus, and became a theatre in 1928. It wasn't a fine building, but the atmosphere as a popular local theatre was marvellous. Helen Fowler was the Musical Director here for years. After service in the Royal Air Force, my father returned to working in the theatre and moved in 1946 to the Gaiety in Leith where his responsibilities grew and he became much more involved in the running of the theatre, alongside Claude Worth, the manager and his wife, Dora. The Gaiety had been a picture house, and was quite a rough place in the early days. It had a colourful history, of melodrama, ciné-variety until the war years when it developed into a good number two theatre.

'With this experience behind him, my father moved to the Tivoli, Aberdeen in 1954 as theatre manager, where he stayed until 1963. He was a gregarious man, and enjoyed meeting people, talking to the regular patrons who came every week. One of the things he is particularly remembered for are the many Sunday concerts and revues he organised for hospitals, and charities.

'After my father died, we received many letters from people who wanted to express their gratitude for his continual service in collecting money and arranging small groups to put on a Saturday afternoon or Sunday revue. He would be pleased to take a show out to the smaller villages around Aberdeen for those who could not travel to the Tivoli Theatre.

'In 1963, my father became manager of the Palladium, Edinburgh until this theatre closed in 1968. Having had experience in several theatres around Scotland, he noted local differences such as the extra length of material which had to be sewn on to the chorus girls' briefs when they played in Aberdeen. In contrast at the Palladium, the comic, Tommy Hope, had to be persuaded by the producer, Hamish Turner, that it *was* quite in order to include a sketch in the Donald McGill seaside humour mould, in which a beautiful young female hitch-hiker asks a deaf old man whether he had seen a pair of picnickers, which is misheard as "pink knickers".

CAREY WILSON

'An indispensable member of my father's touring company was an amazing man called Jimmy Mackie. Jimmy was the road manager, a large gentleman reminiscent of the film actor, Sidney Greenstreet, who always wore a Homburg hat and a raincoat whatever the weather. Jimmy was from Fife, and in his early days had been involved in Circus. He knew every town and village in Scotland; where the hall was, where the best digs were, who the hallkeeper was – a rare and temperamental breed – what football team he supported, who would put the Bills up, when the "half-day closing" was, who had played there recently and how well they had done. The company would arrive at the hall and there would be Mackie at the door asking "whaur huv ye been, Roabert? Ah've been here fur four hoors".

'Certain regular members of the company were notorious for their devotion to the Distillery, and as drinking during the show was forbidden, many ploys were undertaken to grab a quick one. Two raincoated figures scurrying down the fire escape would be greeted by the substantial figure under the Homburg hat, saying ''Get away back up thae stairs, fur there's nae fire here!''.'

JIMMY PARKINSON

'Having trained for three years in theatrical management, I heard from friends of mine that the producer, Hugh Ogilvy had learnt of my work and asked if I would like to get in touch with him for pantomime. I wrote and told him that I was free and went up to start in the pantomime at Dunfermline. I arrived there and was told to meet Mr Harry Gordon who was his partner in pantomime. I went to the theatre on the Saturday night and met Harry Gordon there. I was asked to attend the next day at the dress rehearsal which of course I did. He didn't introduce me to any of the company, none of the company, I didn't know a soul and just sat in front with a little book and took notes. And then after the programme I went round to see Harry Gordon who wanted to discuss the various scenes. I remarked that when the Principal Boy does her number in the cave scene, she hasn't got much of a voice. I said, ''I don't think the number does her justice. If I were you I'd change it, and give her something that's not quite so musical''. ''Oh aye'' he says. I went on and finished all the notes, and then a knock came at the door and in came the Principal Boy who turned out to be Harry Gordon's wife! So I thought I'd put both feet in it, plunk! That would be my job finished. He never said a word, but he changed the number and I liked him from then.

'Of course he had done that purposely when he didn't introduce me to the company beforehand, he knew he'd get a fair crit. So from then I rather liked him. The show ran for three months and we had a good system for the show. Everybody was fined whenever they made a mistake, made a wrong entrance, did something wrong, or if the music was wrong. It was my job at front of the house to pick out the fault and on the noticeboard at the end of the week I put them all up and they were fined from threepence to one and sixpence. Perhaps members of the chorus were fined threepence. At the end of the tour all this money went into a celebration party for everyone. It was rather a good idea, and it kept the show right up on top. I wrote the pantomime from the front page to the back page from memory and I hadn't more than four words wrong, I had seen it so often. I wrote it out because it was different from when it began, and then typed it for them.

'At the end of the pantomime Harry was having a chat with me and asked if I was going anywhere when they finished. I said, ''No nothing definite, I'm just going home. I'll just look around for something else''. So he said, ''Oh aye. Have a nice time''. That's all he said. Then a couple of weeks after I got home I had a letter from him saying would I like to come to Aberdeen for a season. I wrote back to say I would be delighted. By return I got word to come right away to Perth, where he was working and that he would fix digs for me, and from there we would go to Aberdeen. And from what started out as one season's job, turned out to be a ten year job at the Beach Pavilion, Aberdeen, and touring shows.

'I was in charge of all finance, front of house, wages and arrangements for travel, taking the company on tour. That reminds me of a good story. The Castlecary disaster was one of the worst accidents in railway history. This was in the winter of 1937, on 10th December, 1937, when a Glasgow train crashed just past Cumbernauld New Town. We were doing a one-night stand tour and going from Falkirk to St Andrews for the Saturday. We had two shows to do on the Saturday night and a matinee in the afternoon. Harry was going by road while I was accompanying the rest of the cast. So we got to Polmont Station and of course right away we saw long faces at Polmont. There had been this disaster and there were no trains going to St Andrews. And we had three shows to do. "Is there no chance of any transport?". "No". There was absolute chaos and they didn't know what was happening. So I said, can we get to Edinburgh, and we were told we would get to Edinburgh but nowhere else. So I got the company to Edinburgh and jumped off the train and up to the offices at Waverley Station to see one of the managers there who used to be in the theatrical business. I told him the situation and he said, goodness, there is nothing to be done. The place is upside down.

'However, he said, there is a train going to Kirkcaldy from Edinburgh. He said, get on that and I'll see if I can do anything between times. I asked whether we could get a bus, and he said he would find out. So we got on the train to Kirkcaldy and at Kirkcaldy station, running along the platform came the Station master looking anxiously about until he spotted us. "Are you Harry Gordon's company? There are no buses because the roads are blocked with snow. So what we are doing is that I have instructions to send this train on to Cupar with you in it".

'And so they specially sent the train to Cupar and there they held up the Dundee connection from Dundee to St Andrews for us arriving from Kirkcaldy. They took us on to that train and then they had a bus waiting at the station to take us down to the theatre. That was organisation.

'When we went into the theatre, there was Harry on the centre of the stage, dressing gown on, make-up on, pattering away there. He suddenly saw us coming in. "Where the hell have you been? I've been half way around Scotland looking for you". So I told him the story of our amazing journey, and what had happened. I wonder now if the railway company would do that kind of thing again. That was certainly service. But we did three shows that day. We got there at the back of three o'clock and the company dashed in, made up and straight on. We were a little late getting through the first house, and then took a short break and then onto the second house. That was the story of going to St Andrews.

'A happy company makes a happy show. And we always had a happy company. That was one of Harry's successes. Everyone was treated the same; it didn't matter if you were a chorus girl or the comic, you were the same, and that made the success of the company.'

JOHN ROBERTSON
Comedy Script writer.

'I have never been what you might call a stand-up comic writer. It was always sketches, or production scenes. I might crack an odd gag or two but I was never a gag man as such.

'It all started in the early fifties. A chap I knew ran an amateur concert party, and he used to get me involved in writing sketches, things like that. It started from there, but really I felt I was hitting my head against a brick wall, knowing there was not much future in it. At the time Stanley Baxter was appearing at the King's Theatre in Edinburgh, and he was just feeling his way in the business – a bit more famous than I was ever likely to be – but nonetheless starting out as a comedian. When I approached him he said to come and see him, and it progressed from there. I did a few bits and pieces for Stanley Baxter. Within a few years he felt that his niche was in the south and he decided to move to London. He suggested I might go there too, but there was too much at stake at the time. So I pottered on here, and sent material to Rikki Fulton, and was reasonably successful. But you found that comics drifted, unless you could nail them specifically, and they explained to you that this is what I want, or I don't want that kind of material. I could write something which I thought was tremendous and then they would tear it to pieces and you were left hanging high and dry. I moved on to Molly Weir, and she was quite encouraging. Ian McFadyen produced light entertainment shows for the BBC at that time, working with Stan Stennet and Derek Roy, and I would contribute quite a few items for programmes like Workers Playtime. It was quite encouraging for a young man, not so much from the financial angle, because you didn't get paid all that much, but the fact that you heard people laughing at something you'd written.

'From then on I started to write stuff for Sam Cree, on behalf of Jimmy Logan, and Sam would boost my confidence telling me that Jimmy was interested in working for the BBC, radio and television, "So get cracking, this is the big time". But after a few months it was plain that the BBC wasn't interested so that all fell apart. Then in 1955 I spotted a photograph of the comedy double act, Clark and Murray in a performance which gave me an idea. I listened to them on the wireless and I thought, I wonder if they would be interested in my work? I began sending them some material and they responded very positively to this. From then on there was a kindred spirit sort of thing. I would send them sketches and our relationship just developed from there.

'We would have great fun just talking, and going over an idea for a sketch. I would say, "I've got an idea, Grace" and we'd work on it together, and before the night was out, the thing was almost finished. They moulded it to suit their particular requirements, so between the three of us, it was ideal teamwork. Grace and Colin had a gift of bouncing ideas off each other, with a natural wit. I had the original idea, though, perhaps based on some everyday, or topical subject. One of the funniest ones I thought of was a sketch with Colin coming home for tea. These things just come to you in daily life. It was just typical domestic stuff, maybe not earth-shattering, but it was their style of humour:

"What's for tea tonight, hen?"

"I saw it on television, Ricci's biccies."

"I don't like the look of them."

"Well they looked good when I saw them on the telly."

(I would always remember phrases and comments which people would naturally say, "I saw it on the telly", which was the name of this sketch actually.)

"What's this?"

"It's a new egg dish I saw on the telly."

'Then there would be a lot of business playing about with omelettes, which they would add and embellish themselves, which you cannot write down. I just gave them the basic words. Then he finishes his meal and gets up from the table, goes to the drawer and pulls out a gun, and says,

"Do you know what I am going to do? I am going to get your mother, and I am going to throw her out of the window and then I'm going to shoot you."

"What on earth's got into you, dear, what are you doing?"

"I saw it on the telly."

'The ending came about because at the time there was a great row about violence on television. These things just pieced themselves together. We had great fun writing the things and then when you went to the theatre to hear it, it gave you a wee boost.

'There was an amusing incident one year. Clark and Murray had just finished their Metropole show, *Breath of Scotland*, which had been very popular, with bus loads of people coming to see it. The critic, Jack House wrote, "Grace and Colin, there is no-one who can beat them with their Glasgow humour". Every sketch I had written for them, and I don't come from Glasgow, I live in Edinburgh. It gave me quite a thrill to read Jack House, saying it was pure Glasgow humour. But it was the way they presented it. They had a natural gift which is difficult to describe, but they had a great knack of expressing the funny side of married life, in ordinary conversation, never mind the theatre.

'Colin and Grace would do a sketch about buying a suit, the usual occasion when a wife goes with her husband to buy a new suit. It started with the typical nagging scene where Grace would be telling Colin that the price had to be right, and what colour, and style he was to have, before going into the shop. George Rex was the salesman, with gags like "This raincoat is like Poetry in Motion – the Aberdeen Gaberdine". The comments which Grace made in the sketch were really colourful lines such as "That suit certainly fits you where it's landed". People really could identify with that kind of Glasgow humour. Grace would also come out with, "I'll have to go and clash the pan on". There were so many of these wonderful Glasgow phrases which were a joy to use and really made the sketch come alive.

'With comedy sketches it's not the sort of thing you can be continually writing. I couldn't just sit down and write a sketch, just like that. With Grace and Colin, because I got to know them so well, they would phone me up and say, "We're looking for a parody on the song, 'I'm just one of those girls, that you meet now and then' – can you do anything for us, we're opening on Friday?". I would have to work fast but I would be able to do that. But there is never any guarantee that anything I write will be accepted, by anybody. You just live and hope. You have a rough idea. Sometimes I think, that's not very good, but if you labour at it it still doesn't work. It has got to be spontaneous. Quite often I'm sitting on a bus, or passing people in the street, and hear a remark, and think, that will make a good sketch. It's got to be based on truth and simplicity. If it becomes too involved the humour can be lost. Stanley Baxter gave me very good advice, "If a thing is not funny after the tenth time of repeating it, it's not funny". That's true. Stanley Baxter was on stage at that time and he said if he didn't find it funny to say it, it's not really funny.'

BUNTY MACLEOD

'Minnie Simpson was Florrie Forde's dresser and companion for many years. When Florrie Forde died in 1940, I think Minnie became wardrobe mistress for some company. My father heard about her and arranged to meet her telling her that he was in dire need of a good dresser and invited her to join him. Minnie was very good at making outfits and women's costumes which was ideal for my father's role as pantomime Dame.

'Minnie did join him and she was a lovely person, she really was. She wasn't a pro herself but she gave the impression that she was. All pros have a certain air about them, when you have always been connected with the theatre. She could be frightfully stern as well and if someone came to the dressing room who she wasn't keen on, she would say, "Well, if you would like to take a seat outside, I will see if Mr Gordon can see you". She really used to take charge. On the crucial and nerve-wracking opening night of the pantomime I am sure my father used to sack her about three times because a button was off or something. "Minnie, you're sacked", he would shout. But she knew him too well. She really was a lovely lady and such a valuable member of the company. After Daddy died I think she stayed on with Howard and Wyndham as wardrobe mistress, but I believe Minnie died about four years after my father. She was a smashing lady, so caring and committed to her job, a real character to have back stage, and we used to have a lot of laughs together.'

The King's Theatre, Edinburgh

Chapter 10

THE VARIETY THEATRE: SCOTTISH POPULAR ENTERTAINMENT

A common strand which emerges from the reminiscences of comics, dancers, singers, stage managers and musical directors, is an utter commitment to putting on the show. Writing gags until three in the morning, rehearsing a new dance sequence just one more time, or going out on the road for weeks on end, was all part of the job to ensure that the members of the audience who paid to come back and see the show would not be disappointed.

From the 1920s, when the old-time music hall had subsided, there gradually developed a wealth of local talent to suit every taste in light entertainment. Here was a performance style and theatrical expression which reached out to identify and capture an eager and ready audience.

Yet why would people take out a permanent booking and see the same comics perform week after week? What was so popular and distinct about this particular brand of Scottish entertainment, whether in city theatre or seaside pavilion? And why did such a popular form of entertainment so quickly die out after fifty years and more of giving the people a good night out?

INA HOWDEN

Theatregoer in Leith and Edinburgh during the 1930s and 1940s.

'I was brought up in Balfour Street, in Leith and it was a lovely community, quite separate from Edinburgh. It was such a quiet place, and come eleven o'clock at night, the streets were empty because no one was about as the pubs closed at ten. When my sister and I were in our teens we would go up to the town and we thought it was so exciting. Leith was quite tame compared to Edinburgh.

'We went to the Gaiety Theatre in Leith every week and then the Theatre Royal and the Empire about once a month and we all loved it. The Gaiety was very popular and I went there a lot during the war years and I didn't pay any attention to who was playing, you just went along to that week's show and they were all good. The small local shows would have singers, jugglers, comedians and four or six dancers. We saw all kinds of acts; animals, acrobats, and contortionists, maybe two or three double-jointed men, doing incredible things.

'Going to the Theatre Royal in Edinburgh by tram would be a family outing, and as children we used to get impatient with my gran because she would take such a long time to get ready. She had to put her hat pin in and the more we said, come on now, the more she dithered about. We usually went to the second house and didn't want to be late. The theatre was chock-a-block, with long queues for the cheaper seats in the gallery. We didn't book before we went, but would get there early waiting for the first house coming out. You could book tickets but we were never that well-off to do that. There would be a long queue outside and all the way up Little King Street, around the side of the Theatre Royal, but everyone was in good spirits waiting to get in.'

The re-opening of the Theatre Royal, Edinburgh January 27th, 1876:
"The Manager has the honour to announce the re-opening of the Theatre Royal which will take place on Thursday evening January 27th, 1876. The new theatre, although re-erected within the external walls of the old theatre is an entirely new building, different in every way from its predecessor, and specially designed for the comfort and convenience of its patrons.

'The Entrances are numerous and every division of the audience has its own distinct entrance. Commencing at the end of the frontage in Broughton Street, near the Chapel, the first doorway leads to the Amphitheatre; the second to the Pit Stalls; the two centre doorways to the Dress Circle, or Balcony stalls, or the front seats of the Upper Circle Stalls. The Gallery is entered by the old door in Little King Street. The Balcony stalls are fitted up with comfortable armchairs. The Upper Circle and the Pit stalls have well-upholstered seats with backs. The private boxes, of which there are fourteen, are well-fitted and hung with crimson drapery. The theatre seats 2,300 people.''

INA HOWDEN

'Once we had a treat and had tickets for the Pit at the Theatre Royal, and it was lovely to see the show properly, to see the faces and make-up. The pit was at the back of the stalls, and it was rare. We also got taken out for our supper that night.

'At the Empire during the war we had all those famous big bands, Geraldo, Ray Fox, Oscar Raban, which was wonderful. The Palladium Theatre was another place that had a lot of talent. Spoon Willie, he came from just round the corner in Fountainbridge and he used to be a marvel playing the spoons. People really were quite satisfied with fairly simple entertainment like that. The entertainers were terrific; great comics, singers and bands.

'The theatre was really so good in those days. It is so sad we don't have those shows now. We have the Usher Hall for concerts, the Playhouse for pop stars and the King's for plays, but all those old theatres had middle of the road entertainment. Everyone; families, children, old couples, we all went to the theatre every week, it was a regular event. People stopped going when they got a televison.'

JOHN NELSON

'I went to the Palladium theatre at Fountainbridge, every week for years. The queue would stretch to the bus station down the street. The theatre would be packed out, with two performances each night at about 6 pm and 8.30 pm. Lex McLean would play there for months, and would really get the audience going with his typical opening line, "When the choo-choo train comes over the hill, it's going to be Rangers, Two, Celtic, Nil". He was a great Rangers fan and many of the jokes and sketches were about football. The shows were always in good taste with never any bad language. There might be some hanky-panky, with Lex chasing a chorus girl around the stage to pinch her bottom but it was never coarse or offensive. It was a show for a family audience.

'Being a Glaswegian, Lex McLean would have some gags about Edinburgh life. He would tell the story of a woman who lived in Morningside who had asked for a plumber to call, to repair a pipe. He is invited to have a coffee, and he begins to chat to her. "This is a nice house, Mrs McTavish. It must be four or five apartments. Are you worried about the rates?". "Young man", she replies, "we do not have rates here. Only mice". This kind of joke about snobbery and upper-crust accents of certain quarters of Edinburgh would go down well at the Palladium, because the people who went there were local, ordinary men and women who did not live in Morningside. Morningsiders would more likely frequent the King's, or the Lyceum for drama and operetta.

'I think this kind of theatre was so popular during the forties and fifties because of the war and the depressed times which followed. People were willing to go out and pay to have a good laugh. You knew you would have a good time. There were no arguments or bad behaviour. Women and children could come and it was value for money. Half-a-crown for a good night out. Then perhaps it was a fish and chip supper on the way home. No-one went out to eat in those days. There were hardly any restaurants in Edinburgh, unless you went to the expensive hotels, but after paying for our seats, we could just afford to buy some chips.

'If variety theatre came back I'd be the first in the queue. I think if there was another war, people would want variety theatre again. It was the war which brought people together, to be entertained with a community spirit of laughter. It made you forget the suffering and sadness for a couple of hours. You wanted to go out of the house and enjoy yourself.'

EDDIE THOMSON

Theatregoer in Edinburgh, 1940s to 1960s.

'A friend and I had seats A1 and A2 in the stalls, every Monday evening at the Palladium from about 1943 until 1968 when the theatre closed. Mamie and May were the usherettes. Davie was the doorman. Mary ran the paybox. The shows were usually packed out, perhaps not the first house, but Mondays were often busy with bus parties.

'The stage sets were very advanced for the type of show it was. Even waterfalls with real water would flow for Highland scenes. Shows would run for a week, or for a short season, perhaps a fortnight or a couple of months in the summer. Often they would star Lex McLean, Johnny Victory, or Johnny Beattie.

'Johnny Victory was very quick and witty, especially the ad-libbing when certain things happened. One night I had laid my coat over the back of the orchestra pit barrier, near the side of the stage, sitting in A1, and Johnny came over and picked up the coat and keys fell out of the pocket. As quick as a flash he said, "Oh, oh! I see we share the same mistress, keys for No. 2 MacDonald Street," or whatever. He made that gag up in an instant, because he had picked up the wrong coat, and no keys should have fallen out of the pocket. He apologised for the mistake afterwards, but I hadn't minded, it was all in good fun.

'Lex McLean was never regarded as a "blue" comic, but he did enjoy his double meanings. He performed with Ronnie Dale, Glen Daly, Margo Bentley and others. He would always dress well, perhaps in a long coat and top hat. Sketches might be about a hospital scene, with a doctor, nurse and patient, a pub, a place of work, anywhere.

'The Palladium would have cost about 2/6d about forty years ago, and the Empire, about 6d in the cattle pen, and perhaps 7/6d in the stalls. The "Gods" or the Upper Gallery at the Edinburgh Empire was nicknamed the cattle pen because it would be packed out with people wanting to pay the cheapest price, and because it had wooden fencing around it. The gate was opened to let a few people in at a time, when it was busy.

'Denny Willis was extremely funny and changed his humour to suit the audience and theatre he was in. At the Palladium he would shout out, "Sweeties, please" – it was a kind of gimmick and people would throw him a few sweets. He would do the same at the King's Theatre but this time he would shout out, "Chocolates. Does anyone have any chocolates for me!". He always knew his audience. The Palladium was a working man's theatre, as was the Gaiety. A middle-class audience attended the King's, for musicals, musical comedies and plays.

'The Palladium had a wonderful family atmosphere. People would come in all weathers, winter and summer and I remember once arriving one cold, wet Monday night, absolutely soaked and being given a towel to dry myself. It was such a friendly place and if you went every week like I did, the staff knew you very well indeed. I still remember the sadness of the final week in the theatre, when Jim Johnstone and his band were performing in the very last show.'

BARBARA McCALL

'When I was a young girl, in the twenties, I went to every musical comedy at the Lyceum Theatre. On Monday night, we girls from the office used to go to the early doors, as they called it. You got in half an hour early for ninepence, instead of the 7.30 pm price of one-and-threepence. Sixpence less for a seat was a lot of money then when our pay was fifteen shillings a week. We used to stand in a queue and take our knitting with us, and sit at the very front of the balcony; we always got the front seats and we saw every musical comedy that there was.

'I remember being taken to the Pantomime from the age of five to see wonderful Principal Boys like Dorothy Ward. They were very elaborate pantomimes, with transformation scenes. I have gone to Pantomimes all my life and have enjoyed so many kinds of shows in Edinburgh theatres. I saw Judy Garland at the Empire when she was there. It was my parents who influenced me I think, because when I was a child my parents went to the Empire Theatre every Wednesday night. They had a permanent booking on a Wednesday because that was their half-day from their butcher's shop.'

MARGARET BUCKLAND (née Guthrie)

'Over the ten years in the chorus I worked with all the comedians and acts that were on the boards at the time in Scotland. People will always remember the favourites and top liners, but one mustn't forget all the hundreds of supporting acts, without whom there wouldn't have been a show. The singers, dancing acts, accordionists, acrobats, and of course the backbone of every show that was ever put on, "The Chorus". We were proud to be Calder Girls, widely accepted to be the best dancers in Scotland. When working in Edinburgh you could tell which night it was by the regulars who attended every week. Faithful fans who gave everyone their support.

'At the end of the season I've seen the curtain come down at 10.30 on the last night and we would not leave the stage until 11.30 because of the time it took to hand up the last night presents from fans to cast. That sort of thing made it worthwhile. It was a sad day when all the old theatres were either pulled down or turned into bingo halls. The variety theatre was an institution and in my opinion one that never should have been allowed to die. Whatever happened to that old expression, "the show must go on"? It was all very hard work, we were paid very poorly, but those ten years were some of the happiest in my life and if I could turn the clock back I would want to do it all over again.'

ANNE FIELDS

'The entertainment in the old days was a way of life. At the Metropole, Glasgow, there was a Mrs Salmon who came every week, with her son of about fourteen. She would actually bring salmon sandwiches for the cast to eat between the matinee and evening performance. She was so grateful to us for all our work and the entertainment we gave her, that she always brought the sandwiches for us. She was really a wonderful lady. There was another Glasgow woman, Helen Ross, who went *every* night to the Lex McLean show. She was a bit of a nuisance really because she knew the sketches and tag lines and shouted them out before Lex reached the punch line. But she must have loved the atmosphere of the theatre, not simply the show itself, to want to come every night.'

JIM FRIEL

'People went to the music hall every week because it was a cheap form of entertainment. It was an escape from the living conditions in some of those old tenement houses.

'I remember the Queen's Theatre, the Pavilion, the Metropole and cannot recall any bad behaviour. Repartee perhaps, and the entertainers would be able to give as good as they got. It was a warm atmosphere, intimate and cosy and I loved it. I remember Alex Frutin, the owner of the Metropole, standing at the front welcoming his regulars. There was a real family atmosphere.'

Actually going to the theatre and being part of an audience was a ceremony and a social occasion in itself. But the content of the show was special as well. People knew they would see a distinctive kind of local humour and entertainment. And although both performers and audience had an understanding of what the essence of Scottish comedy and popular culture was, everyone defined it a little differently.

WALTER CARR

'I think the key traditions of Scottish comedy lie in homeliness. We are all Jock Tamson's Bairns and this is a thing that you find everywhere. It is an honesty about ourselves, and the variety theatre has been like a mirror on life, showing up our eccentricities. Harry Gordon did it for Aberdeen, and the Will Fyffes, Lex McLeans, Rikki Fultons, and Jimmy Logans turned the mirror on the eccentricities of the lowland Scots. I do the same still. We talk about fat ladies, and the next door neighbours, and all that sort of thing. People still love that kind of local humour. To be successful, a good comic must know the lives and experiences of his audience. You must know what it was like to have a stairheid, and to put white clay round, when you washed the steps. You need to be a constant observer of people and remember what your mother and funny aunties said and did. If you have an understanding of people, then you colour them, and when this is put over in a bigger, exaggerated way on stage, that is the basis of our comedy.'

JOHNNY BEATTIE

'Glasgow has a very down-to-earth kind of humour. It is a strange thing why Glasgow and the West of Scotland, as opposed to other parts of Scotland, should have produced so many comics. Perhaps it's the influx of various ethnic groups over the years, the Irish, they've always had the blarney, and the Highland, the nice gentle humour of the Highlands, and the Glasgow "Tallies". They were awfully amusing, the hoffatalian/hoffaglesga. They weren't trying to be funny, they were simply half Italian, half Glaswegian. But this mixture of cultures has injected something distinct into our language and humour.

'They are a lot more couthy, more gentle in Aberdeen, they really are. That has been proved by the great success of *Scotland the What?* in recent years. Local allusions are always wanted, but you would change gags to suit the audience anyway. Edinburgh and Dundee audiences are different again, and in Glasgow the first house would be totally different to the second house. Just as the Gaiety in Ayr has a different feel to a Glasgow theatre, it is a bigger change from city to city. But that is the fascination of our business. You play around, see what the audience is like and go for it. It keeps you on your toes.'

JIM FRIEL

'Much of the population of West Central Scotland is but a few generations away from Ireland and the West Highlands, so there is a shared attraction in people having a long lost mythical past. That's my theory anyway. Much of the stage entertainment in Glasgow from the early days was Irish-oriented. Because of their Calvinism, Scots disapproved of the stage. Many theatres were temporary edifices around Glasgow Green, the Saltmarket, and the Stockwell, all in Irish areas. The Queen's (originally called the People's Palace), Metropole (the old Scotia), Panopticon, Princess and Palace, were all in this area.'

Extract from *The Irish in Modern Scotland* by James Handley:
'For the lighter moments of the immigrant, the playhouse provided fare with a rich native flavour. In the second half of the nineteenth century, the abundance of Irish melodrama on the boards would indicate that the theatre in Scotland looked to the immigrant for solid support. Edinburgh, Glasgow, Dundee, Paisley, Greenock, and Coatbridge purveyed such robust entertainment as *Savoureen Dellish*, *Dermot*, the *Son of Hibernia*, *Whiteboys*, or *The Lily of Leinster*, *The Bleak Hills of Ireland*, *Handy Andy*, the *Irish Emigrant*, and Dion Boucicault's *The Colleen Bawn*, and *The Shaughraun* which were regularly performed in Scotland well into the twentieth century.
'While the Irish actor was playing Shakespeare to the patrons of the Theatre Royal, Paisley, the Exchange Rooms nearby were delighting immigrant audiences with the spectacle, *Kate of Kellarney* complete with the Irish jig performed by twenty children. At the same time the Scotia music hall in Glasgow (later the Metropole), was offering the attraction of *Donnybrook Fair*, with no fewer than one hundred people on stage. At the Britannia Theatre (later the Panopticon), Messrs Dempsey and McGuinness, *The Unapproachable*, were serving up Irish slapstick to crowded houses. At the circus in Glasgow's Hope Street, patrons had the opportunity of viewing the magnificent Diorama of

Ireland illustrated with the songs, dances, and humorous sketches of Mr J. F. O'Neill, the charming delineator of Irish character with the melodies, duets and choruses of the unrivalled Hibernian minstrels'.[2]

JIM FRIEL

'This Irish tradition continued over the years in the music hall and in drama. The now neglected works of Paul Vincent Carroll were always crowd pullers at the Citizens' and Sean O'Casey's classics still are very popular. A whole number of performers, singers, comedians and actors have come from Glasgow/Irish backgrounds: Tommy Morgan, Tommy Lorne, Jimmy Donaghue, Charles Naughton, of Naughton and Gold, unkindly known as Naughton and Rotton, Glen Daly, Jimmy Neil, and Billy Connolly. Singers like Joe O'Rourke, Master Joe Peterson, the O'Neill Sisters, Renee and Billie Houston, and actors, Joe Brady and John Cairney are among many more.

'In addition to the Irish influences, the Gorbals, just across the river, was the home of the Princess and the Palace and was the district that was home for thousands of immigrants from Eastern Europe, mainly, but not all, Jewish. I believe that pseudo-tartanry was never all that popular in Glasgow and I attribute this to the Irish and Jewish influences.

'I think it is interesting now to hear catch phrases which some of the old comedians used have passed into the Glasgow vernacular. Like Tommy Lorne's "in the name of the wee man", and "I'll get ye, and if I don't get ye, the coos will get ye". There is Sammy Murray's famous greeting, "Hello chinas", which Jack Milroy also uses. Dave Willis would always quote his lovely line, "Way way upa kye", and for many a Glasgow child, that would be the first words he would speak. Then Jimmy Logan is known for his enigmatic phrase, "Sausages is the boys".

'There was an old time act, O'Leary, Tracey and O'Leary, who when "resting", would sing or busk in the streets and backyards. They gave their name to the street ball game rhyme, "1, 2, 3, O'Leary", and in that way they have passed into Glasgow folk lore. When I was young, I was one of the last generation before television so that these street songs and games were still popular. We had one about Tommy Morgan, before we children even knew who he was:

'Tommy Morgan had an organ,
And his father had a drum,
And his sister had a blister,
On the corner of her bum.'

MAE FARRELL

'My mother was in the Salvation Army and she was a good singer, while my grandfather was Irish and had a beautiful voice, so that as a child I was very much encouraged to learn to dance and sing. I remember my mother telling me about the Penny Geggies, a travelling theatre company who would come to perform in a "but and ben" at the top of the Main Street in Pollokshaws when she was young. They travelled gypsy-like, from place to place, with their cart of costumes and props. They came from Pollokshaws and were given the name, the Queer Folk of the Shaws. My mother and her family would love to see these melodramas such as "East Lynne" and she used to say how tears would be streaming down her cheeks, hearing the lines, "Dead, dead, and never called me mother". Even strong, elderly men would have tears in their eyes, watching these actors. That was my mother's time and she loved the visit by the Geggies, because they had so little enjoyment in their lives. My mother began to work with her mother in the fields when she was eight or nine, and then went to the mills at Pollokshaws when she was ten years old. They had nothing else, but just worked from morning to night.'

JACK HOUSE

'I think Glasgow produced such a wealth of entertainers because first of all it is the biggest place in Scotland, so by the law of averages it should have done so. Secondly, as far as comics are concerned, they invariably come from industrial centres, which gives them valuable armour to get through the rough and tumble which existed then in the music hall. I think it is also in the nature of the beast. In other words, Glasgow people are comic. They have this wonderful thing called the patter. The patter is very good, but the thing about it is that it is pronounced with a glottal stop as well.

'There is the famous story of a little boy's first day at school and the teacher is making up the class register. She says "Well, sonny, what's your name?". He replies, "Pa'erson, with two T's". Between this glottal stop and all the wonderful Glasgow sayings, you come across a language which is only spoken in Glasgow and through that individual language, comes the humour of the people themselves.'

STANLEY BAXTER

'It is interesting that the vast majority of Scots comics have come from Glasgow. The notable exception is Harry Lauder, who was much more of a singer of popular choruses than being a comedian. Most have been West Coast for some reason or another. Glaswegian has undoubtedly been the *lingua franca*. Glaswegians laugh with you if you speak in broad Glaswegian, and the rest of Scotland probably laughs more at it. But the laughs are equally big, whether you are playing in Aberdeen or Edinburgh. I have played just as much in Edinburgh as I have in Glasgow. The Edinburgh audiences are just as good for Parliamo Glasgow as they are in the west.'

'Scottish humour has so much to do with dialect. It is all to do with the way things are said. The "dinnaes", the "wees", the "doon the stairs" and so on. Gags translated directly into English can be terribly unfunny. If you take out words like "glaikit", or "stotious", and you have to say "stupid" and "drunk" instead, it is just not the same. It is essentially a thing of language, and the life of the audience. Of course you can take good gags and translate them into Scots and when you do that they are even funnier, because you introduce a Scottish word which beefs it up. The essence of Scottish humour is also to do with our attitude to life. They always used to say that the Scots comic loved death, and I think there was a certain amount of truth in that when I remember Jack Radcliffe's famous "biled ham after the funeral" sketches. It is a very elusive thing to understand what makes Scottish comedy, but it is really language other than anything else.'

PARLIAMO GLASGOW
(A television series created by Stanley Baxter and Alex Mitchell, to explain to the visitor, the niceties of the Glasgow language.) One situation concerns a young lady, Shona, going shopping for a dress with her mother. The lesson is called, SHONABYNAFROAK. When she tries on a very short ra-ra skirt, her mother objects and Shona responds with a phrase, WHISSAMARRAWIRARARA?
Similarly, Stanley Baxter's sketch MATTUROPATTUR gave a glossary of Glaswegian phrases with subtitles for use on television:
HULLAWRERR, or AWSHURSEL?: How do you do?
AMNOTOOBAD or AVFELTWURSUR: I am feeling quite well.[3]

JIMMY LOGAN
Actor, comedian and producer.

'It was predominantly in Scottish theatres that entertainment was for a family audience. The strange thing was that in England you had what was called a Watch Committee and the acts in all variety theatres had to be licensed by the Lord Chamberlain. You were not supposed to deviate and on a Monday the Watch Committee would come and see the show, and if you altered your script or used strong language, or told distasteful jokes, they had the authority to have you removed from the show. We never had that in Scotland, a Watch Committee, it was all under the Chief Constable, and if anyone complained to the Chief Constable then something would be done. Normally this never occurred because we performers depended on the family audience and if you insulted or upset that audience, you would simply lose the very backbone of the theatre.

'The Empire Theatre in Glasgow was well known as the "Graveyard of English comics". The reason was that many of the English comedians came up here and would begin their act with " 'ello, 'ello, 'ello, how are yer? alright luv?". And they didn't attempt to make any rapport with the audience. They did their act which they had done last week, the week before, the month before, the year before. It was like switching on a tape recorder, which is something you have to be careful of. Sometimes the material was cheeky, or attacking: " 'ere, I'm goin' to tell ye something . . . yer gonna listen and I'm gonna tell yer. . .", and the Scottish audiences would sit there and think, "Oh, are you? That's interesting. Away home and work!". So you could get that kind of reaction to comedians who just didn't try and adjust to a different audience.'[4]

The Glasgow Empire: March 17th 1952; Max Wall, Beryl Reid.

BERYL REID

'I performed at the Glasgow Empire, once appearing immediately after the great comic Max Wall, who was actually "getting the bird". I was crying in the wings and didn't want to go on at all. There was Max Wall being told by the crowd, "Away and work you great big Jessie", which was very sad. I was advised by the stage manager to go up very close to the mike, speak quickly and clearly and then go home. I didn't do badly myself and played the Empire many times. But it was not the easiest of houses.'

KEN DODD

Comedian

'I became a stand-up comedian and started off quite well at the Nottingham Empire in 1954, and played Sunderland, Middlesborough, and Barnsley, and then the House of Terror, the Glasgow Empire. Here the audience would say to English comedians, "Awa hame and bile yer heid". When I first went on there, the manager said to me, "No football gags and you'll get the bird on Friday''. So on Friday night I was terrified. I walked onto the stage shaking, my hair all over the place, my eyes popping. My first line in those days – and this was to a Glasgow audience – was ''I suppose you'll all be wondering why I've sent for you''. One man uncoiled himself from the second front row, with a half bottle of whisky in his hand and looked at me. ''Cripes'', he said, ''what a horrible sight'' and fell back in his seat. That was my first laugh of the evening and probably my only laugh. I did a couple more gags and got off as fast as I could.'[5]

JACK HOUSE

' ''Giving the bird'' by the audience meant shouting, screeching, booing, just generally making disapproving noises. Throwing coins certainly only happened in places like the Panopticon and the Palace, theatres of that sort. In these music halls, in the minor league, you would actually get street vendors outside, selling squashy oranges to be thrown at the turns people didn't like.

'Jack Buchanan made his debut appearance in the Panopticon and he hated it. He stood it for a week and the really bad thing was when they threw rivets which could have killed the performers. The following week he was booked into the Palladium, in Edinburgh. There, the audience just sat on their hands and Jack Buchanan said afterwards that he would rather have some reaction like the people gave at the Panopticon than the way they behaved at the Edinburgh Palladium.

'I have seen quite a lot of English comics receiving a good reception at the Empire in Glasgow, but I have never seen anyone faint on stage as one story goes. Actually, the dangerous night at the Empire was a Friday night, when the workers had been paid and they had all had a very good bevvy before they arrived. That was the night when things could happen. If English comics ever did have a bad reception, I think perhaps it was because they were not very good, the same would happen if it was a bad Scottish comic. I remember the Edinburgh comic, Johnny Victory appearing there and he was the first ''blue'' comic that I can remember and he was certainly unpopular. I don't think he got the bird, but people just didn't go, which is a better answer than anything.'

DENNY WILLIS

'Scottish comics have a definite sense of humour. They have a sense of humour in other places but you can't make a name for yourself elsewhere in Scotland, only in Glasgow. No matter how good you are in Edinburgh, or Aberdeen, if you don't make it in Glasgow, then you can't do it. It's the same in Liverpool, where so many people there are harder, rougher, but they have a wonderful sense of humour to balance that out.'

BIG CURT

Ex-Empire stage-hand; now Stall holder, The Barras, Glasgow.

'I started in the theatre business because my uncle was chief electrician at the Theatre Royal in Glasgow. After school I used to go and learn to work the lights. I got the smell of greasepaint there and later went to work at the old Glasgow Empire. I went on to work in the circus, and for years now I have had my market stall. The Barras is show business too, these are all little theatres, these stalls, and you have to be an entertainer to survive here.'

And so the Scottishness of Scottish entertainment is rich and complex. The influences come from far and wide: Italian, Irish, Jewish, Gaelic, all creating a popular culture, and a cultural bond between the people of Scotland. The weekly visit to the theatre had become so important to so many people, that the stage performance and the local community's loyalty to it was initially strong enough to withstand the introduction of television during the 1950s.

But the next twenty years saw the beginning of the gradual demise of long running variety seasons. During the early period of television and Rock and Roll music, in an effort to attract younger people to the theatre, managers began to introduce pop stars and television quiz games of the day on to the family variety bill.

Metropole Summer show 1957
Ma Logan in *Housewives on Parade*, with Alex Harvey, 'Scotland's Tommy Steele', Bert Bendon, Master Joe Peterson, and big supporting company. Weekly shows including *Flashback of Glesca Variety*.

Empire: week of March 21st 1960
Bobby Darin, Duane Eddy and Emile Ford.

Empire: week of April 4, 1960
Cliff Richard.

Empire: week of May 2nd, 1960
Adam Faith and the John Barry 4.

Empire: week of May 7th, 1960
Hughie Green in *Double your Money* and *Opportunity Knocks*.

Kings, Queens and People's Palaces

Empire: week of June 20th, 1960
Liberace in *The Music Box* show.

Through the comparatively affluent decades of the sixties and seventies, values began to change. The regular outing to the theatre had lost its attraction. Many families now owned a car, and began to think of taking their holidays in Spain rather than Saltcoats. But if the era of every little seaside town down the Clyde coast, and every urban district having its theatre with its weekly show, was slowly coming to an end, the demand for spectacular city centre summer shows and pantomimes healthily flourished:

Empire, Edinburgh: January, 1957
Meet Me at the Empire, with Denny Willis, and Dave Willis.

Metropole: March 7th 1960
Heart O' Scotland, with Clark and Murray. (Over 200,000 saw this show.)

Alhambra: June 20th 1960
Five-Past Eight, with Jack Radcliffe, Jimmy Logan, Eve Boswell, and the Bluebell Girls.

Ayr Gaiety: June 20th 1960
Popplewells 31st Dazzling, *Gaiety Whirl* with Johnny Beattie.

King's, Edinburgh: Summer 1961
Five-Past Eight with Rikki Fulton and Jack Milroy, Fay Lenore, Margo Henderson. Stalls 9 shillings; upper circle 5/6d; family circle 3 shillings.

King's, Glasgow: July 5th 1971
The Callum Kennedy Show with Clark and Murray. Stalls, 50p, Saturday, 60p. Children 30p.

Pavilion: Summer Show
Lex McLean's Super '71 show, with Charlie Sim, Una McLean, Walter Carr and the May Moxon Lovelies. From Monday 16th August until November 6th.

Pavilion: Winter 1971–72
Francie and Josie, as *The Pie-Eyed Pipers*, 'The funniest, the fastest moving and the most colourful production the "boys" have ever been in''. *Evening Citizen*.

King's, Glasgow: June–July 1990
King's High: See Culture, See Francie and Josie, 'the third year of this spectacular revue with Jack Milroy and Rikki Fulton'.

King's, Edinburgh: December 1990–February 1991
Cinderella, with Stanley Baxter.

But despite a continuing popularity for a traditional Scottish entertainment, a Summer show and a pantomime alone does not keep the theatre doors open, and the diminishing opportunities for all year round work meant fewer comics and variety acts entering the profession. One by one, theatres began to close down.

JOHN WISHART

'The end of the Empire in 1963 had a lot to do with the rise of Rock and Roll entertainment. It became common for one major singer or band to take over the entire second half and people only came for this headliner act. The youngsters didn't want the other smaller comic and music acts, and the older generation didn't want to see pop stars. In addition, these acts would demand a high fee so that it was more economical to put them in the Odeon for a one night stand.

'There were very few smaller theatres to train up-and-coming acts, so that there were few entertainers to make up the variety bill. It was Rock and Roll which radically changed the variety theatre and ultimately closed the Empire.'

It was actually the Red Army which closed the Empire. Their choir and dancers played the final week's engagement, beginning March 25th 1963. But the last real Empire show took place on Sunday, March 31st, and that show comprised one of the finest variety bills that Glasgow could produce.

Empire: Sunday March 31st, 1963, *The Show of Shows.*
Johnny Beattie, Charlie Carolli, Alec Finlay, Albert Finney, Rikki Fulton, Callum Kennedy, Jack Milroy, Duncan Macrae, Bobby Mcleod, Master Joe Peterson, Jack Radcliffe, Andy Stewart, Dave Willis, Will Starr, Robert Wilson, White Heather Girls.

MAE FARRELL

'The Metropole, the Pavilion, the Panopticon, the Princess, they were theatres for their ain folk. You had to book months ahead for the pantomime at the Princess and sometimes it went on to April or May. The Metropole had these wonderful all-year-round shows. The Met. and the Princess were for the people of the Saltmarket, Townhead, Gallowgate, the Briggate and all the names and places of the Victorian city where they lived. The Met. was right in the centre of all that and the people came from nearby, mostly from tenement closes. This was the Glasgow People's Entertainment. What made it the people's theatre was that the performers came from the same background as the audience.'

JIM FRIEL

'It is certainly true that theatres had their own following, their own regulars, because people lived locally, in the old inner city districts of the Gorbals, Garngad, Govan, Anderston. Glasgow was a city of villages with a fierce loyalty to where you were born. You could live all your life within your community which would have its own football team, local halls, music societies and theatres. I lived in the Garngad area until I was fourteen, but the living conditions in those cramped tenements really were appalling when you look back. Before the houses were demolished during the fifties, we were moved to Easterhouse, a new estate on the outskirts of Glasgow. The clearing of those old communities coincided with the demise of the theatres. The Metropole and the Empress battled on for a while but the huge move of people away from the city centre tore the heart out of Glasgow in many ways. It seemed then that we were moving to Paradise, to houses with bathrooms. It was only later that people realised the mistakes the planners had made and that a lot had been lost in the move. It really has proved quite disastrous.'

MAY MOXON

'I could see the writing was on the wall, so I realised it was time we were packing it in. I retired about fifteen years ago.

'What saddens me today is that there are no young comics coming up as they did in the old days. What happened was that when the theatres closed, the comics went to the working mens', and the social clubs, and that's roughened up the profession. We haven't got the quality of comics we used to have. Theatres used to have a great choice and pick who they wanted but now you can't get them.'

GRACE MACKAY REAY

'When the Variety theatre began going to the wall, and television was starting off, it was the Clubs which became a replacement in many ways. There was the Ashfield Club in Glasgow run by Mr Donald, which took many variety acts from the Pavilion. This was an excellent club and he did a lot for variety pros at the time. Hector Nicol who had been struggling on the theatre circuit as a second stringer to other comics, really made his name at the Ashfield and his solo career took off. Other clubs were "blue" which was a different kind of entertainment. Television definitely closed a lot of theatres.

'I was literally one of the last people to walk on the Glasgow Alhambra stage. This would be the late sixties, and my husband and I just happened to be passing by near the Central Station the day they were demolishing the Alhambra Theatre and we went inside to have a last look. It was a sad and curious experience to stand on that famous stage with no roof above us. They often say that there is laughter trapped in a theatre and that when workmen begin to knock it down, they can hear the audiences of years past. I don't know how true that is, but they said that about the Roxy, Falkirk, the Empire, and the Alhambra, Glasgow. When they start to take away the galleries, there is laughter still there.'

JOHNNY BEATTIE

'There was television, there were the Clubs and then there was the Bingo. They all had an effect on the theatre. They are quite rightly called Bingo and Social Clubs because the old people especially love it. They have all their friends there, they get their hot pies and a cup of tea, enjoy the bingo and have a wee blether. Television, bingo and the social clubs, that's three things chipping away at the Variety theatre, the music hall, as I prefer to call it. I have always maintained that there should be some sort of support, by way of subsidy, say from the Arts Council, for some kind of retention of the music hall as an art form. I see the music hall as much an art form as opera and ballet, or drama. I am for all these things, not promoting one for the exclusion of the others. As an art form, Variety entertainment is obviously in a shaky state and it would be nice if managements could be given some sort of support to put on a traditional Summer show, perhaps to bring in a good troupe of dancers, that kind of thing. I genuinely believe there should be financial support. I have always maintained that.'

JIM FRIEL

'When Lex McLean died in 1975, that brought the era of the long running summer shows at the Pavilion to an end. I don't think there was a summer show after that. The cost became prohibitive. With the demise of the theatres around Scotland, there wasn't the talent coming forward so that it was difficult to mount the shows.

'The tradition of Scottish entertainment has carried on with pantomime. They have never stopped. The tradition for comedy and song is still in the pubs, in Glasgow houses, where people still enjoy a sing-song at parties. A private club circuit built up when there was strict licencing laws, which coincided with the years when the Music Hall was going into decline. Stand-up comics, particularly with blue material for an adult audience were able to continue working in the clubs. But I think there is now a turnaround again, with all day licencing in the pubs, and only the very good clubs have survived. Much of the entertainment has gone back to where it all started a hundred years ago, in the pubs. The Horseshoe is packed every night with musicians, and some very good singers. Many pubs put on live entertainment. There is a couple called Robert and May Miller who have been performing in the pubs and are taking over the Exhibition Centre and I believe it is going to be a sell-out. So we are going full circle again. I saw a twenty-two year old lad the other day, singing all the old music hall songs.

'There is still a great affinity to the variety theatre and the revival of Francie and Josie at the King's Theatre which has been packed out for three summers running, clearly indicates that people still love it, young and old. It is good clean entertainment, a "Good Night Out", as the playwright John McGrath says. There is nothing to beat it.'

ROSS BOWIE

'There couldn't be a revival of the year-round variety theatre seasons. There is no-one to do it. There is nobody left. *King's High* for a month each summer is great and Jack Milroy and Rikki Fulton work tremendously well together. That's one of the oldest sketches in the world that Jack and Rikki did in *King's High* last year (1989), with the couple of girls eating chips coming in Francie and Josie's bedroom window. And of course the landlady comes in and the boys do a lot of business with hiding the chips under their night-shirts, because food is not allowed in the room. That's been played in Rothesay and Montrose till the cows come home, yet it is still extremely funny and today there is a new audience to see it. They really are so very funny and their timing is immaculate. Rikki Fulton now has other interests, in television, writing and production and a month is enough for him. If you can't have him, who else do you have? Johnny Beattie is probably the last of the production comedians who is very experienced in doing sketches. There are not many of them left because the training ground of the summer season has gone.

'The younger actors, if you don't give them the line, or the exact word, they don't know whether to speak or not. 'But you didn't say "When", you didn't give me my cue'. That kind of thing. The training you had in concert parties and revues was that you had to say something. In the old sketches it didn't matter if your cue was who, when or where, the comic would give you hell if you didn't carry on.

'It's a terrible tragedy for me to know that Clark and Murray are not captured on film or television, because they were positively brilliant. Gracie Clark, who is still alive, was the greatest comedienne that I've ever seen in my life. That woman was a comic genius and had a lot to offer in entertainment but television never gave her the chance. She would have been awfully good because her facial expressions were excellent. In television you can have close-ups of faces, unlike the theatre when you might be sitting in Row Z. Television didn't help in any way, but watched the Variety theatre die. Now they are suffering because they are stuck for people and have to take actors who are struggling to be comedians. Some of them are as funny as a night with the toothache.

'I'd like to think there could be a revival but I think what we're seeing now is the last kick of a dying horse.'

BERNARD COTTON

'The theatrical policy, when I came, of a summer Variety season was successful and so there was no conscious decision to change anything. The Council just wanted to let it run on in the way it always had so we just continued to run the Gaiety in the same sort of vein. Circumstances decree that. Even to this day, and that is sixteen years later, we get parties writing in and booking 200 tickets for say, June 9th, because such and such a group is coming down on a day outing. Bus loads still come each year. After booking well in advance, they *then* ask, "Could you let us know what show will be on please?". I am therefore more or less duty bound to provide the kind of entertainment they are looking for, which is light entertainment, not necessarily Scottish performers, but a Variety revue show. The public have determined the policy of what we put on.

'In the early days, if you saw a graph of the theatre business it reached a peak during the Glasgow Fair period in July, and trailed off afterwards. Now, it tends to dip at that time because it's the change of people's holiday habits. The Scottish people, the Glasgow people, do not come to Ayr for a fortnight or even a week's holiday now. Instead we have day trippers, coach parties of the Women's Institute and other groups of people who come to Ayr for some shopping, have tea and come to the Gaiety.

'The difficulty is that there are not the same number of attractions around that were available sixteen years ago. Some of the performers have died or retired. It is just not possible to present the same large show as we did in those days because of costs. While Johnny Beattie has developed into the Gaiety's favourite Panto star and he has very popular Summer Shows here, we cannot afford to have a second comic, so that the training ground is lost. We also have Jack Milroy, but there are so few good Scottish comics who know this type of business. There are more touring companies available so our policy has changed slightly through what kind of entertainment we can still present. We do still do a summer Variety season, and I'm sure that will remain for a long time yet and we do a traditional pantomime. The rest of the fifty-two weeks of the year is selected from what is on offer. Straight drama by touring theatre companies tends to be chosen from who is in it, rather than what the play is. People who are fresh from television will fill the theatre. What people want are today's TV stars, and if I could get a play with someone from a popular soap opera, the theatre would be packed out.

'The market for Variety shows is still healthy and we are benefitting from that demand. If anyone is wanting to come to the seaside and see a summer Variety show, then there is only the Gaiety Theatre, Ayr. There is no choice. People travel across Glasgow, and parties come from Dumfries and further afield to see *The Gaiety Whirl*. The video recorder is becoming quite an asset to theatre going. Those TV viewers are no longer tied to their television set. When there is something at the theatre they want to see, they can record the programme they would otherwise have missed. Also television variety shows have begun to lose their attraction and people are coming back to enjoy live theatre. There is still a market for produced Variety revue entertainment.'

CHRIS POTTER

Manager, Adam Smith Centre, Kirkcaldy, 1974–1987. Currently Manager, Kings Theatre, Edinburgh.

'As soon as I went to the Adam Smith Centre one of the first people I booked was Alec Finlay. Wee Alec was a great performer. They were good shows, no set really, just a bit of tartan hanging about, but because of the presence of Alec Finlay, who had been all those years in music hall, it had a touch of class about it. We had many successful seasons, but then Alec became ill, and had to leave the show. I then stopped having that kind of Variety show, it just didn't seem to have the appeal without him.

'After that I became more ambitious and started putting on these big stars, the great entertainers, not all from England, but a tremendous amount, mainly because there are so few from Scotland. I had Johnny Beattie for two or three seasons, compering. We'd do the first half as a normal Variety show, and then Johnny would introduce our special guest star, who would be someone like Jimmy Tarbuck or Frankie Vaughan. These shows did very well. We had a marvellous week with Tommy Cooper for instance. He presented me with a Fez and a lovely letter thanking me for looking after him. Then about four or five years ago, we had Ken Dodd and the Diddy Men which did twice nightly for a week and was extremely successful. He's very much the old traditional Variety. You won't see anyone more experienced than him, he's steeped in the Music Hall tradition. That week in Kirkcaldy was truly memorable. I hardly ever seemed to get to bed because after he finished his second house – always after midnight – he would stay regaling anyone who was in the bar with even more anecdotes.

'Other Variety artistes who appeared at the Adam Smith during my time include Chic Murray, Clark and Murray, Lena Martell, Lulu, Dickie Henderson, Bob Monkhouse, Harry Worth, Harry Secombe, Frankie Howerd, Matt Munro, Bruce Forsyth, Vince Hill, Leslie Crowther, Rikki Fulton, Larry Grayson, Des O'Connor, Ronnie Corbett, Cilla Black, Jimmy Edwards, Ted Rogers, Tom O'Connor, Bernie Winters, Little and Large plus several "veteran" performers from England such as George Lacey, Leslie Welch (the Memory Man), Tommy Trinder, Cyril Fletcher, and Ben Warris. Not a bad line up for Kirkcaldy!

'I don't think there will be a revival of Variety theatre as we remember it, but it is fascinating to see a return of some first class spectacular Revues. Last autumn the popular television entertainer, Russ Abbot, set out on a thirteen city tour of the country doing a twice nightly show, six o'clock and eight forty-five, which is what it always used to be. It was his lavish Blackpool show with eight dancers, and a big orchestra. When it came to the Edinburgh King's, he was a huge success and played to £70,000 of business. There are not many who can do that today.'

MAIDIE MURRAY

'I really think there could be a revival of Variety, light-entertainment shows. There is a renewed interest for people to go out to the theatre now, because as a contrast to television it is really different to see performers in the flesh; there is a thrill to it. I don't think the local flavour will come back which people enjoyed in their own districts and communities. And without these small halls and theatres to gain experience, there is no grounding for people nowadays, that's the trouble. Talent has got to be nurtured. You have got to perform your act again and again to understand the business. You have got to have the opportunity to perform. Like Chic and I, I can remember the early things we did, how we adapted the content of the act, and what he particularly did to improve his timing. He just had to get on and do it, and with continual performance and practice, it became very good. He had to learn timing. Comedy, singing songs, it's all about timing. Some of the youngsters trying their best on television just now, are frankly terrible. I feel for them sometimes, because it's a big, big audience they're playing to.'

WALTER CARR

'I wouldn't say the training circuit has entirely gone. The young comics used to come out of ordinary jobs and into the theatres and club scene. Now they come out of drama colleges and train in television and radio, through the *Naked Radio, Naked Video* and *City Lights* comedy programmes. We have Gregor Fisher, Gerard Kelly and a vast number of actors, comedic actors coming up who are our future. We have a public who still comes. We have the tradition, the format and we have the young people who could carry it on.

'The problem is that we don't have the summer shows where young people used to get their experience of standing at the front of the stage at the front mike, telling gags and doing all the funny sketches so that when they walked into a pantomime, they would have this kind of background. So we must somehow entice today's comics into pantomime and allow every opportunity to give them the material to work on and let them develop it. They are working a newer style of comedy and they must bring this, which might seem so strange to my generation, but if we have got to move on, they've got to do their kind of comedy. But if they need a few gags of the old time stuff, then we'll be very happy to give it. I do think the tradition is still there and I'm pleased to see recently so many young potentially good comedians coming up through the club and cabaret scene, with several of them moving into pantomime.

'There is that wonderful Glasgow act, Victor and Barry, who are very funny. They have an original kind of comedy, sitting at the piano. The Funny Farm, the Comedy Store, and Tron Theatre in Glasgow and the Traverse, and the Gilded Balloon, in Edinburgh have been staging revues and cabaret evenings to encourage new comedy talent. Television shows on Channel 4 and STV give an opportunity to young alternative comedians, although some of the material is pretty horrendous. It's just not clever to do blue or offensive material. But at least there is still a shop window for potentially funny people, and if they are funny, if they have comedic quality, a kind of humility, and a natural desire to make people laugh, their material can be changed.'

JIM FRIEL

'Very few Glaswegians realise that the city's oldest theatre is in the Trongate, right in the heart of the city. Built in 1857, it was originally called the Brittania, and once owned by A. E. Pickard, an eccentric millionaire and a renowned Glasgow character. The Panopticon Theatre closed in the late thirties and has its own particular place in theatrical history because it was on this stage that the great clown Stan Laurel and the debonair musical comedy star Jack Buchanan made their professional debuts. It was said that the audiences were so tough they would make an appearance at the Glasgow Empire look like a Sunday School outing.

'Glasgow could pay its own tribute to music hall, a form of entertainment which was extremely popular for almost a hundred years. The Glasgow comics were particularly loved, and many of their catch phrases have entered the language and patter of the city. The tradition is still alive especially in Pantomime which is something of a major art form in Scotland. I think it is important to renovate the Panopticon Theatre as a shrine to the Music Hall and Popular Theatre. Variety entertainment is not Grand Opera, but it is indigenous to Glasgow.

'I have interested various people on the Council who support the project, but the problem is finance. Costs would be very high but I have spoken to union representatives and everyone is interested in the idea, but they ask, could the cost be justified? I think that the cost could be justified because the music hall and Variety theatre was so much a part of Scottish social life that it should not be allowed to be forgotten. The Panopticon Theatre is lying there empty, in a state of disrepair, but intact, next door to the Tron, on the fringe of the Merchant City. There has been talk through the years for a Museum of Entertainment in the city, and this is an ideal place for it. Somebody with a wee bit of foresight, possibly commercial sponsorship, could create a perfect theatre museum of cultural history, and I think we could be on a winner. I intend to push this project. I will continue speaking to the council, theatre unions, and see if something can be got off the ground. I'd love to see it in Glasgow. The artistes, the performers, and the people who were involved, in so many ways, working for the Scottish Variety theatre should all be remembered.'

A FINAL WORD

RIKKI FULTON

'I have been asked many times my opinion on what is particular about Scottish humour. I usually refuse to answer this question because it is too complex and broad a subject.

'Glasgow humour is cheeky and nerdlike, born of the character of the people. Language and dialect is very much a part of Scottish comedy and comics tend to emphasise the dialect, and speak very broad Scots. Especially in pantomime this is true when characters become caricatures, and I know I myself completely alter my accent. If people hear my own voice, they say, why are you talking so posh? But this is my natural voice, I have to try and convince them, because they are used to an exaggerated accent.

'I do believe humour is a personal thing which is born in the main when people are under pressure, or are suppressed. Their problems have to be allowed to escape and humour is employed to release this tension. Humour varies from region to region. I have heard that Russian humour is obscure by our way of thinking – it is turgid and slow. In Scotland, humour may reflect the history of Scotland. One of the hallmarks is a preoccupation with death and funerals. The humour of a country or region is about its people and its history.'

REFERENCES

INTRODUCTION

1. Bailey, *Music Hall; The Business of Pleasure*, Open University Press 1986, from the Foreword.
2. Waites, *The Historical Development of Popular Culture in Britain. Unit 5; The Music Hall* (Open University Course) p76.
3. Stedman Jones, *Working Class Culture, Essay in Popular Culture, Past and Present*, Ed. Waites etc. Open University Press 1982, pp103, 108.
4. ibid, p117.
5. McGrath, *A Good Night Out*, Methuen, 1981, pp54–7.
6. Interviews with David McLennan, from *Tuesday Review*, BBC Radio Scotland, 12th July, 1988, and from *Scottish Theatre News*, October 1981.

CHAPTER 1

1. Interview by James Copland with George Clarkson, extracts from *Dear Green Place*, Radio Clyde, October 1974 and from interview by Judith M. Rankin, for Motherwell Community Museums Service Oral History Unit.
2. Interview by Allan Rogers with Alec Finlay, from BBC Radio, Scottish Home Service, April 30th, 1974.

CHAPTER 2

1. Interview with George Clarkson, see Reference 1, Ch. 1.
2. Interview with Alec Finlay, see Reference 2, Ch. 1.

CHAPTER 6

1. From *Why I am a Comedian*, a talk by Harry Gordon, BBC Radio, Scottish Home Service, March 18th, 1949.
2. Interview with Alec Finlay, see Reference 2, Ch. 1.
3. Extract from *The Opening of the Kirk Bazaar*, BBC Radio, Scottish Home Service, September 27th, 1951.

CHAPTER 7

1. Jack House, *Music-Hall Memories*, Richard Drew Publishing Ltd, 1986. p44.
2. Gerald Frow, *Oh Yes It Is: a History of Pantomime*, BBC Publications, 1985, p15.
3. Interview with George Clarkson, see Reference 1, Ch. 1.
4. Colm Brogan, *The Glasgow Story*, Frederick Muller, 1952.

CHAPTER 10

1. J. B. Howard, Manager, Theatre Royal, Edinburgh, from theatre programme, January 27th, 1876.
2. James Handley, *The Irish in Scotland*, Cork University Press, 1943.
3. Stanley Baxter, *Bedside Book of Glasgow Humour*, Richard Drew Publishing Ltd., 1988; Extracts from Parliamo Glasgow and Matturopattur, pp82 and 90.
4. Jimmy Logan, extract from 'Limelight, Chicken Wire and Plush, Red Velvet', BBC Radio Scotland, 24th October, 1988.
5. Ken Dodd, extract from interview on 'Desert Island Discs', BBC Radio 4, 8th June, 1990.

SELECTED
BIBLIOGRAPHY

Bailey, Peter, *Music Hall: The Business of Pleasure* (Open University Press, 1986).
Baxter, Stanley, *Bedside Book of Glasgow Humour* (Richard Drew Publishing Ltd., 1988).
Bratton, J. S., *Music Hall: Performance and Style* (Open University Press, 1986).
Cheshire, D. F., *Music Hall in Britain* (David & Charles, 1974).
Frow, Gerald, *Oh, Yes It Is, A History of Pantomime* (BBC, 1985).
Green, Benny, *The Last Empires, A Music Hall Companion* (Pavilion/Michael Joseph, 1986).
Honri, Peter, *Working The Halls* (Saxon House, 1973).
House, Jack, *Music Hall Memories* (Richard Drew Publishing Ltd., 1986).
Irving, Gordon, *The Good Auld Days: The Story of Scotland's Entertainers, from Music Hall to Television* (Jupiter, 1977).
Littlejohn, J. H., *Aberdeen Tivoli* (Rainbow Enterprises, 1986).
McGrath, John, *A Good Night Out: Popular Theatre, Audience, Class and Form* (Methuen, 1981).
Waites, Bernard (ed), *Popular Culture: Past and Present* (Open University Press, 1982).
Wilmut, Roger, *Kindly Leave The Stage! The Story of Variety, 1919–1960* (Methuen, 1985).
Yule, Andrew, *The Best Way To Walk: The Chic Murray Story* (Mainstream, 1989).

Appendix 1

WHO'S WHO LISTING
OF CONTRIBUTORS

ROBERT AITKEN
Born 19th December, 1925, Glasgow. Fireman with North Fire station, Glasgow. Duty fireman at the Glasgow Empire, The Empress, Pavilion and the Lyric from 1948–1951. He attended the fires which destroyed the Queen's Theatre in 1952, the Lyric in 1953, and which damaged the Empress in 1956.

REG ALLEN
Born 5th November, 1916, Willesden, London. First worked as a scenic artist for the pantomime, Cinderella, at Drury Lane Theatre in 1935. From 1938 he worked as designer and scenic artist at the Gaiety, Palace and Olympia Theatres, Dublin, until he joined the Royal Corps of Engineers in 1942. Invited to Scotland by Howard & Wyndham, to assist in the design of the 1949 pantomime, he remained with the company for thirty-one years as scenic artist and designer and later Production Manager. When Howard & Wyndham went out of business in 1979, Reg Allen became a freelance designer, retiring in 1982.

BETTY BARR
Born 3rd June, 1922, Lambeth, London. Betty Barr became a Terry Juvenile at the age of twelve in the Paramount Variety cinemas, and later joined The Buckley's juggling act, touring variety theatres throughout Britain. When she was twenty she met and later married Charlie Barr, one of the Three Aberdonians, the contortionists, after which she retired from the stage.

STANLEY BAXTER
Born 24th May, 1926, Glasgow. Trained for the stage at the Glasgow Citizens' Theatre, making his professional debut in *The Thrie Estaites* directed by Tyrone Guthrie, at the 1948 Edinburgh Festival. Following several notable stage appearances as a straight actor, he became known as an all-round entertainer

during many successful seasons in *Five-Past Eight* shows and pantomime with Howard & Wyndham, and in the radio series, *It's All Yours*. Moving to London in 1959, he made his name in several long-running television series such as the award-winning *Stanley Baxter Picture Show*. He has regularly returned to Scotland to play Dame in Christmas pantomimes.

JOHNNY BEATTIE

Born 9th November, 1926, at Govan, Johnny Beattie appeared in an amateur concert party in Glasgow in 1950, and two years later was invited by Robert Wilson to be the comedian in his touring revue. Today he is a leading comedian, pantomime Dame, all-round entertainer and compere, and is particularly associated with the Gaiety Theatre, Ayr, where he has appeared in many Summer seasons including the 60th anniversary edition of *The Gaiety Whirl* in 1990.

ROSS BOWIE

Born 29th April, 1932, Glasgow, the son of G. B. Bowie, the theatre producer and entrepreneur. From 1947, Ross Bowie performed in summer season and learnt the business both from his father and as 'gofer', box office assistant and stage hand at the Theatre Royal, Glasgow. After his father's death in 1974, Ross took over the entertainment agency, which is now in his own name.

MARGARET BUCKLAND (née Guthrie)

Born 14th January, 1933, Edinburgh. Having trained at the Madame Ada School of Dancing from 1936–1947, she made her professional debut aged fifteen in 1948 as a Calder Girl in the summer show at Edinburgh's Palladium Theatre. She was a member of the Calders for almost a decade, appearing in many shows before retiring from the business after the 1955–56 revue, *The Just Daft Company*, which played both the Glasgow and Edinburgh Empires. The all-star line-up included Robert Wilson, Duncan Macrae, Dave Willis, Jack Radcliffe, Jack Anthony, and Chic Murray.

WALTER CARR

Born 26th December, 1925, Larkhall, Lanarkshire. Taken as a child to the Hamilton Hippodrome and appeared aged seven as the Plough Boy in an amateur musical revue at the Swinhill Miners Welfare, near Larkhall. Turned professional in 1940, singing, dancing and appearing in comedy sketches at the Ritz Theatre, Irvine. During the war, he was attached to the naval base at Lyness, Orkney and took part in variety concert parties, appearing with such stars as Will Hay and Gracie Fields. In 1947 Walter Carr joined the Wilson Barratt Company at the Royal Lyceum Theatre, Edinburgh, where he trained as an actor, and now appears in straight drama as well as comedy, variety, and pantomime.

CURT COOK

Born in Glasgow and while still at school, trained during the evenings with his uncle, chief electrician at the Theatre Royal. He since worked backstage at the

Empire, the Victoria Palace, London, and at many theatres, including the London Palladium, with Geraldo, the orchestra conductor. He has also been associated with circuses and now runs a stall at the Barras Market, Glasgow, which he sees as a group of small stages, and where he is a well-known personality.

BERNARD COTTON
Born 10th July, 1934, Sunderland, County Durham. Taken to musicals, circus and the Variety theatre as a child, when he remembers watching the number indicating each act change on the board at the side of the stage. In 1955, he became a trainee assistant manager at the Sunderland Empire, which still retained the old number boards. He became the General Manager of theatres for Kyle and Carrick District Council, and thereby manager of Ayr Gaiety, in 1973.

JANET CRAIG
Born in Hampshire but came to live and work in Edinburgh for the Medical Research Council. She regularly visited the Gaiety theatre, Leith, between 1947–48 and remembers Denny Willis as 'the best comic in sketches such as the Four Chelsea Pensioners'.

ISABELLE DICK (née Dowds)
Born 14th November, 1940, Dundee. Daughter of Musical Director, Bobby Dowds, Isabelle was taken to the Palace Theatre, Dundee, at the age of four, and subsequently visited most of the theatres where her father worked, in Edinburgh, Glasgow and Dundee.

MAE FARRELL (married name Stevely)
Born 12th May, 1906, in Pollokshaws, Glasgow. Taken to the pantomime as a child, and when she was eleven performed the title role in an amateur production of the musical *Princess Chrysanthemum* at Pollokshaws Burgh Hall. Became a professional dancer in 1920, working variety theatres, such as Pickard's Maxwell Picture House, Pollokshaws. As a soubrette, she sang, danced and appeared in concert parties and revues in Glasgow and seaside resorts from 1917–1932.

ANNE FIELDS (née Jean Logan)
Born Dalmarnock, Glasgow. Appeared in a talent contest, aged eight, at Perth Pavilion. First professional performance in 1948 as a singer at G. B. Bowie's Summer season at Barrfields, Largs. Her father, Frank Logan, appeared in a double act, Clifford and Clinton. Her sister, Sally Logan, performs with husband Joe Gordon, in a musical act, in which they are occasionally joined by their son, Scott, on drums. George Logan, of Hinge and Bracket, and Margo Henderson, the impressionist and entertainer, are her cousins. She continues today as a comedy actress, and singer.

W. FINLAY

Born 1936, Glasgow, daughter of the late Alec Finlay and Rita Andre. She and her brother spent much of their childhood backstage but their parents did not encourage them to go into the theatre, perhaps because, as Miss Finlay says, 'they probably realised we had no performing talents whatsover!'.

ARCHIE FOLEY

Son of Andrew Foley, bar and later theatre manager in Aberdeen and Edinburgh, 1938–1968; regular weekly attender at Gaiety and Palladium, Edinburgh in the late forties and early fifties. After National Service considered work in the theatre but concluded insurance offered more job security – now a school teacher. Committee member of Sir Harry Lauder Society and a member of British Music Hall Society.

JIM FRIEL

Born 1941, Glasgow, into a family of music hall enthusiasts. As a child, he was taken to the Metropole, the Empress and Pavilion; later visited the Empire and Alhambra Theatres. He is a printer at the *Sunday Mail* and *Daily Record* in Glasgow, and is Labour Party Parliamentary Agent for Glasgow Shettleston constituency. He is campaigning to preserve the Panopticon Theatre in the Trongate, the earliest music hall in Glasgow.

RIKKI FULTON

Born 1924, Glasgow. Began as an amateur actor at the Lyric theatre in Sauchiehall Street, which led to a four year BBC contract in the late forties. Pantomime and scriptwriting gave him a taste for comedy, and his ten year career with the Howard & Wyndham company. Francie and Josie, his comedy double act with Jack Milroy, made them both household names after it moved from stage to television in the early sixties. Subsequently his own BBC Scotland television series, *Scotch and Wry*, in which he appears in many character roles including the famous Reverend I. M. Jolly, has proved perennially popular. He has also appeared as a straight actor in films and as a comedy actor at the Edinburgh Festival. In 1988, he began the highly successful *King's High* summer revue seasons at the King's Theatre, Glasgow, in which he was reunited with Jack Milroy, playing Francie and Josie to great acclaim. He is thought by many to be the finest Scots comedian of his generation.

MRS ANNIE GREEN, 'Greenie'

Born 1st December, 1897, Aberdeen. Began working as a cleaner at the Beach Pavilion Theatre, Aberdeen, in 1932, when her late husband, William 'Billy' Green, became Harry Gordon's dresser and stage lighting assistant. From 1937–1973 'Greenie' ran a boarding house for performers from the Beach Pavilion and later the Tivoli, the Capitol, and His Majesty's Theatres.

JIM HASTIE

Born 28th February, 1938, Bellshill, Lanarkshire. Remembers seeing a pantomime at age three from a box at the Hamilton Hippodrome. First stage appearance in *Babes in the Wood* at the Theatre Royal, Glasgow, in 1947. Trained at the Celtic Ballet College and was later taught modern, tap, jazz and Highland dancing by the renowned Margaret Morris. After a long stage career he is now Director of Training at the Margaret Morris Movement, the international sports association, and teaches at Scottish Ballet.

EVELYN HENRY
Born Aberdeen, and made her professional debut as a soprano in 1944, with ENSA. After the war and during the fifties, Evelyn Henry toured Britain in revues and musical shows, frequently returning to Aberdeen's Tivoli Theatre where she had been taken as a child. She is now retired.

JACK HOUSE (1906–1991)
Born Glasgow. Left school at fifteen, trained as a chartered accountant but gave up to become a journalist. He has contributed to newspapers, the BBC and Scottish Television since 1928, and for twenty-two years was one half of the Scottish team in the BBC's Round Britain Quiz. He was a theatre critic for many years and retained a particular affection for Variety in Glasgow. He has had sixty-seven books published, the first being *Eight Plays for Wolf Cubs* in 1927, which went out of print in 1990 with a final cheque for royalties of 15p.

INA HOWDEN, (née Hill)
Born 1921, Leith. Her mother, a child circus performer and Highland dancer, encouraged her interest in the theatre. She and her sister sang and danced in local talent contests and were taken regularly to the Gaiety, Leith, the Theatre Royal, Edinburgh, and during the war, Edinburgh's Empire Theatre. They saw the leading comics, variety acts and big band dance orchestras of the day.

FAY LENORE
Born 22 March, 1928, Newcastle-upon-Tyne, the daughter of Leon Dodd, theatrical producer, and Babs Gordon, singer and comedienne. First appeared on stage aged eighteen months, in her parents' summer show at Whitley Bay. First worked as a professional dancer in 1940, in Dick Whittington at His Majesty's Theatre, Carlisle. Joined Howard and Wyndham company to play Principal Boy in pantomime and as singer, dancer and comedienne in *Five-Past Eight* shows for many years. Continues career today as actress, theatre director and as private tutor in voice.

JIMMY LOGAN
Born 1928. Son of the famous music-hall double act, Jack Short and May Dalziel. Jimmy learnt the accordion from the age of six and appeared in his parents' touring summer shows in Ireland, and assisted backstage and front of house. For his later solo comedy career he took the name Logan from his Aunt Ella, a Broadway star. Once he had made his name, the 'Logan Family' company under Ma and Pa Logan staged many long seasons at the Metropole Theatre, Glasgow,

introducing several new and established entertainers and the Loganbelle dancers. From the fifties, Jimmy Logan appeared in films, the successful radio series, *It's All Yours*, and joined Howard and Wyndham for pantomime and *Five Past Eight* shows. Established as a top entertainer by 1964, he moved into theatre management, buying the Empress Theatre, Glasgow and re-naming it the New Metropole. With the days of Variety numbered, Jimmy Logan presented a series of musicals, and light comedies before closing the theatre in 1970. Subsequently Jimmy Logan has produced and starred in successful farces during the Summer months, has appeared as Sir Harry Lauder, in a one-man show, at the Edinburgh Festival and toured Scotland as Archie Rice in John Osborne's *The Entertainer*.

BARBARA McCALL
Born 1904, Edinburgh, Barbara McCall visited the theatre, pantomime and musical comedies from a young age. Her late husband, Tommy McCall, was manager of the Marine Gardens Dance and Concert Hall in Portobello from 1922–1939. They assisted Donald Peers in his early career at Letta's Pierrots in Portobello, and were close friends of the comedian Lex McLean.

PAT McCANN
Born 19th July, 1926 in London, the son of a semi-professional club act, Doris Arnold and Pat McCann. He was taken at the age of ten to the Hackney Empire. After working in music publishing, he moved to Edinburgh in the early fifties, to be Music Librarian and arranger with Howard and Wyndham, later becoming Musical Director. He works as a freelance musical director, conducting many shows including *King's High* with Rikki Fulton and Jack Milroy in Glasgow. In 1990 he conducted *Cinderella*, with Stanley Baxter as Dame, his 21st consecutive pantomime at the King's Theatre, Edinburgh.

CATHIE MacDONALD
Born 15th August, 1924, Edinburgh. Daughter of M. J. McHale, producer of the touring concert party, The Melody Makers. She danced as a child in dancing school and charity shows. While she did not take up a dancing career, she worked in the bar at the Theatre Royal, Edinburgh, during the war, where she was able to see all the shows and meet the entertainers.

NANCY McILROY, (née Dick)
Born 13th July, 1931, Edinburgh. Trained as a dancer with Madame Ada School of Dancing and first performed in pantomime at the Glasgow Pavilion, with Jack Anthony, in 1945. So began a twenty year career in the chorus, first as a Calder Girl, then as a Moxon Lady and finally as a White Heather Club dancer. She married Hugh McIlroy, the baritone. Retired from the stage she is now a qualified keep-fit teacher.

GRACE MACKAY-REAY, (nee Pagan)
Daughter of Variety dance act, Douglas Pagan and Babs Ross, the first dancers to appear on British television on 12th February, 1938. After the war, Grace,

also a dancer, joined her mother in the act which then became Babs Ross and Grace. After her marriage to Jimmy Logan, she assisted him with the administration of company tours. Grace would often prepare meals for the entire cast of a show, as during the fifties and early sixties few Glasgow restaurants remained open after eleven o'clock. Grace is now married to Tom Mackay-Reay, with whom she ran an artistes agency.

BUNTY MACLEOD, (née Gordon)
Born 3rd November, 1927, Aberdeen, daughter of Harry and Josie Gordon. Introduced to pantomime and given dancing lessons from the age of three. In 1943, Bunty appeared with her father when she joined the chorus of the *Half Past Eight* show at the King's Theatre, Edinburgh. Two years later, she became a Tiller Girl and in 1946 was promoted to captain of her troupe. In 1948 she appeared in the first Royal Command Performance after the war. She retired from the theatre in 1951 when she married Norman MacLeod, co-founder of the Canadian singing group, The Maple Leaf Four. Their son, Rory Gordon, is in the theatre profession.

MAY MOXON
Born 1906, Glasgow, into a theatrical family and made her stage debut at the age of ten. With her two elder brothers, she was trained by her mother and joined her in the Four McLeans comedy act, appearing in cine-variety shows during and after the First World War. As a dancer, May Moxon toured in Variety revue for many years until, when she was 28, serious injury ended her career. She founded her own troupe, The Moxon Ladies, which quickly became established as a highly successful company. She retired in 1975.

JUNE MURRAY (stage name June Don)
Born 19th June, 1929, Scarborough, daughter of Roy Don and Phyllis Ward who performed from 1915 in a trampoline, song and dance act, The Bouncing Dillons. They later settled in Edinburgh and Roy Don became manager of the Palladium Theatre, during the early forties. June Don's professional debut was in a Hope and Lang show at the Victory Theatre, Paisley, in 1944. She was in the chorus of many troupes until 1960, working with Short and Dalziel; Johnny Victory at the Gaiety, Leith, and on tour from 1945 for four years; with Lex McLean from 1949 to 1958; and Clark and Murray at the Pavilion, Glasgow, the Palladium, Edinburgh, and the Palace, Dundee. From 1958 June toured the Moss Empire circuit for two years with the Great Lavante, the Australian Illusionist. Today she teaches tap, jazz and keep-fit.

MAIDIE MURRAY, (née Dickson)
Born 1922, Edinburgh. Appeared as a child in concert parties, talent contests and Variety shows in Edinburgh and Leith. Singing to her own accompaniment on the accordion, Maidie appeared with Letta's Entertainers, Portobello, for an eight-week season when she was twelve. She was billed as 'The Discovery of the Year' on a tour of *Vaudeville Parade*, and at fourteen was appearing in pantomime

at Newcastle and in shows around Scotland. She married comedian Chic Murray in 1946, forming a musical-comedy double act, Chic and Maidie, affectionately known as 'The Tall Droll and the Small Doll', Chic being six-foot-two, and 'Dainty Maidie', a neat five feet. After many years touring Scotland, the agent Billy Marsh took them to London, beginning a successful stage, television, and recording career for them both.

JOHN NELSON
Born 5th April, 1933, Edinburgh, he visited the Palladium, the Empire, and other Variety theatres twice or sometimes three times a week during the fifties and sixties with his wife Margaret. He remembers seeing Chic Murray, Lex McLean, Johnny Victory, Johnny Ray, the Deep River Boys, and Frankie Lane.

LENA NICOL, (née Sweetman)
Born 1922, Edinburgh. She and her three sisters and two brothers were all trained to dance. She was taught at the Madame Ada School of Dancing and made her first professional appearance at the age of fourteen when she was one of the Babes in the Edinburgh Theatre Royal pantomime *Babes in the Wood*, starring Harry Gordon. From 1936 to 1948 Lena Sweetman was a dancer in the Adeline Calder troupe touring in revues throughout Scotland. Her husband was the comedian and comic 'feed' Hector Nicol, who died in 1985.

JOAN NICOLL, (née Joan Spiers McKee)
Born 15th June, 1920, Dundee. Taken to the King's Theatre, Dundee, as a child to see plays. In 1938 she joined the Palace Theatre, Dundee as a box office clerkess and worked there until she joined the Women's Royal Naval Service from 1940–1945.

MARJORIE O'DONNELL, (née Dowds)
Born 25th March, 1936, Glasgow, the elder daughter of Bobby Dowds, Musical Director. Taken to the pantomime for the first time in 1940, and spent much of her childhood backstage at the Palace Theatre, Dundee, and the Empire Theatres in Edinburgh and Glasgow. She is now married with five children and lives in New Jersey, USA, and uses her musical background by singing soprano in the church choir, specialising in classical sacred music.

JIM PARKINSON
Born 24th August, 1908, Heseldon, County Durham. First job was from 1925–1928, as trainee manager for Frank E. Franks Productions. Harry Gordon invited him to manage the Beach Pavilion summer season at Aberdeen. This was the start of a ten year contract as business manager to Harry Gordon. After the war he managed a hotel but returned to the theatre when Harry Gordon requested his services to organise a tour of one-night stands during the fifties, a tour marred by the death of Harry Gordon's straight man, Jack Holden. Within a year or so, Harry Gordon too had died.

SEAN PATCHELL
Born 1940 in Donegal, Ireland, and first worked in a show, *Is the Priest at Home?* in 1952. He literally ran away to join Batty's circus in 1958, touring Ireland before moving to Scotland to work in circus and Variety theatre. He began the Smallest Travelling Circus in the World in the sixties, virtually a one-man production. Touring the Highlands of Scotland in the summer and Glasgow theatres in the winter, Sean performed many tricks such as fire-eating, lying on a bed of nails, and working with animals from foxes to snakes.

DOROTHY PAUL
Born Glasgow. Trained as a soprano, appeared as a Variety artiste before becoming a television and theatre actress, and pantomime entertainer. One of her most acclaimed performances was in 1989/90 as Margrit in Tony Roper's play about Glasgow wash-house life, *The Steamie*.

CHRIS POTTER
Born 27th February, 1939, Heswall, Cheshire. He saw his first pantomime, *Dick Whittington*, starring George Formby, at the Liverpool Empire when he was five years old. He joined the profession as an assistant stage manager for *Babes in the Wood*, in 1959. After thirteen years as manager of the Adam Smith Centre, Kirkcaldy, where he wrote and directed twelve pantomimes, Chris Potter became Manager of the King's Theatre, Edinburgh, in 1987, choosing a year-round programme of plays, musicals, revues, dance and opera. He continues to write and direct pantomime: *Cinderella*, starring Stanley Baxter, in 1990–91, marked his fifteenth production.

BERYL REID, O.B.E.
Born 17th June, 1920, Hereford, of Scottish parents. She began her career in concert parties and pantomimes; her own radio show, *A Quarter of an Hour with Beryl Reid*, and her Monica sketches in *Educating Archie*, established her as a leading comedienne. During the late 1940s, she appeared in the *Half-Past Eight* shows with Dave Willis in Edinburgh and on the Empire circuit. This led to her London debut in 1951 in the revue, *After the Show*, at St. Martin's. Her film career began in 1954 with *The Belles of St Trinians*. She is a renowned stage actress, won a Tony award for her performance in *The Killing of Sister George* on Broadway in 1967, and has appeared at the National Theatre, in London. She also stars regularly in television drama.

JOHN ROBERTSON
Born 21st February, 1927, Edinburgh. Attended Variety shows and pantomime as a child and in 1952 began writing comedy scripts for Stanley Baxter's appearances in the *Half-Past Eight* shows at the King's Theatre, Edinburgh. After working for several other performers, he began a long association as script-writer for Grace Clark and Colin Murray, while also working in the paper industry.

ALEC RODGER
Born 30th March, 1928, Alloa. At the age of eleven he began working as a stage hand, controlling the 'limes' (spotlights), at the Metropole Theatre, Glasgow. After the war he became stage manager of the Empress, probably the youngest in any Glasgow theatre, where he worked until the late fifties.

ILONA ROSS
Born 22nd October, 1918, Godalming, Surrey, the daughter of Charles Ross, theatre producer and singer. From the age of four she was taken to all her father's musicals, and rehearsals. Her first professional job was in the chorus at Drury Lane, in which she was the youngest chorister, at seventeen, to understudy the star – although she never went on. At nineteen, she joined her father working for the Howard and Wyndham company. Her father was producer, while she was choreographer and ballet mistress for all the *Half-Past Eight* shows and pantomimes in Edinburgh, Glasgow and on tour, for twenty years. After retiring from the theatre she wrote short stories, articles and pantomime scripts.

MAY ROSS
Born 25th November, 1907, Rhynie, Aberdeenshire. She visited His Majesty's Theatre, Aberdeen, in 1913 to see Harry Lauder and saw Harry Gordon many times at the Beach Pavilion.

PHILIPPA SAUNDERS, (married name Mackay)
Born 6th June, 1918, London. Trained as a dancer from a young age, and first worked professionally in 1933. She joined the Tiller Girls and appeared in Harry Gordon's Beach Pavilion shows, toured Scotland with Dave Willis, and appeared in the Royal Variety Performance in 1938. She retired from showbusiness in January 1940, when she married and settled in Aberdeenshire.

DAVID SMITH
Born 1925, Glasgow. Started working in the wardrobe department at the Pavilion Theatre, aged twelve, graduating to stage-hand at fifteen. In 1953 he moved to the Empire Theatre where he became senior stage-hand, remaining there until it closed in 1963. This was always part-time evening and weekend work in addition to a day job in the printing inks industry. He is now retired.

ROZA LOUISE THOMPSON
Born 1916, Colliers Wood, London. Her mother, Glenice Louise, was a dancer, billed as 'England's Highest Kicker'. Roza was taught dancing and acrobatics as a child and began her professional stage career, aged thirteen in 1929 in a concert party at Burnham-on-Sea. The show was Freddie Fay's Frolics and she was one of four girls in an acrobatic dance act called The Dinky Dots. At fourteen she joined the two Barr Brothers, Charlie and Tom, in their contortionist act, and, as the Three Aberdonians, they performed together for almost twenty years. They appeared at the Royal Variety Performance in 1938.

EDDIE THOMSON
Born 14th October, 1923, Edinburgh. He remembers being taken to the Theatre Royal, Edinburgh as early as 1935. From 1943 until 1968 he had a permanent booking in the front row at the city's Palladium Theatre.

RUBY TURBERVILLE
Born 24th December, 1922, Aberdeen. First visited the Palace Theatre, Aberdeen as a child to see Sir Harry Lauder and Harry Gordon on the same bill. In 1940 she appeared as an amateur actress and dancer with the Carl Rosa Opera Company at His Majesties Theatre. She then moved into journalism, becoming Woman's Editor of the *Aberdeen Evening Express*, and working for BBC Scotland and World Service. She is now a freelance writer.

DOROTHY TREWHITT, (née Ward)
Born 15th February, 1907, Liverpool. Trained at the Faulkner School of stage dancing and appeared in cine-variety shows as a young girl. Her first professional appearance was in 1923 in pantomime as a dancer at the Theatre Royal, Handly, Staffordshire, and thereafter she toured in Variety shows throughout Britain. Her future husband, Jack Trewhitt became resident stage manager of the Theatre Royal, Edinburgh in 1929. After their marriage in 1931, Dorothy worked there in the wardrobe department and continued as a dancer in every pantomime until 1938. She and her husband also ran theatrical digs for almost forty years until the late seventies. Her husband's sister, Kitty Evelyn, was a leading Principal Boy in Glasgow pantomimes during the 1920s and 30s.

AILEEN VERNON
Born in 1923 in Newcastle, of Scottish parents. She was taken to the theatre as a child and first performed at the Curtain Theatre, Glasgow, while still at school; first professional role was with the BBC Drama department during her last year of school. After the war, she joined the Little Theatre, Stockton, and also had small parts in films. She joined the Harry Hanson Repertory company, the Wilson Barrett company, and appeared in television drama, such as *Dr Finlay's Casebook*. She became Stage Director/Assistant Producer on Duncan Macrae and Jimmy Logan tours, Tom Arnold Productions and the Howard & Wyndham company, from 1955–1966, and the production department at Thames Television from 1968–1979. Now retired and living near Salisbury.

BEN WARRIS
Born 29th May, 1909. First stage performance 19th October, 1919, at the Hippodrome, Stockport, and, when he was twelve, appeared on Marie Lloyd's last bill. Between the ages of ten and fourteen, while touring, he attended almost 300 schools throughout Britain. In 1934, he joined his cousin Jimmy Jewel in a cross-talk comedy double act, Jewel and Warris, and became stars of the Moss Empire circuit at £35 a week. In 1937, they turned down a new contract with Moss, while doing very successful business in Glasgow. Moss promptly offered them £100 a week. The Jewel and Warris partnership lasted

thirty-six years until 1970. Recently, Ben Warris toured England as Archie Rice, in John Osborne's play *The Entertainer*.

JOHNNIE WILLIAMSON
Born 16th November, 1914, Perth, and taken to pantomime and Variety shows in Perth from five years old. All his life, he has continued to visit theatres throughout Scotland. More recently in Fife and Tayside he and his wife travel to see the *Breath of Scotland* revues produced by Ron Coburn, which play one-night stands for summer visitors and which subsequently tour the Highlands and Islands.

DENNY WILLIS
Born 27th May, 1922, Glasgow, the son of Belle and Dave Willis. He was taken to the Variety theatre as a child and first worked professionally as a comedian in 1946, touring the UK. He has appeared in twenty countries, from the Far East, Middle East, West Germany, and all over Europe, including six months at the Lido, Paris. He has also performed in the Royal Variety Performance and appeared in films in Italy. Denny Willis still works as a comedian and played Dame in the pantomime *Robinson Crusoe*, at the Pavilion, Glasgow, 1989–1990, with Andy Cameron.

CAREY WILSON
Born 4th April, 1944, Ayr, the son of Robert Wilson, the singer, and Margaret MacDonald. He first performed as a child of nine in summer season at the Palace Theatre, Dundee. In 1967, as a professional singer he appeared in the *Black and White Minstrel Show*, at the Victoria Palace, London, and continues today as a singer and actor.

JOHN WISHART
Born 1942, Glasgow. Began working at the city's Empire Theatre, aged fourteen, as a trainee stage electrician, working the 'limes'. He continued there until the theatre closed in 1963, and now works in the newspaper industry.

A WHO'S WHO GUIDE
TO THE VARIETY
BUSINESS

Jack ANTHONY (1900–1962); Light comedian.
Born Glasgow, John Anthony Herbertson was never known as anything other than Jack Anthony, a name his father, also an entertainer, adopted in America. He began singing and dancing in the Kinderspiel, charity concert parties in Glasgow. Fyfe & Fyfe shows in Rothesay, lead to the Millport Entertainers in 1926 where he became a good all-rounder, singer, dancer and comedian, often made-up with the white face and outsize clothes of a clown. He partnered G. H. Elliot, billed as 'The Chocolate Coloured Coon', at the Pavilion. His comic feeds were Bertha Ricardo and, from 1929, Bond Rowell.

Arthur ASKEY (1900–1982); Comedian.
Diminutive British music hall comedian who began in 1924 in concert parties. He became popular through the radio series, Band Wagon from 1938, and moved into films and television during the fifties. Also regularly appeared in pantomime throughout Britain.

Charlie and Tom BARR (see 'The Three Aberdonians')

Dr Walford BODIE (1870–1939); Speciality act.
Born Aberdeen; apprentice electrician and appeared at Stonehaven Town Hall in 1886 demonstrating electricity. From 1904, with his wife as his partner, he appeared as a Variety entertainer, billed as an electrical conjurer, hypnotist, cartoonist and ventriloquist. He was an uncle of Helen Norman, the comic feed.

G. B. BOWIE (?–1974); Theatrical agent.
Variety show impresario and producer from 1932 when he began leasing seaside

resort pavilions for summer shows. He built up a circuit of fourteen theatres all round the Scottish coast. Under the Bowie management, revues were also staged in many theatres from the Roxy, Falkirk to the Empire, Inverness.

Jack BUCHANAN (1891–1957); Singer, dancer, actor-manager.
Born Helensburgh; debut at the Glasgow Panopticon, before appearing in London in 1912, where he established himself as a stylish song-and-dance man and actor in musical comedy shows such as *Top Hat and Tails*, and *Kings Rhapsody*, visiting the Edinburgh Lyceum in 1925 in *Boodle*. First pantomime, 1940, as Buttons in *Cinderella*. In America he appeared in many films including *Band Wagon*, with Fred Astaire. He also directed films and managed the Garrick Theatre, London.

Freddie CARPENTER (1908–1989).
Born in Australia and came to Britain as a dancer. In 1951 he became Chief of Productions for Howard & Wyndham. By 1960 he had produced twenty-six spectacular pantomimes and was commissioned by Rodgers and Hammerstein to produce *Cinderella* at the London Coliseum in 1959, which starred Tommy Steele. That year he staged five pantos in the space of forty-four days, in London, Glasgow, Edinburgh, Liverpool and Newcastle. He staged the first all-Scottish pantomime *A Wish for Jamie*, in 1960, which he devised and created, and was an outstanding success for the company.

Sir LEWIS CASSON (1875–1969); Actor-manager and producer.
Born in Birkenhead. Married Sybil Thorndike in 1908, and together they acted and produced plays, frequently on tour. He was knighted in 1945. Their son, John Casson, was a director at the Citizens' Theatre, Glasgow.

Charlie CHAPLIN (1889–1977); Film comedian and director.
Born London, of theatrical parents but his father died early leaving the family in financial straits. At the age of eight he became a stage performer and was trained in comedy acting by Fred Karno who took him to Hollywood in 1914. He achieved world wide fame as the 'little tramp' in many silent films (*The Kid*, *The Gold Rush* etc.) and unlike many stars, made the transition to sound, finding new audiences with films such as *Modern Times*. He then acted in, directed and composed for the film *Limelight*. He was knighted in 1975.

Grace CLARK (1905–   ); Musician and comedienne.
In 1926, Grace, who performed a solo piano act, met Colin Murray, a baritone, when they shared the bill at a Dunbar Concert Party. They began a musical double act, and married in 1931. They appeared with Sir Harry Lauder, Will Fyffe, Sophie Tucker, Tommy Lorne, Harry Gordon and Max Miller. In 1948, Alex Frutin, owner of the Metropole, suggested they introduce comedy into the act. They became increasingly popular, touring throughout Scotland during the fifties and sixties, their winter Metropole seasons often being extended until April. In 1976, they celebrated their golden anniversary as 'Mr and Mrs

Glasgow'. They were awarded the BEM in 1984 in recognition of their contribution to the Variety theatre. Colin Murray died in 1989.

George CLARKSON (1894–   ); Song-and-dance man; producer.
Born Motherwell into a family of eighteen children, the son of a railwayman. Was taught singing as a child and joined The Five Jocks, a music, comedy, dance act, in 1918, touring almost every theatre in Britain for two years. Worked as a solo dancer in summer seasons around Scotland, and from 1940 produced G. B. Bowie's summer revues for twenty-five years. He gave many pantomime performances at the Queen's Theatre, Glasgow. His son, George, trained with him and in 1934, when he was fourteen, until the war, appeared with his father in a double act in which they would be dressed in top hat and tails with a white bow tie.

Fred COLLINS (1877–1931); Variety agent.
Managing Director of the Collins Theatrical Agency which ran five theatres in Britain: Edinburgh Theatre Royal; Pavilion, Glasgow; Palace, Dundee; Tivoli, Aberdeen; and the Shakespeare, Liverpool.

Horace COLLINS (1900–1947); Variety agent.
The son of Fred Collins, christened Horace Horatio Nelson. Trained by his father and took over the family business after his death in 1931. The personal manager of Sir Harry Lauder and Dave Willis, he tirelessly sought out new talent, and like his father before him, made many an entertainer a star. He was awarded the OBE.

Billy CONNOLLY (1942–   ); Comedian and film actor.
Born Glasgow; began as a folk-singer and became a stand-up comic, his frank, sometimes outrageous monologues appealing to young people, paved the way for the so-called 'alternative' comedians emerging through clubs and the Comedy Store in London.

Tommy COOPER (1922–1984); Comedian, magician.
Born Caerphilly. A barrackroom comic during seven years in the Home Guards. On stage and television he developed a famous comedy routine of fumbled conjuring, punctuated by genial patter and manic laughter. Judged by many in the business as one of the greatest stage comics.

A. Stewart CRUIKSHANK, Senior (1877–1949); Theatre manager.
The son of a builder, he joined the Howard & Wyndham company in Edinburgh in 1906, and became Managing Director in 1928, when the company owned several theatres including the Royal Lyceum and the Kings in Edinburgh. He was regarded as an astute business man and a good employer, known amongst the staff as 'the Guvnor'. Under his management, the *Half-Past Eight* shows and pantomimes became renowned productions during the thirties and forties. He was killed in a road accident in 1949.

Stewart CRUIKSHANK, Junior (1908–1966); Theatre manager.
He joined his father in Howard & Wyndham, succeeding him as Managing Director after his death in 1949, and moving the company headquarters from Edinburgh to London. The business continued to expand during the next twenty years. He took over the Alhambra Theatre, Glasgow, and presented spectacular revues, pantomimes and Royal Command Performances.

David DEVANT (1868–1941); Conjurer.
Began as a child entertainer and later became a highly accomplished stage illusionist. In 1904, he assisted John Maskelyne, regarded as the doyen of British magicians, before establishing himself as a solo performer. He created some ingenious tricks and illusions, including one called Vice Versa, in which it seemed that he could turn men into women.

Ken DODD (1931–   ); Comedian.
Born Liverpool, Kenneth Arthur Dodd made his professional debut at the Nottingham Empire in 1954. Twelve years later he starred in his own show for a record forty-two week season at the London Palladium. He has appeared in over twenty pantomimes and travels widely in his ambition to play every theatre in Britain. He was awarded the OBE in 1982.

Bobby DOWDS (1903–1987); Musical Director.
Born Alexandria, one of six brothers and one sister, all of whom were musically gifted. Began professional career playing violin in the orchestra at the La Scala cinema, Dumbarton. From 1936 until 1949, apart from war service, was musical director at the Palace Dundee, thereafter moving to the Empire, Edinburgh, 1949–1951, and finally to the Empire, Glasgow, 1951–1958, when the post of resident MD ended. He then taught violin and music in Dunbartonshire schools. Just before he died he passed on his violin to his grandson Robert Dick who is now a talented young musician.

Jack EDGE (1891–1977); Comedian.
Born Manchester, he made his first stage appearance in 1904 in pantomime in Birmingham. He trained with the famous Lancashire Lads, alongside Charlie Chaplin, J. W. Jackson and others. He developed a solo act in 1908, touring in shows and revues, and appearing as principal comedian for producer Julian Wylie for twenty years. He was the leading comic in the first *Half-Past Eight* show in Glasgow in 1933, produced by Wylie, and also in the first Edinburgh *Half-Past Eight*, in 1935.

G. H. ELIOT (1883–1962); Light comedian.
Started as a child actor, and became one of the earliest and most famous 'blacked-up' entertainers, billed as 'The Chocolate Coloured Coon'. Black-faced performers were an extremely popular novelty, and troupes of seaside pierrots would often put on a swanee minstrel show. There was no racist intent, and none was seen before Britain became a more cosmopolitan country. This

style of singing continued with the *Black and White Minstrels* on television during the sixties.

Alec FINLAY (1906–1984); Comic actor, singer.
Child singer of Lauder songs, 'The Pocket Harry Lauder', at charity concert parties. He made his professional debut in Millport in 1928, formed a double act with his wife Rita Andre, and first appeared in London in 1931. They toured Britain and South Africa, returning to Scotland in the late thirties, when Alec began his 'Scotland's Gentleman' act, wearing top hat, tail coat and kilt. An accomplished musician, he also became a successful all-round entertainer, in pantomime often starring with Harry Gordon; and in revue, and as a character actor, known for his portrayal as the wee Free Kirk elder.

Andrew FOLEY (1911–1975); Theatre manager.
First entered theatre business in 1938 when he became bar manager, Palladium, Edinburgh. After the Second World War he took the same job at the Gaiety, Leith. Manager of Tivoli Theatre, Aberdeen, 1954–1963, moving to the Palladium, Edinburgh as theatre manager, 1963–1968, when the theatre closed down.

Florrie FORDE (1876–1940); Music hall singer.
Born Florence Flanagan in Melbourne. First appeared on stage in Sydney in 1893, singing 'He kissed me when he left me and told me I had to be Brave'. Joined revue and pantomime companies, touring as 'the Australian Marie Lloyd'. Came to London in 1897. She was a large, buxom lady, her costumes beautifully adorned with feathers and sequins, and became popular with her renditions of pub songs, 'Down at the Old Bull and Bush', 'Hold Your Hand Out Naughty Boy' and, during the First World War, delighted audiences with, 'It's a Long Way to Tipperary'. She toured Britain extensively, appearing as Principal Boy in dozens of pantomimes, even when she was sixty. At the start of the Second World War, she entertained the troops with songs like, 'What's the Use of Worrying'.

Bruce FORSYTH (1928–   ); Entertainer.
Born Bruce Forsyth Johnson, London. Made his debut at Bilston Theatre Royal in 1942 as Boy Bruce, a dance act. He made his name as compere of the television show, *Sunday Night at the London Palladium*, in the 1960s. Although he is an accomplished song-and-dance entertainer, he is principally known as a regular presenter of television quiz shows.

Ray FOX (1901–?); Dance Band leader.
Born Denver, Colorado, but brought up in Hollywood. In 1920 he made his debut leading a band at Santa Monica. Invited to bring an eight-piece band to London's Café de Paris for a season in 1930, resulting in recording contract with Decca, and BBC radio performances. During the thirties he toured Britain and became extremely popular. Travelled overseas during the war but returned to

tour Britain in 1946. He was nicknamed the Whispering Cornetist, after his signature tune, 'Whispering'. Later he began an entertainment agency.

Ike FREEDMAN; Singer and comedian.
Born Gorbals, Glasgow. Jewish comedian and singer appearing in the forties and fifties, whose well-known songs included 'I'm only a Jew', and 'The Emerald Isle'. He was extremely popular, especially in his own local sou'side district of Glasgow, his performances always given a rousing reception.

Will FYFFE (1885–1947); Character actor and comedian.
Born Dundee and toured in 'Penny-Geggies' – troupes of travelling players – in Shakespearian productions and melodrama. At the age of fifteen he played Polonius. Having developed his rather English-styled, song and patter act, he appeared in the 1922 Royal Variety Show. He was famous for the song 'I belong to Glasgow', played as a typical Scots drunk, and numerous character studies such as 'I'm ninety-four today'. He was also a natural pantomime performer and from 1941 was partnered by Harry Gordon for a notable series of six consecutive shows at the Alhambra Theatre, Glasgow. He died suddenly at the hotel he owned in St Andrews.

Alec FRUTIN; Owner, Metropole Theatre, Glasgow.
Born at the turn of the century, the son of Bernard Frutin, a Russian emigree who came to Scotland, with his wife and baby son, in 1902. Bernard had worked in Russia as a make-up artist, touring with a travelling company of players, but the only associated work he could find in Glasgow, was as a barber. Sixteen years later he returned to show business, becoming manager and owner of the Metropole Theatre. Alec took over after his father's death in 1940. All the great entertainers performed there and it is said that no other theatre reflected the rich, warm essence of Glasgow life to quite the same extent. Alec was a familiar figure in the foyer each evening. After fire destroyed the theatre in 1961, he bought the Empress Theatre, renamed it the Falcon, and later sold it to Jimmy Logan.

William R. GALT (1881–1972); Theatrical agent.
Managed his own theatrical agency at 13 Sauchiehall Street, Glasgow, booking artistes in to a large circuit of variety theatres around Scotland, also under his control. Rather than dealing with the performers personally, Mr Galt employed an assistant, Nellie Sutherland, who was known by every artiste on the Galt books, not only as an eccentric and forceful personality, but someone who knew showbusiness in Scotland better than anyone else.

GERALDO (1904–1974); Big band/orchestra conductor.
Born Gerald Bright, London, and was a child prodigy at the piano. Professional debut as relief-pianist at a cinema in the Old Kent Road. During the twenties, led the resident band at the Hotel Majestic, St Annes-on-Sea. Later, formed his own dance band, broadcasting frequently and performing at the Savoy, during

the thirties. During the war, as Geraldo and his Sweet Music, he managed the ENSA Band division. This led to theatre orchestral management including the *Five-Past Eight* shows for Howard & Wyndham. He became musical director for Scottish Television and was the first bandleader to appear on television after the war. He retired from leading an orchestra in the mid-fifties.

Harry GORDON (1893–1957); Comedian, pantomime dame, producer.
Born Alexander Ross, in Aberdeen, but as a boy reversed his initials, calling himself Harry ('R.A.'). After appearing in talent contests at the Beach Pavilion, Aberdeen, when he was 15, he joined a pierrot troupe in Banchory where he met his future wife, Jessie Dudgeon, who appeared as the Highland dancer Jose Goray, and they subsequently toured as the Two Elmas. There followed pre- and First World War seasons in Aberdeen, Stonehaven, and Burntisland, during which time he met Jack HOLDEN (1893–1955), who became his most accomplished stage partner and comic 'feed' for the rest of his career. Harry Gordon took over the lease of the Beach Pavilion in 1924, beginning his popular resident summer shows which ran until 1940. Thereafter, he played seasons in Glasgow and Edinburgh in *Half-Past Eight*, toured Scotland and overseas, and from 1937, also appeared in the Alhambra, Glasgow pantomimes for sixteen years.

Dickie HENDERSON (1922–1985); Singer, dancer, compere.
Born London, and made his debut as a dancer at the Empire, Middlesborough, in 1938. He toured the Variety circuit for many years but made his name nationally after compering the *Sunday Night at the London Palladium* television show in the sixties.

Billie and Renee HOUSTON; Comedy double act.
Sisters from Renfrewshire, Scotland, of music-hall parents, (James Houston and Company). Renee, born Katerina Valorita, (1902–1980) and Billie (1906–1972) first appeared in 1920 as a precocious girl and boy act, Billie as the Eton-cropped boy and Renee the little girl. In 1924 they appeared in Tommy Lorne's revue, *Froth*, and from there went into pantomime. In 1926, they were in the Royal Variety Show, and continued until 1935, when Billie retired. Renee continued to appear on stage with her husband, Donald Stewart, and made a successful move into straight drama in the theatre, radio and television.

HOWARD & WYNDHAM Ltd; Theatre company 1895–1979.
Actor-manager J. B. Howard, and the former actor, turned manager F. W. P. Wyndham, founded the Royal Lyceum Theatre, Edinburgh in 1883, and formed a limited company in 1895 to run their new acquisitions, the Theatre Royals in Edinburgh and Glasgow, and the Royalty in Glasgow. J. B. Howard died within a few weeks, aged fifty-four. Ten years later, the company owned the King's Theatres, Glasgow and Edinburgh, and by 1912 Howard & Wyndham controlled theatres in Dundee and Aberdeen as well as six across the North of England. In 1928, Wyndham retired (and died in 1930), and A. Stewart Cruikshank, manager of the King's, Edinburgh, became managing director of

Howard & Wyndham. Under his management, the nationwide touring of plays, revues and musicals expanded, while the business owned seven British theatres and controlled another eleven. In 1949, Stewart Cruikshank Junior succeeded his father as managing director and moved the head office to London. Until the late sixties the company's spectacular revues and pantomimes filled the theatres summer and winter, but after Stewart Cruikshank's death in 1966, the slow demise of Variety shows, and the closure of some theatres, the company ceased operations in 1979.

Gertie GITANA (1889–1957); Music hall star.
A child performer, she made her debut in 1900 as Little Gitana. She toured the number-one halls as one of the most popular comediennes of her day, succeeding Marie Lloyd. At the end of her career, she toured in the *Thanks for the Memory* shows, with G. H. Elliot, Nellie Wallace and many others.

Dick HURRAN (1911–   ); Director, musical shows, revues.
He was a successful London director before coming to Scotland in 1957 and joining Howard & Wyndham to produce the *Five-Past Eight* shows. Dick Hurran transformed these summer revues into spectacular shows, with extravagant stage design such as a swimming pool, and an orchestra which was lifted from pit to stage level. For the Alhambra Starlight Room shows, he brought in international stars and immediately broke box office records during long-running seasons. Dick Hurran produced the pantomime at Wimbledon, starring Cilla Black, in the 1989–1990 season.

Jimmy JEWEL (1909–   ); Comedian, actor.
He worked with his father, a Yorkshire comic, from the age of ten. In 1934, he teamed up with his cousin, Ben Warris, to form their cross-talk double act Jewel and Warris which lasted thirty-six years. They were extremely popular in Scotland in *Half-Past Eight* shows and pantomime. By the seventies, the Variety circuit had ended and Jimmy Jewel made a successful move into straight drama roles on stage and television. He was particularly notable in the 1983 National Theatre production of *You Can't Take it With You*, by Kaufman and Hart.

Danny KAYE (1913–1987); Singer, and film actor.
Born Brooklyn, New York. Abandoning a medical career, he entered the Vaudeville business, touring America. In 1938, appeared in cabaret at London's Dorchester Hotel, and then toured the UK number-one circuit. At the London Palladium in 1948, he played for forty-five minutes, rather than the usual twenty, starting the trend for top (American) performers to take over the second half of the bill. Also starred in films: *The Secret Life of Walter Mitty* and *Hans Christian Anderson* etc.

Hetty KING (1883–1972); Male impersonator.
Appeared in Variety shows as a debonair man-about-town, with songs such as *All the Nice Girls Love a Sailor*, and *Piccadilly*.

Harry LAUDER (1870–1950); Singer, comedian.
Born Portobello; he entered Band of Hope talent contests, and charity shows, as a schoolboy, later becoming a miner and flax millworker for ten years. He decided to try his luck in the music hall when he saw Dan Leno appearing at the Glasgow Empire, singing English songs for £100 a week, and thought he might get £20 a week in London singing Scots songs. His first London appearance was in 1900 and within a few years he was touring America and regarded internationally as the most successful artiste the Variety stage had ever known. He was knighted in 1919 for services to the theatre, especially for his work as a wartime entertainer.

Stan LAUREL (1890–1965); Stage and film comedian.
Son of Arthur Jefferson, owner of the Scotia (later Metropole) music hall in Glasgow. He made his debut at the Panopticon in 1906 and soon after went to America where he became a silent film comedian. The partnership of Stan Laurel and Oliver Hardy became one of the most celebrated comedy double acts of all time. They visited Scotland on several occasions, appearing at the Playhouse, Edinburgh, and the Empire, Glasgow. Oliver Hardy died in 1957.

Tommy LORNE (1890–1935); Comedian, pantomime dame.
Born Hugh Gallagher Corcoran near Glasgow. As a boy joined a local troupe, The Port Dundas Court Juvenile Minstrels, making his music hall debut in a George Formby Senior Talent competition at the Queen's Theatre, Glasgow. After touring Scotland in a burlesque and dance act, Wallace and Lorne, he became principal comedian at the Princess Theatre, Glasgow in 1920. Now an established solo performer, he developed his own comic style, with eccentric clownish make-up, a kilt, glengarry bonnet, high collar with a bootlace tie, a short jacket, long white gloves and large boots. In 1928 he played Dame for the first time at the King's Theatre, Edinburgh, launching a successful pantomime career. Among his professional admirers were Harry Gordon and Will Fyffe.

Carroll LEVIS (1910–1968); Theatre impresario.
Born Toronto, the son of a murdered policeman. In 1935 he came to London and began managing touring talent shows, *Carroll Levis and his Discoveries*, and *Teenage Discoveries*. Aged 25, he was twenty-three stone and looked older than his years. He started many a talented youngster on the Variety circuit, his signature tune being 'Stardust'. He died in Scotland aged fifty-eight.

LIBERACE (1919–1987); Pianist.
Born Vladziu Valentino Liberace, Wisconsin, USA. Billed as 'The Rhinestone Rubenstein', he was a flamboyant piano virtuoso, wearing outrageous sequined suits, rings on each finger, a candelabra on his grand piano. He became a top-class professional 'showman' of cabaret and Variety theatre and television.

Marie LLOYD (1870–1922); Music hall comedienne and singer.
Born Matilda Alice Victoria Wood. Regarded as the epitome of the spirit of

pre-First World War music hall entertainment, her famous song being 'The Boy I Love is Up in the Gallery'. Her performance often portrayed an innocent sexuality, with its mixture of naive girlishness and blatant flirtation in songs such as 'Every Little Movement has a Meaning of its Own' and 'Then you Wink the Other Eye'. She also realistically played the part of a drunken woman, in which sketch at the Edmonton Empire, in 1922, she collapsed, and while the audience believed this to be part of the act, she was carried off, never to recover.

Lex McLEAN (1908–1975); Comedian.
Born Alexander McLean Cameron, Clydebank; was an apprentice at John Brown's Shipyards before entering the theatrical profession. He worked in the Pierrot show in Girvan, and with Jack Radcliffe and George West, before embarking on a solo career as a comic in 1947, at the Empress Theatre, Glasgow. While he was often described as 'earthy' and nicknamed 'Sexy Lexy', his material only had a touch of the double entendre and he filled the Pavilion Theatre, Glasgow, the Tivoli, Aberdeen and the Palladium, Edinburgh, for many seasons during the fifties and sixties with family audiences. He was a popular television entertainer with his own comedy series, regularly assisted by Walter Carr. Regarded as the last of the old-style music hall comedians, his death in 1975 is said to mark the end of the traditional summer Variety season at the Pavilion.

Max MILLER (1895–1963); Music hall stand-up comic.
Born Thomas Henry Sargeant and called 'the Cheeky Chappie' due to his loud suits, ostentatious diamond rings and a seaside humour which relied on obvious double entendre. He was never explicitly 'blue', as he would plant an idea in the audience's mind, the audience would laugh before the punchline and he would blame the audience for their 'shocking sense of humour'. He wore flat pink make-up and enjoyed making rather effeminate, 'camp' gestures. Miller is traditionally thought to be the inspiration for Archie Rice, the music-hall comic, in John Osborne's play *The Entertainer*.

Jack MILROY (1920–   ); Comedian.
Born Glasgow. Made his name in the summer seasons at the Tivoli, Aberdeen, as a solo comic in 'Whirl of Laughter', from 1950–1952. That year he married Mary Lee who sang with Ray Fox and his Band during the thirties. In 1953, they starred in a twenty-two week Tivoli 'Whirl' season and this success began a stage partnership lasting over thirty years. More recently they starred in *King's High*, a series of summer revues at the Glasgow King's in which Jack Milroy revived his role as Francie to Rikki Fulton's Josie. The characters Francie and Josie, Glasgow wideboys of the fifties, as played by Milroy and Fulton, made their first appearance in 1960 and their double-act has since become one of the most celebrated of the Scottish Variety stage.

Eric MORECAMBE (1926–1984); Stage and television comedian.
Born John Eric Bartholomew, in Morecambe. Appeared as a 'gormless' comic

at the Empire, Nottingham in 1939. His partner of long-standing, Ernie WISE, was born Ernest Wiseman in Leeds in 1925, and appeared aged seven at a local working men's club. Morecambe and Wise teamed up in 1940, playing in the wartime revue, Garrison Theatre, and in Juvenile shows. Their partnership continued on stage and television until Morecambe's death. Their first television show was in 1954 and in 1960, they appeared at the London Palladium.

Tommy MORGAN (1898–1958); Comedian.
Born Bridgeton, Glasgow. First stage appearance 1920, the Panopticon; London debut, 1924, Shoreditch Empire. His foil for over thirty years was Tommy Yorke, with whom he slowly worked his way up in the Variety Business, until they enjoyed record-breaking six-month seasons for many years at the Pavilion, Glasgow. Other feeds with whom he was associated were Margaret Milne, George Daly, Arthur McBride and Arthur Rogers. He appeared in pantomime and his own shows, and encouraged many promising young entertainers including Jimmy Neil, comic; Anne Fields, singer; Roy Castle, dancer; and Ruby Murray, an Irish singer. His catch phrase was 'Clairty, Clairty', derived from the phrase, 'I declare to Goodness'; he was renowned for his character study of the G. I. Bride, 'Big Beanie McBride, the Pride of the Clyde'.

Sir Edward MOSS (1852–1912); Theatre owner.
Moss founded the Empire circuit, the most prestigious chain of Variety theatres. The first Empire Palace, designed by Frank Matcham, opened in Nicolson Street, Edinburgh, on 7th November 1892. Thereafter, Moss opened theatres in almost every major city in Britain, creating a nationwide touring circuit; to play the Moss Empires, was to have 'arrived' as a Variety artiste. Moss died in 1912, but the business survived and expanded. In 1932, the company owned thirty-eight theatres and merged with the General Theatre Corporation, with George Black as managing director and Val Parnell, as general manager. Parnell imported top American performers to the Palladium during the fifties and sixties, when British Variety was losing ground. In 1960, Moss Empires was taken over by the Stoll circuit, to form the Stoll-Moss company.

Chic MURRAY (1919–1985); Comedian.
Born Charles Thomas McKinnon Murray, Greenock. His father William Murray, was gassed in the Battle of the Somme in 1916 which permanently damaged his lungs. As a boy, Charles (Chic) learnt the piano, organ, banjo, mandolin and guitar and enjoyed singing and yodeling. At fifteen he began a five-year marine-engineering apprenticeship and started The Whinhillbillies, a part-time amateur musical duo with Neilie McNeil. During the war, they were joined by two friends, and the act became Chic and His Chicks, specialising in songs like 'China Doll' and 'Tin Can'. When he was 21, Chic met the singer and accordionist, Maidie Dickson, who was performing at the Greenock Empire. They married in 1946 and over the next few years, developed their own immensely successful comedy/musical act, Chic and Maidie, 'The Lank and the

Lady'. In later years, Chic became a solo comic and personality on stage, radio and television.

Charles NAUGHTON (1887–1976), and Jimmy GOLD (1886–1967); Comic double act.

Both born Glasgow; the double act, Naughton and Gold began at the Glasgow Hippodrome in 1908. Their style of traditional humour was based on two British working men, their catchphrase being 'Turn it around the other way'. They were extremely popular throughout Britain, appearing in the Royal Command Performance on several occasions during the thirties, forties and fifties. They were best known as part of the Crazy Gang, which consisted of a solo, 'Monsewer' Eddie Gray, and three double-acts, Nervo and Knox, Flanagan and Allen, and Naughton and Gold, providing a riot of knockabout fun, slapstick, and cross-talk sketches. The Crazy Gang shows were made into a series of films during the late thirties.

Jimmy NEIL (1918–1976); Stand-up comic.

Born Townhead district, Glasgow. Encouraged by the comedian Tommy Morgan, Jimmy Neil became popular throughout Scotland as a front-cloth comic excelling in quick-thinking repartee, verse and song.

Hector NICOL (1920–1985); Comedian.

While appearing in the Rodeo Three cowboy act at the Edinburgh Palladium in the late thirties, Hector Nicol met the dancer, Lena Sweetman, and they married in 1948. He wrote scripts for Stanley Baxter and Jimmy Logan; was comic 'feed' to Johnny Victory for eight years, and for Johnny Beattie for five years before establishing his own solo career as a club comedian and recording artiste during the sixties and seventies. He appeared at working men's clubs such as the Ashfield, Glasgow, and built up an excellent reputation as a comic original, his fast delivery and rather 'blue' material finding a ready audience. He was named 'the Comic King of Clubland', and worked the circuit with great success until his death.

Helen NORMAN (1907–   ); Comedienne and feed.

Born London; stage debut, 1919 at the Theatre Royal, Glasgow. London debut, 1925, Collins Music Hall, Islington. As a young girl, she appeared with her uncle, Dr Walford Bodie, the 'electrical wizard'. Early acting roles included character and comedy parts with the Scottish National Players and, aged 17, she appeared as principal boy in pantomime. In 1935, Helen Norman joined Jack Radcliffe, and became his 'feed' for many years in his resident shows in Scotland and the north of England.

Des O'CONNOR (1932–   ); Entertainer.

Began his career as a holiday camp entertainer, appeared on the Moss Empire Circuit and established himself as an all-round comedian and singer, later known principally for his television appearances.

Donald PEERS (1910–1973); Singer.
Born Donald Rhys Hubert Peers, Ammanford, South Wales. Early appearances singing and playing the ukelele in Lowestoft, and Portobello, near Edinburgh. Reached the height of his fame in 1949, when he gave a one-man concert at the Albert Hall, began his broadcasting career on the BBC, and won a recording contract with HMV. Later, he recorded with Decca.

Oscar RABAN (1899–?); Big-band leader.
Born Riga, Russia; came to Britain as a child. In 1925, he formed a partnership with musician Harry Davis, performing in Southend as 'Oscar Raban and his Romany Band with Harry Davis', and within ten years achieved broadcasting and recording contracts. During the war they toured Britain, building up a popular following.

Jack RADCLIFFE (1900–1966); Character comedian.
Born Cleland, near Glasgow; a former miner, he made his first stage perfor-mance playing the violin and telling jokes, at Airdrie in 1926. Made his name in Scottish summer shows and revues, specialising in character sketch roles, working men and drunks. From 1935, he was partnered by Helen Norman as his comic 'feed'. After his London debut ten years later, he had a successful career throughout Britain, appearing at the Palladium, and playing several resident seasons at Blackpool.

Bond ROWELL; Light comedian and comic 'feed'.
Born Robert Rowell; first stage appearance in 1914, Empire, South Shields; London debut, 1919, Empire, Shepherds Bush. Toured with Warner's agency and Stoll theatres. In 1929 while appearing in Scotland, he met Jack Anthony and they formed a long-lasting stage partnership in Variety and pantomime.

Sir Oswald STOLL (1866–1942); Theatre owner.
In 1904, Stoll opened the London Coliseum as a first-class Variety theatre. By 1920, the Stoll Circuit consisted of seventeen theatres. Within ten years there was intense competition from the Moss Empire chain (thirty-eight theatres), General Theatre Corporation (fifteen theatres), and the smaller circuits run by MacNaghten, Fred Collins and Howard & Wyndham. In 1960, the Stoll company took over Moss Empires to form Stoll-Moss, although within a few years, many theatres began to close.

The THREE ABERDONIANS; Contortionist act.
Having trained as acrobats with Duffy's Circus in Ireland, two Scottish brothers, Tom and Charlie Barr, a former weight-lifter and miner, toured Britain during the twenties as the Barr Brothers double-act. In 1930, they recruited Roza Louise Thompson to join the act, changing their name to The Three Aberdonians after appearing at His Majesty's Theatre, Aberdeen. Within a few years, they were touring the Number One circuit, and after appearing in the Royal Variety Performance in 1938, travelled overseas and were extremely

successful. Roza Louise left the act in the early fifties, while the Barr brothers continued to appear in pantomime and summer season at Blackpool until the early sixties. Tom Barr died in 1964 and Charlie in 1978. (See entry for Roza Louise under list of contributors.)

Tommy TRINDER (1909–1989); Music hall comedian.
Born Streatham, London. First London appearance in 1922, at Collins Music Hall. He worked continuously in Variety and pantomime for many years, becoming recognised as one of the greatest Variety comedians. For his act he wore an ordinary suit, with a battered trilby hat. His catch-phrase was 'You Lucky People'. He appeared in several Royal Variety Performances, and at Command Performances at Balmoral, Buckingham Palace and Windsor.

Frankie VAUGHAN (1928–   ); Singer.
Born Frank Abelsohn; stylish British song-and-dance man, particularly noted for his 'signature' performance, carrying top hat and cane, of the song, 'Give Me the Moonlight', written by Fred Barnes and which he found in a music shop in Sauchiehall Street, Glasgow. He is held in great affection locally for his charitable work for the Poor Boys' Clubs, and community centres in the city.

Johnny VICTORY (1923–1968); Comedian.
Born Edinburgh, son of the manager of Victory's Taxis. He specialised in often serious and moving monologues commenting on topical issues. His famous character was the pseudo Frenchman, Pierre, 'ze great lovair'. He was a Bing Crosby enthusiast, and had a St Bernard dog called Bing. A familiar figure about town he drove a yellow Rolls Royce, which had belonged to Harry Lauder. Married to the dancer, Betty King, who was also his comic 'feed', they appeared together for most of his career. Also associated with the comics Hector Nicol and Betty Nolan, and the singer Ron Coburn, he led many seasons of touring summer and winter revues, at the Tivoli, Aberdeen; Palace, Dundee; and the Palladium, Edinburgh.

Max WALL (1908–1990); Comedian, actor.
Born London, Maxwell George Lorimer, son of Jack Lorimer, the Scottish comedian. Max Wall played Jack in the pantomime, *Mother Goose*, when he was fourteen and became a speciality dancer from 1925. After twenty-one years touring the Variety circuit, he developed his famous 'grotesque' act, Professor Wallofski, in which he walked with bended knees, wearing black coat with tails, ballet tights and large boots, and played the piano. He will be remembered as one of the great music hall entertainers. In 1974, he played Archie Rice in John Osborne's play, *The Entertainer*, and in his later career extended his range as a serious actor in plays by Samuel Beckett, such as *Waiting for Godot* and *Krapp's Last Tape*.

Dave WILLIS (1895–1973); Comedian.
Born David Williams, Cowcaddens, Glasgow; first appeared on stage as a child,

under the name Funny Clive, assisting his brother Claude, a conjuror, at the Panopticon and other Glasgow theatres. At thirteen, he appeared in the Theatre Royal chorus in pantomime, while beginning an engineering apprenticeship. After the First World War, he gained experience in amateur concert-parties and joined Galt's Agency, regularly working in ciné-variety in the west of Scotland. He began to be noticed during the early thirties in pantomime at the Theatre Royal and Pavilion, and in the next five years developed his unique clowning humour, starring in *Half-Past Eight* and pantomime in Edinburgh and Glasgow. He was particularly popular during the War, when his famous character sketches included Hitler, Ghandi, and the A.R.P., in which he sang the comic song 'In My Wee Gas Mask'. After a period of financial difficulty following an unfortunate investment, he broke back into the Empire circuit, touring throughout Scotland, and continued working until late in life. A small man who wore a toothbrush moustache, his looks and the enormity of his talent led him to be nicknamed the Charlie Chaplin of Scotland. His son, Denny Willis, is also a comedian.

Robert WILSON (1907–1964); Tenor.
Born Cambuslang, Glasgow; sang in a local choir before joining the Rothesay Entertainers in his early twenties. Having trained and toured with the D'Oyly Carte Opera Company for five years, he abandoned an operatic career to establish himself during the forties as the leading singer in revue. Billed as 'The Voice of Scotland', his repertoire was a popular blend of light opera, and Scottish ballads, 'Down in the Glen' and 'Here's to the Gordons'. He appeared with Jack Anthony and Jack Radcliffe in road shows across Scotland, before managing his own touring companies in the early fifties, choosing comedians such as Stanley Baxter and Johnny Beattie, and often giving young entertainers their first 'break'. In the mid-fifties, he founded the White Heather Group which, during the following years, proved a training ground for young singers, including Andy Stewart, Sydney Devine and Joe Gordon.

WILSON, KEPPEL and BETTY: Speciality sand dance act.
Jack Wilson, an English dancer, met the Americans, Joe Keppel and Betty Knox, in the United States in 1909, where they formed their burlesque Arab sand-dancing act. They came to Britain in 1932, and toured Variety theatres for many years, becoming recognised by many as the finest speciality act in the business. The first Betty was replaced by her daughter, Betty, in 1932, and in 1941, by her daughter, Patsy. The trio retired in 1963.

Appendix III

MUSIC HALL
SOCIETIES

THE BRITISH MUSIC HALL SOCIETY
c/o The Honorary Secretary,
Brodie and Middleton Ltd.,
68 Drury Lane,
London, WC2B 5SP

The aims of the Society are to preserve theatre and miscellania, including properties and photographs, to keep alive the tradition of this particularly British institution and to actively support this entertainment wherever and whenever produced.

President: Louis Benjamin Chairman: Jack Seaton Historian: Max Tyler Membership Secretary: Wendy Lunn.

THE SIR HARRY LAUDER SOCIETY,
c/o 61 Craiglockhart Road,
Edinburgh EH14 1HF

Formed in May 1979, in Portobello, the aims being to immortalise the name and works of Sir Harry, to encourage the appreciation of his works world-wide, and to co-operate with such bodies willing to further this. In November 1980, a committee was formed with Jimmy Logan as Honorary President and Miss Greta Lauder Fraser (a great-niece of Sir Harry) as Chairwoman. Lauder Festivals, dinners, lunches, musical evenings and exhibitions of Lauder photographs, have been held on a number of occasions.

Patron: Lord James Douglas-Hamilton, M.A., LL.B., M.P.
Hon. President: Mr Jimmy Logan.
Hon Vice President: Miss Greta Lauder Fraser.

Chairman: Mr George Gillespie.
Secretary: Mrs Connie McVey.

THE WINTER GARDEN TRUST LIMITED
The Winter Garden,
Victoria Street,
Rothesay,
Isle of Bute, PA20 0AH

The Winter Garden theatre was completed in 1924 and was the venue for first-class Variety revues throughout the heyday of holiday summer seasons of the thirties, forties and fifties. The building was closed in 1976 but demolition was refused owing to a Grade 2 listing being imposed by the Historic Buildings and Monuments Department in 1978. Four years later an action committee, the Winter Garden Trust Limited was founded in order to preserve and restore the theatre as a heritage centre. The refurbishment of the Winter Gardens was completed in May 1990, providing a unique audio/visual exhibition illustrating the traditional seaside holiday at the Clyde resort, travelling by train from Glasgow to catch the steamer to the Isle of Bute, the Punch and Judy shows, and penny in the slot machines. There is now a 97 seat theatre for video presentations and current films, a restaurant and an open air tearoom. Funding for this ambitious project has been given by The Highlands and Islands Development Board, Strathclyde Community Business Ltd., Scottish Tourist Board, Scottish Development Agency, several other public bodies as well as many private donations.

Patrons: The Marchioness of Bute and Magnus Magnusson.
Hon. Presidents: Johnny Beattie and Jimmy Logan.
Administrator: Rhona Sutherland.